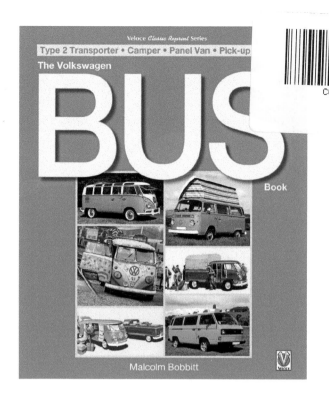

Veloce *Classic Reprint* Series

Type 2 Transporter • Camper • Panel Van • Pick-up

The Volkswagen

BUS

Book

Malcolm Bobbitt

First published in January 2007 by Veloce Publishing Limited, Veloce House, Parkway Farm Business Park, Middle Farm Way, Poundbury, Dorchester DT1 3AR, England. Fax 01305 268864 / e-mail info@veloce.co.uk / web www.veloce.co.uk or www.velocebooks.com. Reprinted July 2016 and October 2016. ISBN: 978-1-845849-95-5 UPC: 6-36847-04995-9.
© 2007 and 2016 Malcolm Bobbitt and Veloce Publishing. All rights reserved. With the exception of quoting brief passages for the purpose of review, no part of this publication may be recorded, reproduced or transmitted by any means, including photocopying, without the written permission of Veloce Publishing Ltd. Throughout this book logos, model names and designations, etc, have been used for the purposes of identification, illustration and decoration. Such names are the property of the trademark holder as this is not an official publication. Readers with ideas for automotive books, or books on other transport or related hobby subjects, are invited to write to the editorial director of Veloce Publishing at the above address. British Library Cataloguing in Publication Data – A catalogue record for this book is available from the British Library. Typesetting, design and page make-up all by Veloce Publishing Ltd on Apple Mac. Printed and bound by CPI Group (UK) Ltd, Croydon, CR0 4YY.

Veloce *Classic Reprint* Series

Type 2 Transporter • Camper • Panel Van • Pick-up • Wagon

The Volkswagen

BUS

Book

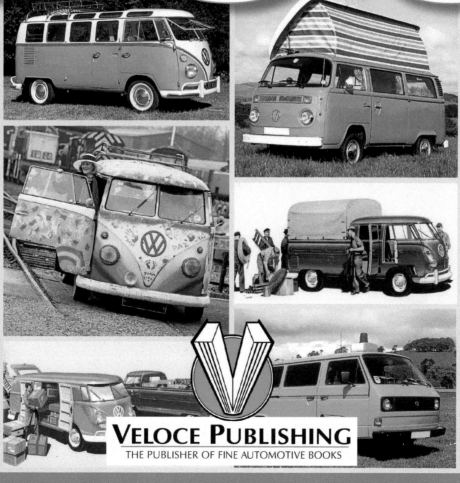

VELOCE PUBLISHING
THE PUBLISHER OF FINE AUTOMOTIVE BOOKS

Malcolm Bobbitt

Contents

Acknowledgements & Introduction

Acknowledgements

Compiling the first edition of the book proved to be a daunting task; because of the huge number of vehicles that have been produced over the decades, and because of the complexity of the specification changes made during that time. I thought that preparation of this entirely new edition would have been relatively easy since much of the original research remains in place: how could I have been so wrong? Revisiting the Transporter in all its guises has been a pleasurable exercise, and how satisfying it is to know that, as this book goes to press, the classic Bay Window model (albeit with a 1.4 litre Total Flex water-cooled engine) is still being produced in Brazil. A production run approaching sixty years must be something of a record!

I am grateful to so many people who have given up their time; imparting enthusiasm, advice and knowledge in helping me to produce the two editions of this book. Mark Reynolds of Just Kampers and Robin Taylor for checking my manuscript regarding technical matters; the late Roger Lister; Brian Screaton for the loan of archive photographic and publicity material; Geoff Wiltshire of the Split-Screen Van Club for organising a get-together of owners for my benefit; Neil Barker, Phil Bunting, Harry and Judith Cook, Robert Corker, Nick Gibbons and Keith Hocking for the loan of photographs and allowing me to photograph their vehicles.

My thanks, too, to Volkswagen Group United Kingdom Ltd. for furnishing production figures and related information, and, in particular, Kate Thompson (Press Office manager) and Fabricio Mendonça Migues (Brazil); Rod Sleigh of VW Books; Dorival Piccoli Junior for photographs, publicity material and information concerning Transporters produced in Brazil; Charles Trevelyan of Auto Sleepers; Herr Witzleben at the Stiftung Auto Museum; Richard Copping; Ton Roks, Bill Wolf and Jonathan Day; and the librarians at the National Motor Museum, Beaulieu.

Many of the photographs that appear in this book are the work of Ken Cservenka. The production of this edition would have been all the poorer had it not been for Ken's help, and I am grateful to him for allowing me to access his vast photographic library. Ken is well known within the Volkswagen fraternity, and his photographic collection, numbering in the region of 30,000 slides, is the product of some thirty years' work. Ken has also contributed to a number of Volkswagen related books, and has co-edited VW Motoring magazine.

I'm also grateful for the enthusiasm and advice given by automotive historian and researcher Andrew Minney who read through my manuscript in depth and made many pertinent suggestions.

Last, but not least, my appreciation to my publisher Rod Grainger who suggested this book in the first instance and encouraged me to prepare this new edition; to the many enthusiasts I have had the pleasure of meeting, and to the forbearance of my wife Jean who has come to recognise all the different Transporter models.

Introduction

There is something very comforting about seeing a classic VW Bus sedately going about its business. Not only does such a sight reflect a social era that is, for some people, receding all too rapidly in a world where everything is executed with great haste, it is reassuring to know that particular values continue to have importance. For those people of a certain age, the Bulli, as the Transporter has become universally known, has been around for a lifetime. The Split-Screen Bus – Splitties to Volkswagen aficionados – helped change the face of the global motor industry by heralding the multi-purpose vehicle, the MPV in modern parlance. Multi-purpose and practical it certainly was, efficiently acting out the role of delivery van, builder's pick-up truck, school bus, campervan, and so much more.

The Bulli is not exclusively for those generations of people keen to rediscover their youth and who want to take to the road in search of renewed freedom. It is very much a vehicle for young people, so ageless is its concept and design. Never mind that the Bulli made its debut in a fragile world recovering from being torn apart by war; the demand for this incredible vehicle, half a century or so later, has never been greater. In an age which has been witness to a rapid shrinkage of the automotive industry, where choice is being eroded and there is too much conformity, the humble Bulli affords the means of escaping the confines of modern living. There is reassurance, however, in knowing that the classic Transporter, which went into production in 1950, is still built in Brazil, fifty six years on.

To a lot of people this rather odd Volkswagen, which is said to have been inspired by the once ubiquitous Dutch Bakfiet, a pedal-powered delivery vehicle, will forever be the hippie bus. Because of its ability to suffer extremes of climate and a penchant to conquer diversities of terrain, the Transporter became synonymous with youth seeking spiritual fulfilment as well as satisfying desires to wander

Volkswagen released a series of illustrations aimed at promoting the Transporter, this evocative example depicting the diversity of models, including the Samba Microbus, Kombi, Panel van and Pick-up. There is a wonderful ambience, the artist having successfully portrayed the excited atmosphere and the level of interest directed at the vehicles. There is an element of propaganda about the scene, especially as there's no hint of Germany's postwar austerity. (Author's collection, courtesy Volkswagen)

the world. Freedom of expression, therefore, allowed the Bulli to become the symbol of flower power, radicalism and protest; quite simply, it afforded the means of travelling the world incognito, with minimum fuss but maximum resourcefulness.

Bullis painted in lurid colours and bedecked with graffiti and nationality stickers were once a frequent sight, not only in Britain, but throughout Europe and beyond, to Asia and the Indian

The familiar face of the Transporter as so often seen on roads throughout the world, in this instance the Road to The Isles, in the north west Highlands of Scotland. (Author's collection)

subcontinent.

America, too, was another of the Bulli's spiritual homes, and as well as serving as a hippie bus it was essential to surf culture.

Splitties were followed by Bays, which were so called because of their styling, the most distinctive aspects being their wide and curved front panels and panoramic windscreen. Even when the third generation Transporter arrived, its image being further removed from that originally sculptured, the Wedge, as it affectionately became known, could not belie the vehicle's ancestry. With more than six and a half million Transporters taking to the roads over a forty-two year period, the recipe for success is there for all to see.

Had it not been for Ben Pon, an entrepreneurial Dutchman who fought to sell the Volkswagen Beetle in his native country, and to export it around the world, the likeable, comfortable and iconic Bulli probably would never have been conceived.

Like most successful ideas, the Transporter was born out of simplicity. Visiting Wolfsburg immediately after WW2, and seeking to negotiate a VW franchise, Pon was impressed at seeing flat-bed trucks being used to convey equipment around the factory. The trucks, which had been designed on the instruction of Major Ivan Hirst and built from Beetle components simply because fork-lift vehicles were unavailable, inspired Pon in 1947 to sketch in his notebook an idea for a commercial vehicle. The motorised bakfiet principle had emerged as nothing more than a box on wheels: at the front sat the driver, at the rear was the air-cooled motor, and in between a vast cargo hold.

If the Dutch bakfiet was the inspiration that produced the Bulli, it was the Bulli that inspired development of the modern commercial vehicle. Needless to say, the emergence of the Transporter wasn't as simple and straightforward as it might seem. Had it not been for Major Ivan Hirst and other senior officers of the British Occupying Forces in the immediate postwar Germany, and the foresight of Heinz Nordhoff, Volkswagen's first chief executive, all of whom recognised the soundness of Ben Pon's idea, the Transporter story would have been very different.

In addition to being the world's favourite cargo carrier, the Bulli can be credited with kick-starting today's massive motorhome industry. The Bulli wasn't the first motorhome, but it did help make the ubiquitous campervan accessible to a wide market. In Germany and throughout Europe the arrival of the Campingbox provided the means of taking vacations in style and comfort; Americans delighted in the Sportsmobile, while Britons freed themselves of conventional holidaying with the Devon and Dormobile.

Take a visit today to any of the world's tourist resorts, national parks, or venture somewhere off the beaten track. Before long there will appear a Bulli, its occupants happily enjoying the autonomy and independence this vehicle provides. Nothing changes!

Malcolm Bobbitt
Cumbria, England

Chapter

A Dutch affair

There can be few places in the world that have not at some time been visited by that most iconic of vehicles, the VW Transporter. The growling engine sound and the unmistakable bread loaf profile of what surely must be one of the most familiar of vehicles are characteristics that essentially make the VW Bus both comforting and practical. Visit any resort from the Highlands of Scotland to Cornwall's surfing paradise, from Europe's North Cape to Africa's Cape of Good Hope, California's surf culture or Australia's Gold Coast to appreciate the exceptional following that the Transporter enjoys.

Though the Transporter has become a symbol of independence and carefree travel for today's young and young-at-heart adventurers, the vehicle was serving exactly the same purpose for motorists in the fifties, sixties and seventies. Then, as now, the Transporter was perceived as a vehicle without boundaries or frontiers.

From its debut in 1949, this functional and highly practical VW set a trend that would not be emulated to any degree until the arrival of the ubiquitous people-carrier in the

More than half a decade after the Transporter's introduction, the Bulli remains a firm favourite with young people determined to enjoy the freedom and independence the vehicle promises. The well travelled Splittie illustrated, a Dormobile conversion which dates to between 1960 and 1963 and is owned by Geoff and Kath Lee, was pictured at Kirkby Stephen in Cumbria on Easter Sunday 2006. (Author's collection)

seventies and eighties. That's not to say that manufacturers like Bedford and Commer in the United Kingdom, Citroën, Fiat, Borgward-Hansa, Peugeot and Renault from Western Europe, along with a number of Eastern European

The Transporter is truly universal, this Bay Window 1974 Devon Eurovette looking quite at home in an idyllic location. By the time the MPV made its impact on the motoring scene, the Type 2 Volkswagen had been in production for more than thirty years. (Courtesy Ken Cservenka)

vehicles, and Dodge and Ford of America, did not produce some interesting ideas.

By the time that MPVs with their flexible seating and interior layouts, not to mention easy conversion from passenger carrying to commercial and utilitarian use, had made a mark on the world's motoring scene, the Bulli, as the Transporter was often known, had already been in production for some 35 years. This long production run ensured a supreme reputation, and customer demand resulted in world-wide sales of more than 5 million examples.

The emergence of the Volkswagen Transporter at a time when Europe was deeply engulfed in postwar austerity would not have been possible without the dedicated efforts of a number of people of several nationalities. It also

goes without saying that had it not been for development work undertaken before World War II to produce an affordable car designed for mass-ownership, then the Transporter would not have materialised. The matter is all the more complicated in the sense that circumstance also played a specific and essential part in the project's conception.

Prewar origins

The origins of Volkswagen and the emergence of the Beetle in prewar Germany are well documented, as are the ambitions of two people in particular to enable large numbers of German people to enjoy the independence that motoring afforded. Ferdinand Porsche and Adolf Hitler shared these aspirations, though their political leanings were quite unrelated.

Without Porsche's passive expertise in innovative engineering, and Hitler's campaign to change the face of Germany by constructing a network of Autobahnen – no doubt with the aim of mobilising the nation in war – it's doubtful whether the 'People's Car' could have been developed.

Hitler, who was obsessed by motorcars, first became aware of Porsche in Berlin on 11th July 1926 on the occasion of the German Grand Prix, which was won by Rudy Caracciola driving a straight-eight Mercedes. The engineer was busy supervising his team's activities at the meeting, and was quite unaware of the future Chancellor's presence.

When Hitler and Porsche were introduced to each other it was on 1st March 1933 at Berlin's Old Chancellery. The meeting had been convened through the efforts of junior

Audi board member Baron Klaus Detlof von Oetzen to discuss the prospect of Auto Union – a consortium comprising Audi, DKW, Horch and Wanderer – entering motor racing (and therefore rivalling Mercedes). It's quite possible that Hitler knew of Von Oetzen's motorsport activities, particularly his leadership of the Auto Union team of Porsche-designed Wanderer sports cars which competed in a series of road rallies organised by the Nazi-inspired Vehicle Drivers Corps.

Porsche was accompanied to the meeting by Von Oetzen and racing driver Hans Stuck, the aim being to secure German government funding in order to build a suitable car. Armed with details of the proposed vehicle, and possibly unconvinced as to the meeting's successful outcome, Porsche was shocked to know that Hitler knew all about him. Porsche's engineering credentials were assets when it came to winning the Chancellor's support, particularly as Hitler was an ardent Mercedes enthusiast, and could, therefore, have readily turned down Auto Union's approach. Whilst being interviewed by the Führer the trio would have been somewhat intimidated by the sight in the room of an oil painting depicting Hitler at the wheel of a Mercedes-Benz ...

It was from that meeting that the long course towards developing the Volkswagen began. Hitler gave Auto-Union the government funding that was sought, though it was apparent that such approval had depended upon Porsche's association with the project. Porsche had long desired to build an

Had it not been for the emergence of the Volkswagen, the Transporter would not have materialised. Adolf Hitler's dream that the Volkswagen would provide inexpensive and reliable motoring for millions of German families was made possible by Ferdinand Porsche's design which met the Führer's exacting demands. After a search to find a suitable location, the Volkswagen factory was built at Wolfsburg, the construction of the factory depicted in this archive illustration. (Courtesy Volkswagen)

affordable small car that was easy to maintain and inexpensive to run, ideals that were close to Hitler's plans for the development of a national 'People's Car'.

Support for the Auto-Union programme meant that the German government had effectively bought into an arrangement whereby the country's motor industry was able to expand. Before the Nazis were elected to power in January 1933 with Adolf Hitler at the helm, it can be safely said that the German motor industry lagged behind that of mainland Europe, Britain and America. It was Hitler's intention that ,as part of revitalising Germany's economy, the nation's motor industry should be substantially boosted, and, to do this, tax concessions were introduced in respect of car ownership. The incentives were aimed mainly at the working and middle classes who generally were deprived of car ownership. The inter-war period had seen Germany's economy decline, and whilst there were some people who could afford large, powerful and expensive cars, a far greater number were unable to afford the more modest, mass-produced vehicles, hence the proliferation of inexpensive yet often innovative cyclecars.

Hitler's enthusiasm for the motorcar, and his edict that it should be widely accessible to as many people as possible, led to the adoption of the 'Volksauto' scheme. The Führer was adamant that a People's Car should not display any of the characteristics associated with the fragile-looking machines, such as Hanomag's loaf-shaped open tourer and Golliath's three-wheel Pioneer, which were gaining in popularity.

The Volksauto project

With mass car ownership on the agenda, Hitler summoned Porsche to a further meeting at Berlin's Kaiserhof Hotel in May 1934. The engineer was invited to discuss ideas for a Volkswagen (People's Car) along with

some specific details regarding fuel economy, maximum speed and engine configuration. Rather than being able to put forward his own ideas, Porsche discovered that Hitler had definite ideas of his own, which Porsche was expected to put into practice. The ideal car, the Führer insisted, should be air-cooled, so as to be impervious to freezing in winter; it would be capable of travelling at 60mph (100km/h) on Germany's new autobahns; it had to accommodate two adults and three children in comfort; and consume petrol at no more than 6 litres per 100km (33mpg). Hitler was adamant that the car's selling price should not exceed 1000 Reichmarks, an amount, Porsche opined, that was virtually unachievable.

For Hitler, the development of the Volkswagen served an alternative purpose to that of an affordable means of transport. He believed that such a

vehicle could be employed in a military capacity to provide armed transport for German troops as well as having commercial applications.

Determined to get the car into production at the earliest date, Hitler arranged for the German Society of Motor Manufacturers (RDA) to enter into a contract with Porsche who would design and develop it. Dated 22nd June 1934, the contract allowed for the construction of 50,000 vehicles within the almost impossible timescale of ten months, at the end of which time experimental cars had to be running. Design work, conducted with the aid of Porsche's son Ferry, began immediately in garage outbuildings in the grounds of the engineer's Stuttgart home. The drawings, completed by Erwin Komenda as Ferry recalls, were annotated with the word geheim (secret) and depicted a vehicle displaying a

Adolf Hitler, having secured Ferdinand Porsche's expertise in motor design, ordered that the Volkswagen should not demonstrate any of the characteristics of the fragile-looking economy cars that proliferated in Germany during the early to mid-thirties. The Type 32 shown here was one of several prototypes created by Porsche in the search for the definitive vehicle. (Courtesy National Motor Museum)

Early Volkswagen development was conducted within the garage at Porsche's Stuttgart home before work was transferred to new premises, seen here, built at Zuffenhausen in the northern part of the city. (Courtesy Volkswagen)

similar outline to the car that eventually went into production.

In his autobiography, Ferry Porsche recalls the work that surrounded engine development: all configurations were considered, including two- and four-strokes, twin- and four-cylinder types, horizontally opposed and in-line. The choice was the now familiar air-cooled flat-four of 985cc developing 23.5hp at 3000rpm.

There was opposition to the Volksauto project from the RDA which considered that Hitler's proposals undermined its own efforts to design and produce a small and affordable car. There was, however, little that the RDA could do about the situation, because of Hitler's extensive involvement in the assignment, and ultimately had to accept the arrangement. One particular opponent to the scheme was Opel's Heinz Nordhoff who, during WW2, managed the firm's Brandenburg factory, which at the time was the largest producer of trucks in Europe. Ironically, Nordhoff was to become

Volkswagen's postwar chief executive who directed Volkswagen to become Europe's leading motor manufacturer.

The Pon brothers

Showing interest in Germany's Volksauto project were former Opel dealers the Pon brothers, whose Opel franchise was lost when the car maker was taken over by General Motors in 1929. General Motors acquired Opel with the aim of producing in Germany a small car that would sell in large numbers, as the marque was Germany's largest car maker and supported an extensive dealership. Ben and Wijn Pon from Amersfoot in Holland were among some 500-600 Opel dealers invited to Frankfurt following General Motors' acquisition of the German manufacturer. Despite the euphoric mood of the occasion there was an underlying problem in that General Motors viewed the Opel dealer network (there were 736 agencies in Germany alone) as being detached from the main business operation. GM's management

discovered that because Opel did not have a system of interchangeable parts, many dealers had established elaborate machine shops to produce their own components, a system not in keeping with General Motors' practice. Unwilling to be encompassed within General Motors' sales organisation, the Pon brothers were forced to surrender their franchise.

Looking for alternative business, the Pon brothers became agents selling American Federal Trucks. However, when news reached the Netherlands about the proposed Volksauto, the Pon brothers saw this as a unique opportunity and immediately began campaigning to become the first agency selling the vehicle outside Germany. The brothers first indicated their interest in 1937, presumably to the RDA and Dr Porsche since Hitler had already made it known that the high-ranking engineer had been commissioned to design the vehicle which was to enter production at the earliest opportunity.

Porsche's design team included a select number of motor industry personnel, including Karl Rabe and Josef Kales, both of whom worked closely with the engineer at the Steyr company, Austria's most prolific car maker. Rabe was Porsche's senior engineer and chief designer, while Kales was responsible for engine design. Other team members, again known to each another since Steyr days, included bodywork expert Erwin Komenda, transmission specialist Karl Fröhlich, Josef Zahradnik whose chassis design and engineering experience was invaluable, and Josef Mickl who was responsible for calculations.

By the time the Pon brothers had established their interest in the future Volkswagen, prototype cars had been undergoing trials for several months, testing having officially commenced on 12th October 1936, though there is evidence of preliminary assessments

Assisting with Volkswagen development, Ferdinand Porsche's son Ferry was instrumental in much of the testing programme. Ferry Porsche is seen here at the wheel of a prototype cabriolet vehicle that was built by Reutter in 1936. (Courtesy Volkswagen)

before that date. The tests, which meant each of three vehicles covering in excess of 31,250 miles (50,281km), were conducted by the Automobile Manufacturers' Association and were the subject of a lengthy and involved report showing them as fulfilling the criteria expected of them. The satisfactory report summoned the building of a further 30 prototype cars, each of which, driven by a squad of SS drivers, completed more than 62,500 miles (100,563km) to amass a total of some 1.5 million miles (2.4 million kilometres).

The creation of Wolfsburg

The definitive Volkswagen was presented to Adolf Hitler on 20th April 1938, the Führer's 49th birthday. A little more than a month later, the 26th May, three pre-production cars

Prototype Beetles were subjected to extensive testing by officers of the German army. The vehicles shown here were pictured on test, and quite clearly the definitive shape of the Beetle can be appreciated. Each of the cars on test was required to complete 50,000 miles (80,000km), during which time Ferry Porsche kept comprehensive records to show how many times the brake pedal was depressed and the rate at which different controls were used. Such reliability meant that when the Transporter was designed, there was no hesitation in employing the Beetle's running gear. (Courtesy Volkswagen)

The date is 20th April 1938, Adolf Hitler's 49th birthday. The occasion is the official presentation of the Volkswagen. Surrounded by his Nazi colleagues, Hitler is obviously enthralled by the design; on the far left of the picture Ferdinand Porsche explains some of the car's finer points. (Courtesy Volkswagen)

were displayed at the ceremony for the laying of the cornerstone of the Wolfsburg factory. Watching Hitler perform the ceremony, an occasion used to promote the Nazi regime and display the swastika emblem, were 600 distinguished guests and 70,000 spectators. Hitler used the event to announce that the Volkswagen would be known from then on as the KdF-Wagen to associate it with the Strength Through Joy (Kraft durch Freude) movement, a decision that was unpalatable to the Porsches.

The task of finding a suitable location for the Volkswagen factory fell to Dr Bodo Lafferentz, the Gesellschaft zur Vorbereitung des Volkswagens mbh (VW Development Company) commercial manager and prominent member of the German Labour Front.

Lafferentz was deputy to Robert Ley, a close associate of Hitler and joint pioneer of the movement leading to the establishment of the Third Reich. A chemist by profession, who, it was claimed, was being a habitual drunkard, Ley keenly anticipated adoption of a People's Car to compliment his establishment of the Volksempfänger, Volkskühlschrank and the Volkswohnung – people's radio, people's refrigerator and people's dwelling, respectively.

Following Hitler's demand that the factory be sited in central Germany and be accessible by road and rail for the easy conveyance of materials and products into and out of the works, Dr Lafferentz scoured the region by aeroplane. A suitable location was eventually found near the village of Fallersleben, adjacent

the Schulenbergs. Another significant landowner was the Wense family, and between them and the Schulenburgs, along with a number of other smaller landowners, some 15,000 acres were given over to the Volkswagen factory.

The building of the Wolfsburg factory was conducted at great speed, the intention being that it would be completed in stages so that ultimately more than 30,000 workers would be employed building more than a million vehicles annually. Extending for almost a mile along the banks of the Mittelland Canal, the Volkswagen works would ultimately encompass an entire town, accommodating workers' families totalling 90,000 people in all. According to Ferry Porsche, the vast complex, which was constructed by a mainly Italian labour force, was designed to have a production capacity dwarfing all other automobile factories around the world.

It was American technology that benefited the design of the Wolfsburg factory. Porsche, along with those whose responsibility it was to build Wolfsburg, was influenced by Ford's Dearborn motor factory south of Detroit, which he visited on several occasions, Henry Ford having ensured his guests be shown the full extent of his operations. By European standards Dearborn was vast, and, whereas it was normal for car makers to import many components and castings, these were produced in-house. During their visits to the United States the regime accountable for Wolfsburg ordered machine tools from suppliers in Chicago and elsewhere, so impressed were they by American mass-production methods.

Planning the town adjacent to the Wolfsburg factory was the responsibility of the young and newly qualified architect Peter Koller, but it was Robert Ley who influenced its identity. Several appellations were

A little more than a month after the Volkswagen was officially presented to Hitler, the Führer presided over the laying of the cornerstone of the Wolfsburg factory. On the right of the picture, Hitler is seen discussing with Porsche the car and its derivatives that would be built at the works. (Courtesy Volkswagen)

to the Mittelland Canal and the Hanover-Berlin autobahn. Although the Count of Schulenburg owned much of the land which had been in his family for 500 years, and on which was built the 14th century Schloss Wolfsburg, the site was commandeered by the Nazi regime without heeding protests raised by

Hitler sitting in a prototype cabriolet with Ferdinand Porsche looking on, the occasion being the cornerstone laying ceremony held on 26th May 1938. (Courtesy Volkswagen)

Another view of the cornerstone laying ceremony at Wolfsburg, but this time showing Hitler about to try out a saloon. Looking on, Porsche explains the car's interior design and layout. (Courtesy Volkswagen)

suggested, Volkswagenstadt being one, Porschestadt and Neu-Fallersleben being others. The final choice was Hitler's: he named it Stadt des KdF-Wagens, thus connecting it with the Strength Through Joy movement, though he did agree to the abbreviation KdF-Stadt.

The creators of Volkswagen, known as Gezuvor, wanted to hire two of Ford's key planners, Charles Sorenson and Harry Hanson, to design the Wolfsburg factory. Ford refused to the arrangement on the grounds that there was much work for them at Dearborn, and Gezuvor was forced to look elsewhere. Instead, it employed a team of architects comprising Rudolf Mewes, who had previously worked on Ford's projects, Karl Kohlbecker, and the partnership of Schupp & Kremer.

A gift to Porsche

Wolfsburg was energised in August 1939 when Ferdinand Porsche was invited to switch on the factory's power system. The date for commencing production of the Volkswagen had been set a year previously when Robert Ley proclaimed that the first cars would leave the factory in the autumn of 1939 and that 10,000 vehicles would be completed by the year end. Further predictions were for 100,000 vehicles in 1940 and 200,000 in 1941, building up to nearly half a million annually. Production was expected to rise to more than a million vehicles annually after further development of the works. Ley's schedule depended on the punctual delivery of machine tools from America, and when there was evidence of serious delay, the programme was deferred by a year, by which time political events in Germany had summoned the onset of war ...

By the time Porsche had performed the 'switching-on' ceremony his team was installed in premises in the wooded hilly countryside to the south-east of

Fallersleben overlooking the factory with its rapidly growing town alongside it. What had once been a single-storey hunting lodge was adapted for use by Porsche so that he could be on hand to oversee Volkswagen development. The premises became more than a Wolfsburg out-post, especially when Anton Piëch, Porsche's highly qualified lawyer son-in-law, was recruited to manage the KdF works, making the 'hut' as it was called, his wartime abode.

Watching events very closely, whilst maintaining his interest in Volkswagen development, Ben Pon lost no time in sending a significant gift of 10,000 Dutch tulip bulbs to Ferdinand Porsche. Pon, who had already acquired a reputation in motorsport, also arranged for the planting of the bulbs in the grounds surrounding the hut so that the fields of colourful flowers served as a constant reminder of his generosity.

Pon's gift to Porsche is claimed by Walter Henry Nelson in his book *Small Wonder* as being the key to the Dutchman's role in becoming the first exporter of Volkswagens. Whilst elsewhere it is said that Pon was first able to drive the car at the time of the 1939 Berlin Motor Show, Nelson is adamant that it was through Porsche's efforts that the Dutchman had a meeting with Robert Ley at a somewhat earlier date. Ley, it appears, was amenable there and then to him acquiring the franchise to sell the car in Holland, though, of course, at the time production was nowhere near commencing. An experimental car, it appears, was made available at the time of the meeting, and it is recorded that Porsche and Pon drove around Berlin's ring road, the former said to be very relaxed about the affair even to the point of wearing brocaded slippers.

At the onset of hostilities the Wolfsburg factory was enlisted as part of Germany's war effort, producing armaments in addition to components for the nation's aircraft industry. Limited production of Volkswagen cars also got under way and records show that between 1941 and 1944 the 630 civilian vehicles that were built were used mainly by Nazi personnel, including high ranking officials, Robert Ley among them. A number of other vehicles were presented to selected industrialists, and some were used for experimental purposes by the Porsche design team.

The Kübelwagen

A derivation of the Beetle intended for military use also went into production at Wolfsburg during the war, the vehicle having a significant bearing on the development of the Transporter. Commercial and military variants of the KdF-Wagen had been proposed as early as 1935, the most favoured of the latter being an open vehicle with bucket (kübel) seats that allowed personnel to enter and leave with ease. Hence such vehicles were known as Kübelwagens

A vehicle with a significant relevance to the development of the Transporter was the Kübelwagen, a derivation of the Beetle that was intended for use by the German military. The proposal for a military version of the Beetle dates from 1935, but it was not until the spring of 1940 that the vehicle entered production at Wolfsburg. By allowing for adequate ground clearance in order for the vehicle to traverse rough ground, it was necessary to fit reduction gears on each of the rear hubs, a detail employed on the Type 2 Transporter. A number of Kübelwagens were built at Wolfsburg under British command during the aftermath of WW2. (Courtesy National Motor Museum)

An indication of the engineering expertise within Volkswagen during its formative years is the emergence of the amphibious Schwimmwagen, a derivative of the Kübelwagen. (Courtesy National Motor Museum)

when they entered production in the spring of 1940, the 1000th example leaving Wolfsburg in December that year, and the 5000th in 1942.

Putting the Kübelwagen into production was a slow and involved process which was not without many difficulties. At one time so much harsh criticism existed about the vehicle's basic KdF-Wagen design that the success the Porsche team had anticipated appeared to be denied. It was only when modifications to the vehicle's design were undertaken that its agility over rough terrain was at last recognised, thus allowing for more exhaustive testing to be carried out. Ferry Porsche records that initial enthusiasm on behalf of Germany's Military Ordnance Office for the Kübelwagen was only lukewarm, and that it was Hitler and his officers who were insistent on its ultimate production.

Revisions to the Kübelwagen's basic specification required raising the ground clearance, an exercise that involved some innovative measures. Fitting larger diameter wheels was not a success, as the modification resulted in the vehicle being too highly geared. The aim had been to lower the gearing in order that the vehicle could be driven at a pace commensurate to a soldier's walking speed when carrying a regulatory backpack. Raising the front axles and fitting a pair of reduction gears on each of the rear hubs had the desired effect of lowering the overall gear ratio, reducing the vehicle's road

Pictured at Wolfsburg during the initial days of the British occupation of Germany, when the British army had the responsibility for the future of the Volkswagen factory, Major Ivan Hirst is seen with an early Beetle saloon. It was Major Hirst who had the foresight to see the value of the Volkswagen, something overlooked by senior motor industry personalities. Production of the Beetle under British command led to a series of events that culminated in the emergence of the Transporter. (Courtesy Volkswagen)

speed while improving power, and achieving greater ground clearance. It was these modifications that heralded the debut of the Volkswagen Type 82. The Kübelwagen theme was then extended, and, while not entirely pertinent to the Transporter story, the developments gave rise to the introduction of an amphibious derivative, the Schwimmwagen.

Pon and the British Occupying Forces

Although Ben Pon had helped promote the concept of the Volkswagen, and had connived to obtain the franchise to sell the car outside Germany, he was not a Nazi collaborator. During the war Pon was conscripted into the Dutch

army where he was commissioned as a colonel. In the book *Small Wonder,* Nelson qualifies Pon's regard for the Nazis by writing that he had developed such a violent hatred for them that by the war's end he was unwilling to pursue the VW franchise awarded to him. Owing to Holland's close proximity to Germany there is evidence that eighty per cent of wartime Dutch business was conducted with Germany, and this no doubt convinced Pon that, with hostilities at an end, there simply was no reason not to continue trading with the neighbouring country.

With Pon's enthusiasm for the Volkswagen as strong as ever, when the Dutchman returned to Wolfsburg following Germany's surrender, it was

the British he met. On 10th April 1945 the United States Infantry discovered the Volkswagen factory and the town of Wolfsburg, neither of which were shown on the Allies' maps. Ultimately, it was the British who had responsibility for the administration of that sector of Germany, their occupation of the zone being effective from May 1945. The factory had been extensively damaged by Allied bombing raids between 1943 and 1944, evidence remaining of large holes in the roof and extensive craters along the factory's southern extent for some time after the British occupation.

It became evident to the British Occupying Forces that the Wolfsburg factory, with its power generation and machine tooling, ideally offered

Major Ivan Hirst at the wheel of the 1000th Volkswagen to leave the Volkswagen assembly line. When the British Occupying Forces took control of the Volkswagen works in May 1945, Wolfsburg was in a bad state following Allied bombing raids of 1943-4. Despite the extensive damage and the lack of resources, production of the Beetle commenced, and, within nine months, the scene was as depicted here. (Courtesy Volkswagen)

provision for the salvage of military vehicles. Moreover, Wolfsburg's facilities would make it possible to produce the much needed means of transport, not only for military purposes – the British army's resources having been seriously depleted – but for use by the Red Cross and other essential organisations. Throughout the war the Allied troops had first-hand experience of the Kübelwagen's effectiveness, and it's known that examples were, from time to time, captured for examination. It was during the early days of US and British occupation of Wolfsburg that the opportunity was taken to complete a number of Kübelwagens for British Army use.

The fact that vehicle production could be reinstated at Wolfsburg with the minimum of expenditure did not go unnoticed by the occupying forces. Investment in retention of the Volkswagen factory and protecting it from destruction by looters became the responsibility of old-Etonian Colonel Michael McEvoy, a Rolls-Royce trained engineer whose successful apprenticeship at the Derby car and aero-engine manufacturer led him to pursue motorcycle racing and the establishment of a company building racing motorcycles. From these beginnings McEvoy became much involved in the preparation of cars for racing and rallying, before turning his attention to supercharging technology. Regarding the latter, Mercedes Benz employed McEvoy as a consultant when it was preparing its Grand Prix cars between 1937 and 1938. Like Ben Pon, McEvoy, having been invited to drive the Beetle whilst visiting the 1939 Berlin Motor Show, was no stranger to the Volkswagen. Pon, too, had participated in motorsport and was a very capable driver (an expertise which his racing driver son inherited), and it is most likely that he and McEvoy were known to each other.

Colonel McEvoy had served as a Territorial Army Officer before the war, thus at the onset of hostilities he was enlisted as a serving officer, his engineering expertise and the fact that he was fluent in German putting him in good stead for a role in charge of German workshops at the Rhine Army HQ. McEvoy's tenure at Wolfsburg, though brief, was highly significant. In establishing the need to resume vehicle production, such a task fell outside Army jurisdiction and was a matter for the Military Government, hence the appointment of a suitably qualified officer to oversee the factory's management.

Major Ivan Hirst was the officer selected by the Control Commission to fill the position, his engineering background and university (Manchester) education making him the ideal candidate. Serving with the Royal Mechanical and Electrical Engineers (REME), Major Hirst had been sent to Brussels as Second-in-Command of the Central Tank Workshop, his experience there being an important factor in his Wolfsburg assignment. Hirst's immediate superior officer at Wolfsburg was Colonel Charles Radclyffe CBE DSO, whose experience in the motor industry was considerable, having worked for companies as diverse as White Trucks and Alvis.

Hirst, a Yorkshireman born 1st March 1916 and who died aged 84 on 10th March 2000, had the remit to maintain production of the Kübelwagen, a vehicle which he had come to respect after closely examining examples that were captured during the war in Normandy. Hirst had been impressed by the vehicle's design, and not least by its all-independent suspension and

lightweight alloy boxer engine. The Major was well placed to opine on the Kübelwagen's engineering for he understood motor vehicles and loved nothing better than to get behind the wheel of a sports car.

Without Major Ivan Hirst's dedication and belief in the Volkswagen, it's doubtful whether the marque would have survived to become the leading motor manufacturer it is today. Certainly, without Hirst's enthusiasm, and the foresight of Ben Pon, the Transporter would not have materialised.

When he returned to Wolfsburg in postwar years, Pon saw a factory that had been saved from certain destruction. It had been Colonel Radclyffe's brief to dismantle the production line and machine tools and make the Volkswagen available to Britain's motor manufacturers, none of which were in the least bit interested in what was seen as an eccentric and ugly motor vehicle with little or no commercial potential. An official British investigation of the Volkswagen carried out by AC Cars Ltd, Ford Motor Co Ltd, Humber Ltd, Singer Motors Ltd and Solex Ltd, failed to produce the same level of satisfaction with the car as did the British Army. Concluding a

Major Ivan Hirst's confidence in the Volkswagen assured the vehicle's future. The same belief in Volkswagen was not shared by Billy Rootes, who told Hirst he would never get vehicles built at Wolfsburg! Born 1st March 1916, Hirst died March 10th 2000. (Courtesy Volkswagen)

detailed report, the official document claimed the Volkswagen as lacking "the fundamental technical requirement of a motorcar", and that it was "unattractive to the average buyer". There was more: the report stated, "to build the car commercially would be a completely uneconomic enterprise".

It was the view of Billy Rootes of Rootes Motors, who was offered the German plant as war reparations, that the Volkswagen was nothing but a travesty, an opinion shared in similar vein by others. The evaluation of the Volkswagen on behalf of Rootes Motors was undertaken by Humber, using a prototype Hillman Minx Mk III model for comparative purposes, and, though a jaundiced review and somewhat contrived, it was, nevertheless, outwardly meticulous. Rootes was allegedly most derogatory towards Hirst and his endeavours at Wolfsburg when visiting the factory: he told the Major "If you think you'll ever get cars built here you are a bloody fool, young man".

Without venturing into the politics surrounding the Volkswagen affair, the views expressed by Britain's motor manufactures in the immediate postwar era must surely have been the cause for some misgivings in later years when the success of VW and its products were clearly evident.

A famous notebook

Ben Pon, who, in the aftermath of war was keen to re-establish the rights bestowed to him to trade the Volkswagen in Holland and elsewhere, made a determined effort to impress the British management at Wolfsburg. It is recorded that he arrived at the factory in 1946 dressed in full Dutch Army uniform but was unable to elicit an interview with any of the commanding officers. Walter Henry Nelson refers to Pon as being "an extroverted, snuff-sniffling, ebullient Hollander", a character description penned no doubt as a result of Pon's own account of how he tried to get into Wolfsburg and make a suitable impression. "I covered my chest with phoney ribbons I'd made myself, got a Dutch corporal to act as a chauffeur driving an old Mercedes, and drove into Germany in high style, puffing a cigar and waving at passers-by." Such revelations would seem to indicate a plausible reason for Pon not being received!

Undeterred, Pon undertook

Dutch motor dealer Ben Pon, once an Opel agent, had been enthusiastic about the Volkswagen since 1937 and strove to become the first agent to have a franchise. Pon was driven in a prototype Beetle by Ferdinand Porsche at the time of the 1939 Berlin Motor Show, and he presented the engineer with a gift of 10,000 tulip bulbs. Postwar, Pon was made VW agent general for Holland and, in 1949, was responsible for sending the first Beetle to America. That car, with Pon on the left of the picture, is shown being loaded aboard the Holland America Line vessel Westerdam. (Courtesy Volkswagen)

another visit in April 1947, and, though there is no indication of any degree of previous flamboyancy, his visit was all the more successful. There are differing accounts as to Pon's behaviour on this occasion. Nelson refers to him posing as a high-ranking Dutch officer keen to see for himself the progress being made at Wolfsburg and being met by Major Hirst who arranged for him to meet with Colonel Radclyffe. According to other sources, Pon's approach was all the more sophisticated, his meeting with Radclyffe instigating further visits to Wolfsburg, culminating with the Dutchman importing a batch of ten Beetles to Holland in the first half of 1947. The business relationship between Radclyffe and Pon finally ratified, a contract between Volkswagen and Autobielhandel, Pon's company,

made the Dutchman agent general for Holland.

The arrangement with Ben Pon was satisfactory since it had been Radclyffe's aim, once production at Wolfsburg commenced, to find suitable export markets. Any thoughts of concentrating on Kübelwagen production were dashed when it became clear that the necessary body components could not be sourced. The few Kübelwagens that were produced were built from existing materials found within the factory. The obvious course of action was to perfect the Beetle and get it into production at the earliest opportunity. Had the Military Government not placed an order for 20,000 Beetles in September 1945, the whole plan for getting Wolfsburg operational could have been jeopardised. Had it not been for Pon's perseverance and his business acumen, the success of the Beetle worldwide, and the vehicle's popularity in America could, too, have been otherwise.

Ben Pon became a regular visitor to Wolfsburg throughout 1947 and, in late 1948, he took a Beetle to America aboard the Holland America Line vessel Westerdam, sailing from Rotterdam to New York. The grey painted vehicle with its blue trim arriving on American soil in early January 1949 was the first Volkswagen to enter the USA, but even Pon's enthusiasm for the Beetle could not summon buyers. Not only had it been extremely difficult to obtain a franchise to sell the car in the United States, his advance and extensive publicity campaign proved to be a total flop. Car dealers were generally reluctant to trade in European vehicles, particularly those from Germany. The message was clear; according to the dealers he met, Pon was told that American motorists wanted large and powerful saloons that incorporated up-to-the-minute styling trends with acres of chrome. American motorists were besotted with the new designs, not merely prewar makeovers, that were emerging from Ford, Studebaker and Chevrolet.

Pon returned home in a dejected state of mind having not sold a single car. His marketing resulted in disappointing press reviews claiming the Volkswagen to be quaint and out-of-date. It wasn't all bad, however, because, as American servicemen returned home from Germany, a few took the Volkswagens they had acquired with them. Others, having had experience of the Beetle while serving in Germany, had come to appreciate the car's qualities and sought to buy examples, despite the motor trade's lack of enthusiasm for it. It was not until 1950, when New York foreign car dealer Max Hoffmann was appointed America's first Volkswagen distributor, that the Beetle was officially sold in the USA. That year Hoffman sold 330 Volkswagens; other agents were signed up and enjoyed a ready market for the car. So began the American love affair with Volkswagen.

Nelson's caricature of the flamboyant Pon differs to the character of the man George Pearson remembered. Pearson was a member of the REME inspection team at Wolfsburg in the immediate postwar period, and his memories of Pon indicate a man whose effervescent attitude hid a strong regard for the Volkswagen. Pon had a clear understanding of the vehicle's engineering and quality and, moreover, Major Ivan Hirst's quest for perfection in respect of administration and production methods. Pon, it seems, showed intense interest in Wolfsburg and was keen to see the results of ongoing developments concerning the Beetle. Pon's visits to Wolfsburg in the first months of 1947 and his amenable business relationship with Ivan Hirst were fundamental to the Transporter's development.

Pon was also aware of the many constraints that were imposed upon Major Hirst mainly as a result of materials shortages. In the early days of the REME's occupation of Wolfsburg, Hirst had at his disposal a number of forklift trucks he had borrowed from the British Army to convey components and supplies around the works. When these were needed for more urgent work elsewhere they were commandeered, thus very nearly bringing to an end vehicle production at Wolfsburg.

Had it not been for Major Hirst insisting that it should be not impossible to devise an alternative method of transporting the all-essential materials, the cessation of vehicle manufacturing could well have been a reality. The answer to Major Hirst's problem was the modification, using tubular steel sections, of a Kübelwagen chassis and drivetrain to support a flat platform, the operator being located at the extreme rear of the vehicle above the engine and steering the motorised trolley via a long drag link. The arrangement proved to be very satisfactory, so much so that a number of plattenwagen remained in use for a number of decades, with one at least working at Wolfsburg as late as the mid-1970s.

Seeing these flatbed trolleys in use gave Pon the idea of devising a commercial derivative based on the Beetle chassis and running gear. The design reminded him of a simple three-wheeled delivery vehicle that was commonly used in Holland, and being pedal-propelled via the single rear wheel it was an efficient yet inexpensive means of transport. Similar machines, known as bakfiets (these are still used in Holland mainly by 'hippies' and students), were commonplace throughout Denmark and some other countries, including the United Kingdom, where they were akin to the ubiquitous 'Stop Me and Buy One' tricycles used by traders, and which became a familiar sight in every town and city.

A limited number of plattenwagen were constructed, sufficient for Wolfsburg use only, but this did not deter Ben Pon, always the entrepreneur, from trying to get the vehicles put into production for sale to Dutch companies. His efforts were thwarted, however, when the Dutch authorities wouldn't allow a road vehicle to be controlled by a driver seated at the rear of the machine. The sight of the plattenwagen persuaded Pon to pursue his idea of a commercial variant of the Beetle, and, taking the matter further, he met with Colonel Radclyffe, who was based at the Occupying Forces Trade and Industry Division at Minden to the west of Hannover, on 23rd April 1947. Taking his notebook from his pocket Pon roughly sketched his ideas for a 750kg enclosed vehicle with forward control. The driver was positioned at the very

Pon made regular visits to Wolfsburg, often meeting with Major Hirst. It was on one of those visits that he was fascinated by the sight of flat-bed trolleys used for conveying materials around Wolfsburg. The trolleys were devised by Major Hirst to replace fork-lift trucks which had been commandeered, and were built from Beetle components. The flat-bed runabouts, or plattenwagen, reminded Pon of the many pedal-powered delivery vehicles (bakfiets) that were used extensively throughout Holland, and it was this connection that gave the Dutchman the idea for a Beetle-based commercial vehicle. (Courtesy Volkswagen)

front; the engine and transmission were located beneath the floor at the rear, above the back wheels, and accessed via a top-hinged hatch in the rear panel; and the body was 'loaf'-shaped, with a sloping cab roof.

Happily, Pon's notebook with the now famous sketch and accompanying notes made at the time of his meeting with Colonel Radclyffe has survived. Although the meeting was just the beginning, and not an entirely promising one at that, the future of Ben Pon's box on wheels was, nevertheless, secure.

Ben Pon sketched his idea for a Beetle-based commercial vehicle in his notebook, the date 23rd April 1947 clearly visible. The rough sketch outlines a 750kg forward control vehicle with the engine positioned above the rear axle that closely anticipates the definitive design. Pon discussed his idea at length with Major Ivan Hirst who was supportive about the idea but lacked the resources to develop it further and put it into production. (Courtesy Volkswagen)

Chapter 2

Shaping the Transporter

With Wolfsburg working to the fullest capacity that the factory's limited resources allowed, Colonel Radclyffe could easily have dismissed Ben Pon's idea which would eventually emerge as Volkswagen's Type 2 model. Pon left the meeting with Radclyffe at Minden without receiving the approval he had hoped for, yet he was grateful that his proposal had not been entirely rejected.

Behind the scenes, Colonel Radclyffe was quite aware as to the benefits a vehicle such as Pon had envisaged would offer. Known to be cautious and not to commit himself or others to an arrangement that might ultimately not be as successful as had been first predicted, the Colonel told Pon that, as good as his idea was, it was impossible for him to sanction it owing to Wolfsburg's limited production and manpower resources. When Hirst received Radclyffe's deliberations about Pon's idea he was disappointed but not surprised at the decision, though had it been left to the Major he would almost certainly have given it the go-ahead.

Hirst, having already studied Pon's initiative at length, had come to appreciate that a commercial vehicle of the type proposed would not only be feasible to produce, it would also present itself as a much needed vehicle at a time when Germany was struggling to emerge from the ravages of war. The pragmatic Hirst let it be known to Pon that as soon as his endeavours to increase production at Wolfsburg were accepted and put into practice, the likelihood was that the Dutchman's idea would materialise.

There had been numerous problems at Wolfsburg during the early postwar period, not least of which were materials shortages, labour relations and there being little alternative at having to work in less than acceptable

Major Ivan Hirst referred Ben Pon's idea for the Transporter to Colonel Charles Radclyffe, his senior officer, who was based at Minden. Radclyffe, pictured here, was equally enthusiastic to get the vehicle into development, but declined to give it the go-ahead owing to limited resources and the manpower that would have been required. (Courtesy Volkswagen)

conditions owing to war damage. For Major Hirst there were constant worries about quality control, to the extent that vehicles were sometimes leaving the factory in a deplorable state; health and safety issues were forever provoking arguments about working practices, and all the more desperate were tensions between the British administrators and the German workforce.

In order to resolve at least a number of the problems a German trustee had been appointed at Wolfsburg in August 1946, a position commensurate to that of general manager, which was assigned to business lawyer Dr Hermann Münch. The arrangement mirrored the German model of company structuring, and with Münch's appointment it was hoped relationships between the workforce and British management would be significantly improved.

However sympathetic Dr Münch was to the regime at Wolfsburg, he lacked the technical expertise that was essential to his assignment; to the extent that he found himself being reprimanded by Hirst at increasingly frequent intervals. Clearly the situation could not be allowed to continue, and Radclyffe, having studied Hirst's report as to the situation decided that Münch needed a competent, capable and charismatic engineering aid to assist in overseeing the technical side of the factory's trusteeship. Whereas Münch lacked the personality to command discipline among the factory workforce, such a candidate for the appointment would adroitly demonstrate man management skills.

Given the task of finding a suitable nominee for the post, Hirst did not have to look far: recommended to him was Heinrich Nordhoff who had wide experience of Germany's motor industry having managed Opel's Brandenburg factory during the war. Nordhoff's motor industry career began at Munich when

When plans to hand over Wolfsburg to the German authorities were scheduled, changeover meant taking down signs installed by the British Occupying Forces and putting up new ones. One sign was left in place, however, and went unnoticed for some time. It now has a place within the Volkswagen museum. The changeover to German control signalled the go-ahead for Transporter development. (Courtesy Bill Wolf)

he joined BMW's design department, leaving there for Adam Opel's works at Rüsselsheim, which by then had become incorporated into the empire that was General Motors. Within a year or so, Nordhoff was promoted to head Opel's service organisation before being appointed a board member of Adam Opel AG. Because he'd been an executive of a factory supplying equipment for the German Forces, Nordhoff was, after the war, prevented from taking employment other than in a manual capacity. Never a collaborator, nor Nazi supporter or party member, work was, nevertheless, not forthcoming: he was, in effect, unemployed, and survived only through the generosity of family and friends.

Having made contact and invited him to Wolfsburg, Major Hirst was quick to realise that Heinrich Nordhoff (he was generally known as Heinz) possessed all the credentials and qualifications that the job at Volkswagen required.

There are, however, conflicting reports as to the business relationship between Hirst and Nordhoff; some suggesting that the two didn't agree, others, in fact, implying that there existed a strong rapport between the two. When interviewing the late Ivan Hirst, Ralph Richter recorded the Major's reminiscences of the occasion when the two men met, and it would seem absolutely clear that they had a high regard for each other. Nordhoff was a cold and calculating person, his strong personality having consequences in terms of his later working relationship with Hirst.

Nordhoff spent two days at Wolfsburg, during which time he toured the factory and got to know Major Hirst. When he was introduced to Hirst's wife Nordhoff made a good impression, and she confirmed her husband's belief that he was the ideal candidate for the job.

It was on the second day of

Nordhoff's tour of Wolfsburg that Hirst had some harmless fun at the candidate's expense by telling him he was not going to recommend him for the post, at which Nordhoff promptly prepared to leave. Hirst then qualified himself by saying that he was going to suggest that he take over Münch's job on his imminent retirement. Hirst then arranged for Nordhoff to go to Minden and meet Colonel Radclyffe who immediately agreed his suitability for the post.

Heinz Nordhoff was appointed general director at Wolfsburg on 7th November 1947, the appointment being effective from 1st January 1948. There was much antagonism on behalf of Dr Münch at Nordhoff's engagement, and within three weeks the former resigned his position. Within two years of Nordhoff's appointment at Wolfsburg the British Occupying Forces handed over Volkswagen to the Federal German Government, which, in turn, confirmed the general director's post as that of managing director.

The Transporter theme revived

During the period between 1st January 1948 and the British hand over of Volkswagen, Hirst and Nordhoff worked closely together, though not always harmoniously, owing to the latter's belief that he should have overall charge of company policy, including vehicle production, sales and marketing, and exports. Ironically, it was Hirst's enthusiasm for Nordhoff's appointment that was to signal a process that eventually led to the conclusion of the Major's term of office at Wolfsburg.

As part of Hirst's efforts to increase Volkswagen's engineering capacity, the Major had received permission to provide for additional drawing office personnel. In charge of the drawing office was Josef Kales who had endured a most demanding era in Volkswagen history

As part of the changeover of administration of Volkswagen, the position of general manager became available, the appointment bestowed upon Heinz Nordhoff as from 1st January 1948. Nordhoff, who began his motor industry career with BMW, and later worked at Opel, is pictured here in the early to mid-1960s at Wolfsburg with a consignment of Beetles. The relationship between Major Hirst and Nordhoff during the British handover of Volkswagen is said to have been difficult at times, but this did not prevent the latter from ensuring that Transporter development went ahead. Heinz Nordhoff died suddenly in 1968. (Courtesy Volkswagen)

with vastly inadequate resources, but at last the appointment of Alfred Häsner had given an opportunity to develop new ideas.

Having previously worked for the Zittau-based Phänomen company, a firm specialising in air-cooled commercial vehicles marketed postwar under the Robur name, Häsner was well versed in air-cooled engine technology. Nordhoff, with his Opel commercial vehicle background, sanctioned Häsner's appointment, understanding only too well the urgent need of producing a light goods vehicle which had the potential to sell in large numbers, and with Häsner's engagement the time was right to consider Ben Pon's idea for a box-on-wheels.

Throughout the initial period of expansion at Volkswagen, Pon maintained contact with Ivan Hirst and Colonel Radclyffe to ensure that his idea of a Beetle-based commercial vehicle was not forgotten. He also insisted that, following Nordhoff's arrival at Wolfsburg, the new general director was made aware of his proposal. The time for Pon's idea was certainly right: since the spring of 1947 the output of vehicles from Wolfsburg steadily increased from 1000 to a little under 5000 per month by the autumn of 1949. With greater productivity and improved manufacturing facilities, not to mention enhanced personnel resources, it was on Nordhoff's instruction that Alfred Häsner's first assignment at Wolfsburg

in the autumn of 1948 was to develop Ben Pon's idea.

On taking up his appointment at Wolfsburg, Häsner was immediately concerned that there was insufficient personnel at Wolfsburg with the expertise necessary to staff the design department, a matter that, for the time being at least, remained unaddressed. Nevertheless, on 20th November, and within a few weeks of taking up his appointment as Volkswagen's chief designer, Häsner was able to present Nordhoff with two design outlines; one having a flat front and side aspects along with a menacing roof overhang, the other a slightly raked and curved shape. The former design Nordhoff instantly rejected: the latter, which

Development of the Transporter commenced in the autumn of 1948, two designs being available by November, and a prototype model ready for testing the following March. The likeness of the definitive vehicle to that which Ben Pon had sketched is apparent. (Author's collection)

was all the more in keeping with Pon's initial sketch, he liked, and immediately authorised the production of prototype vehicles.

When Häsner submitted a scale model of the preferred design for wind tunnel testing, the results were unfavourable. Following experiments aimed at reducing the wind resistance coefficient from 0.75, it was discovered that by adopting a rounded and, therefore, more streamlined profile, the figure substantially dropped to 0.44, thus dictating a definitive styling.

Nordhoff was anxious about the spartan appearance of the cab interior, and, instead of the two seats that were proposed, suggested a modification to allow three people sitting abreast. The design department personnel were not impressed at what they viewed as interference by Nordhoff but eventually gave way to his seniority and introduced the modification once the vehicle was in production.

In design and engineering terms, the prospect of installing a box-like structure onto a Beetle platform complete with the standard Volkswagen 25hp air-cooled engine with the crash-type gearbox and torsion bar suspension as fitted to the saloon cars might now seem too simplistic. Yet this was how the design department approached this early stage in the Transporter's evolution.

Disaster

The first prototype Transporter was made ready for testing on 11th March 1949, just two days after it was submitted for Nordhoff's approval. Ivan Hirst later recalled the debacle that ensued, an affair that ultimately led to the termination of Häsner's employment at Wolfsburg.

In order to maintain a measure of secrecy surrounding the project it was decided to undertake testing of the prototype van at night. Less than

The, by now familiar, air-cooled Beetle engine powered the prototype Transporter. Though the engine proved completely adequate, sadly, the vehicle's platform was far from strong enough to take the Transporter's weight. After only a short test period the chassis collapsed, after which Heinz Nordhoff ordered the vehicle to be redesigned within the shortest possible time. (Author's collection)

a month after trials began it soon became evident that the stresses caused by the vehicle's body weight and its load capacity were too great for the Beetle chassis to withstand, and when the van was returned to the test department on 5th April it was a sorry sight. The chassis had collapsed at its centre section, causing the vehicle to be some six inches lower in height than it had been before it had embarked on its test programme.

When news of the prototype Transporter's apparent design fault reached Wolfsburg's engineers there was dismay and disbelief. The episode could easily have delayed the vehicle's development by a significant margin had it not been for Heinz Nordhoff's interjection and insistence that the Transporter be in production by the end of 1949. The pressure that Volkswagen's engineers were under to design a new

vehicle can only be imagined, and it is a measure of the strict timescale they were afforded that a completely revised model was ready for testing on the 19th May, the date chosen by Nordhoff to announce that production of the vehicle would commence on 1st December.

The notion of using the Beetle chassis, even in strengthened form, was abandoned in favour of devising a unitary arrangement with chassis and body welded together as a single unit on a subframe. The strength necessary to support the vehicle was addressed by the subframe's design, which consisted of two robust longitudinal rails and a series of crossmembers between the front and rear axles, together with outriggers, to provide further reinforcement. On the frame were welded steel floors in the cab and cargo areas, and to the base of the rear luggage section above the

The redesigned Transporter employed unitary construction, the ladder-type subframe comprising two robust longitudinal rails and a series of crossmembers. There was minimal difference in styling between the first and later prototype vehicles (pictured). (Courtesy Volkswagen)

engine compartment, all of which provided for an immensely rigid construction. There was a disadvantage, however, in that the additional strengthening resulted in increased vehicle weight, but this was far outweighed by the design's resilience to flexing.

Although having an entirely different chassis arrangement to that of the Beetle, the prototype Transporter shared its sibling's 94.5 inch (2400mm) wheelbase. Other dimensions, however, were significantly different to those of the saloon: the track was wider, by 2.7 inches (68.58mm) at the front and 4.3 inches (109.22mm) at the rear, and the overall length of 165 inches (4190mm) was greater by no more than 8 inches (203mm), which illustrates what a masterly exercise in styling this was, considering the vast amount of interior space the vehicle afforded.

There was minimal difference between the appearance of the first and second prototype vehicles. Both had split windscreens and sliding cab windows, features that were seen on production Transporters until 1967. The

characteristic vee at the vehicle's frontal centre point, plunging to just above the rudimentary bumper, was also evident, as was the now familiar VW roundel. Semaphore direction indicators were positioned aft of the door pillars, and provision of a single windscreen wiper in front of the driver illustrated the degree of economy employed by way of accessories. Vertical cooling louvres were positioned either side of the rear box section, but these were eventually replaced with horizontal types, the fins outwardly protruding and rearward facing.

Viewed from the rear, there was a strong resemblance between the prototype vehicles and those which entered production. There was no bumper, and the large top-hinged engine compartment cover (hence its 'barndoor' epithet), gave access to a commodious area which, as well as housing the running gear, accommodated the spare wheel. A large fuel filler was located on the rear offside corner of the vehicle, and the

rear-mounted central lamp served a dual purpose, illuminating the numberplate in addition to acting as a stop light.

Refinements over the original prototype included modifying the cab interior to afford greater space, improving the pedal arrangement, and providing better and more comfortable seating. Owing to the lack of a rear window, and the absence of rear access to the vehicle interior, of particular importance was the provision of twin, outward-opening side doors to facilitate loading and unloading the cargo area.

When the revised prototype Transporter underwent testing it was subjected to rigorous trials at Volkswagen's proving ground, as well as enduring thousands of kilometres over Germany's notoriously poor road surfaces. The vehicle's performance was closely monitored over some 7500 miles (12,000km), the encouraging results leading Heinz Nordhoff to sanction the building of further three prototypes, eight being constructed in total.

Expanding the theme

Having been instrumental in furthering Ben Pon's idea, Heinz Nordhoff kept the Dutchman involved throughout the entire development of the Transporter. Though Pon had initially envisaged the vehicle as being nothing other than a simple box van, he began to share Nordhoff's view that the basic design offered the potential for a range of body styles. There were numerous adaptations to which the concept could be applied, so that a basic cargo carrier might evolve as a pick-up truck, travelling shop, ambulance, fire tender or mobile police unit; even a camping car, though such coachwork would be contracted to specialist converters. An application which particularly excited Nordhoff was that of a minibus, which, in addition to carrying some luggage, could easily accommodate up to nine people in comfort while representing running costs lower than that of a normal service bus. Being convinced of the Transporter's potential success, therefore, Nordhoff arranged for demonstration vehicles, one a Microbus, to be made available to Volkswagen dealers for evaluation.

Intensive testing was responsible for a number of modifications that were applied to later prototype Transporters: a wiper was fitted to the passenger windscreen, and the heating and ventilation system improved; brakes were made more powerful, and the front suspension strengthened with modified shock absorbers and axle tubes. Cab doors were made lighter and more rigid, and the luggage space above the engine compartment was reconfigured to make it larger. An insignificant revision, perhaps, the external fuel filler was relocated to within the engine bay as a means of deterring thieves from siphoning petrol, which at the time in postwar Germany was a valuable commodity. The most significant problem trials had exposed was the

Following satisfactory testing, the Transporter theme was extended to include Microbus and Kombi variants in addition to the Panel van. The first-mentioned is shown here, complete with single windscreen wiper and one external mirror. (Author's collection, courtesy Volkswagen)

Transporter's sluggish performance, especially its lethargic acceleration. The Beetle's 1131cc engine was hardly adequate for a vehicle the size of the Transporter, especially when fully laden. As far as road holding and handling characteristics were concerned there was no reason for anxiety, the balance and weight distribution of the vehicle was virtually perfect owing to its forward control, central cargo area and rear engine and transmission layout. Of immense satisfaction to both Nordhoff and Pon, not to mention the prospective customer, was the vehicle's 162 cubic feet (4.59 cubic metres) load capacity, which was two-thirds of the vehicle's total volume. Moreover, the vehicle was capable of accommodating loads commensurate with its own weight. Overcoming the Transporter's lack of power could have been problematic and expensive to resolve had it not been

for Porsche's experience perfecting the Kübelwagen. By fitting reduction gears in the rear hubs, Volkswagen engineers successfully widened the Transporter's transmission ratio to appreciably improve acceleration, but at the expense of limiting the vehicle's top speed to 50mph (80kph).

Of the eight prototype vehicles that were built, six were panel vans. In addition to a Microbus, Nordhoff was keen to offer a vehicle capable of fulfilling a number of roles, and instructed the design department to devise a model having complete flexibility in terms of interior layout. The answer was the Kombi, a panel van with side windows and provision for seats that could be easily removed when conversion to a load carrier demanded.

With Nordhoff's influence, developing the Microbus became a huge priority within Volkswagen's

The Microbus interior was, at first, most austere. The left-hand image shows seats that are simply fitted to the floor, while that on the right depicts the front of the passenger compartment and the cab, the latter with minimal instrumentation. Note the bell pushes, one adjacent to the middle row of seats, the other on the cab bulkhead.
(Author's collection, courtesy Volkswagen)

design department. The prototype vehicle had similar styling treatment to that of the panel vans, and it was originally fitted with a single windscreen wiper, there also being a single external mirror which was located at high level on the thin front pillar. Finished in a two-tone colour arrangement, the bus had an attractive appearance, the three large side windows allowing for a light and airy interior. A door either side of the cab, and twin doors on the vehicle's near-side provided for easy entrance and exit for passengers.

The prototype Microbus was given an interior styling arrangement that was quite utilitarian: a division, from the floor to the bottom of the windows, separated the cab from the passenger accommodation, whilst the seats were typical of those found on commercial buses at the time. Grab handles located on the division and adjacent to the twin side doors facilitated passenger movement, and two bell pushes alerted the driver to stop as required. The cab, with its upright driving position, offered little in the way of luxury or comfort, and comprised the most minimal instrumentation located in a console positioned between the steering column and the front bulkhead. Expedient though the prototype vehicle was, the frugal instrumentation consisted of no more than a speedometer; even a fuel gauge was considered as being an unnecessary extravagance.

From prototype to production
The time between Alfred Häsner having produced his first design drawings for the Transporter and the unveiling of the definitive vehicle to journalists on 12th November 1949 (the date originally had been set for a week earlier, on 6th November) was a mere fifty-one weeks. By motor industry standards, then and now, developing a vehicle in such a short time is remarkable, especially when it's considered the degree of testing that is required to ensure design thoroughness.

Getting the prototype vehicles ready for their media launch proved problematic, and as early as late September Häsner was experiencing difficulties in getting the roofs manufactured to the correct profile. The roofs that had been prepared for experimental purposes had been crafted manually rather than formed by machine, and as a result were flat rather than curved. The required tension was missing, so that under test conditions they fluttered. Ultimately, the roofs, correctly tensioned, did arrive, though it was necessary to work around the clock to have them painted. By then it was 4th November, just two days before the planned launch, and Nordhoff was still insisting on specification changes, hence the need to defer the debut by a week.

Problematic, too, was deciding on a model name for the vehicle. Several names were considered but these were deemed unsuitable for a number of reasons: either they were inappropriate or were too similar to existing trademarks to be comfortably adopted. As much out of choice as desperation, Nordhoff conceded there really wasn't any need for a dedicated name other than the Volkswagen Type 2 Transporter.

News of the Transporter didn't reach subscribers to *The Autocar* until 9th December, by which time motoring journalist Gordon Wilkins had already bemoaned the evolution of the station wagon from a highly practical vehicle capable of seating up to nine passengers

By the time the Transporter went into production, the specification included two windscreen wipers but still only one external mirror. This early vehicle has been restored and, in the process, has been given an additional mirror along with discreet turn indicators in the interest of safety. (Courtesy Ken Cservenka)

Early Transporters lacked a rear window and had a large engine compartment hatch, hence them being known as 'barn door' models. Note also the large VW roundel at the rear. Rear windows were fitted from April 1951. (Courtesy Ken Cservenka)

and swallowing vast volumes of leisure impedimenta to something all the more stylish and car-like. Had he seen the Transporter before penning his piece, Wilkins might have chosen a different approach for his feature.

Motoring journalists invited to the Transporter's launch at Wolfsburg were genuinely enthusiastic towards its appearance and versatility. They might have been expecting a typical commercial vehicle with its cab above the engine and hardly impressive handling when empty and in wet weather or over poor road surfaces. Heinz Nordhoff made such a point when introducing the vehicle by assuring that it would not, like forward control British military vehicles serving in Germany, display horrendous handling characteristics with a propensity to leave the road in wet conditions. To further illustrate his point, Nordoff commented how one had only to look at the roadside trees in Germany's British Zone to see how well the British vehicles handled!

The invited audience was, therefore, delighted to see a purpose-built vehicle with an interior layout that allowed an uninterrupted flat cargo space between the front and rear axles. When describing the Transporter's development process, Nordhoff stressed that should any other design configuration have been considered to work to better advantage, then he would have had no hesitation in adopting it.

It was the Transporter's driving position and handling that was most impressive: quite unlike any other commercial vehicle, there was sophistication about the commanding driving position and passenger comfort, the lightness of steering, effortless gearchanging and easy application of the clutch and brake pedals. The vehicle's performance was appreciated, as was its fuel economy and attention to safety features, to the extent that even the frugal instrumentation could be forgiven.

The Transporter's media launch was the first step in the vehicle's production process. The following three

Though a single type of Transporter had initially been envisaged, a range of body styles was produced, some of which, including the Panel van and Kombi, are seen here under construction at Wolfsburg. (Courtesy Volkswagen)

months were given over to installing the necessary tooling at Wolfsburg, and it was not until February 1950 that the first vehicles, destined to selected customers for evaluation purposes, began leaving the production lines. A month later vehicles began arriving at Volkswagen dealerships to coincide with an appearance at the Geneva Motor Show held between 16-26th March. Three models, Panel van, Kombi and Microbus, were shown at Geneva, the Panel van being the first to enter production, the Kombi and Microbus being available from May and June, respectively.

The Transporter officially entered production on 10th May 1950 at the rate of ten vehicles per day, rising to 60 per day by the end of the year. Heinz

This view of a Kombi fitted with a rear window illustrates the large cargo area and the ease of loading afforded by the wide, side-hinged doors. Few vehicles could offer such facilities in the early fifties. (Courtesy Brian Screaton)

Nordhoff had every reason to be proud of Volkswagen's efforts, for 1950 was an auspicious year for the company, its 100,000th car produced since the re-establishment of vehicle manufacturing after the war left Wolfsburg in March. A ceremony to commemorate the event was attended by 10,000 Volkswagen employees, with the car raffled amongst the company workforce.

The unveiling of the Transporter

marked a change in Volkswagen's fortunes, and, as a manufacturer, the company was in a very different position than it had been when the British Occupying Forces had taken over administration after the war. Production at Wolfsburg had increased from a handful of cars in 1946 to more than 19,000 in 1948, increasing to 45,000 at the end of 1949. An upward trend accounted for a car leaving the production lines every three minutes, so that for 1950 production was estimated at 70,000 vehicles, building the Transporter having much to do with boosting these figures.

In his capacity as general director, Heinz Nordhoff oversaw a revision of production techniques that diminished the number of man-hours taken to build each vehicle: to produce a vehicle in 1947 had taken 180 man-hours, this figure reduced to 129 two years later. Fixed-price servicing and repair arrangements were introduced early in 1950, while a new marketing strategy, which decades later was widespread in the motor industry, promoted a wide range of consumer items, such as wallets, desk calendars, pens, pencils and cigarette cases bearing the manufacturer's emblem.

The first production Transporters

to leave Wolfsburg incorporated a small number of modifications compared to the pre-production model that had been shown to the media. The most significant of these was the relocation of the spare wheel, from its vertical position on the right-hand side of the engine compartment, to horizontally above the engine. The roof of the engine compartment remained to form the floor of a storage hatch capable of accommodating small objects, access to which was from inside the vehicle.

The Transporter was favourably priced when it went on sale, and, costing 5850DM, was only 150DM more expensive than the Beetle Deluxe saloon. It made, therefore, an affordable and attractive proposition for business users who were devoid of a purpose-built commercial vehicle that was compact in size yet capable of carrying significant loads. At that time in Germany reliance was largely on small utilitarian vehicles, often two-strokes, some built as three-wheelers, which enjoyed little in the way of sophistication or traction and roadholding abilities. In Britain, the best that the motor industry could offer was the Morris J-type van with its precarious handling, or Trojan's two-stroke 15cwt van; still two years away was the debut of Bedford's CA van – dubbed the 'roundsman's joy', along with the Morris LD forward control 1-ton delivery vehicle. In France, Citroën's corrugated H-Type van with its front-wheel drive and 2-litre engine derived from the Traction Avant was that nation's workhorse.

The first Transporters to be produced were available in a variety of colours, customers having a choice of Pearl or Medium Grey, Dove Blue, Chestnut Brown or Brown Beige. Vehicles were also specified in two-tone colour schemes: Brown Beige as an upper body colour and Light Beige for the lower body; additionally there was Chestnut Brown with Sealing Wax

This early barn door Kombi features the single external mirror, but note the auxiliary driving lamps and retrospective turn indicators. (Courtesy Ken Cservenka)

Pre-1955 Transporters (identified by the smooth cab roof, thus predating vehicles having a peaked roof above the windscreen) are rare. This Kombi, which looks smart in its white and grey two-tone colour scheme, is used to the full: note the roof rack complete with bicycle and camping gear, along with turn indicators fitted to the base of the bumpers. (Courtesy Ken Cservenka)

Red while Stone Grey was reserved for both upper and lower body colours. As time progressed, the range of colours widened, some specific to a particular model and period of production. Apart from a few exceptions wheels and bumpers were painted Silver White, and hubcaps were painted Light Grey, though Dove Blue coloured vehicles were supplied mainly with hubcaps painted Dove Grey. Microbus and De Luxe models were usually fitted with chrome hubcaps, a cost option often available to other vehicles.

Exports began as soon as production commenced, and, in 1950, vehicles were shipped to Austria, Belgium, Brazil, Denmark, Finland, Holland, Luxembourg, Portugal, Saar Territory, Sweden, Switzerland, Uruguay and the USA. The United Kingdom did not officially receive vehicles until 1953, when a single example entered the country, the figure rising to 786 the following year and 1054 in 1955. From two Transporters destined to the USA in 1950, 50 were delivered the following year, 93 in 1952 and 75 in 1953, numbers rising dramatically from then on with 827 in 1954 and 3189 in 1955.

For Volkswagen, and particularly Heinz Nordhoff, there was the distinct satisfaction that the Transporter had been developed in the main from within the company, in a very short timescale, and without the direct involvement of the Porsche studios. It was considered very much Volkswagen's own product and, as such, has proved to be among the most popular and successful commercial vehicles of all time.

There is much enthusiasm for early publicity brochures which depict the Transporter in the unique style of Reuters, the artist who so successfully depicted the vehicle with an often exaggerated technique. With the Reuters treatment, curves became all the more expressive, some appearing when they were clearly not evident on the actual model! Characters were made larger than life, and while many of the Transporter's features were made somewhat pretentious, the overall effect was typical of the advertising style of the period. Needless to say, such publicity material has become very collectable, and early examples of Transporter in original condition even more so.

Dating from 1955 this publicity item is typical of that issued by Volkswagen. Not only does the image suggest the seating capacity of the Kombi, it also clearly shows the amount of luggage that can be packed into the vehicle. (Author's collection)

wei Wagen in einem –

VW-Kombi

Chapter 3

Technology and evolution – the 'Splittie' era

Customers who bought the Transporter when it was announced were quick to appreciate the vehicle's many qualities, not least its distinctive shape and generous carrying capacity. There is no doubt that, at the time of its introduction, the Transporter offered a radical alternative to anything that was available in the small commercial vehicle market sector, thus giving it particular appeal. The Transporter did, however, reflect the austere nature of the immediate postwar period, to the extent that chromium-plated brightwork was limited to the headlamp and tail light bezels, along with door and engine compartment handles. Not even the single brake light was considered inadequate.

Though the Transporter went on sale in March 1950, a batch of pre-production vehicles was completed a

Before the Transporter went into production a series of vehicles were built and supplied to selected customers for evaluation. This pre-production example survives in Volkswagen's museum. (Courtesy Keith Hocking)

One of the first modifications made to the Transporter was the addition of a rear window. Compare the window size of the vehicle nearest the camera with that on its left.
(Author's collection)

month before, with examples delivered to specially selected, potentially major customers for evaluation and feedback purposes. It's known that some of these pre-production Bullis were returned to Wolfsburg following their trial period, but the fate of others is unknown. Of those that were delivered back to the factory some were used

Volkswagen technology is illustrated with this cutaway diagram, the key as follows: 1, sun visor; 2, parcel tray; 3, defrost vents; 4, brake wheel cylinder; 5, telescopic shock absorber; 6, torsion bars; 7, ventilator; 8, loading compartment lamp; 9, gearbox; 10, flexible heater pipe; 11, rear axle; 12, spur reduction gearing; 13, fuel tank; 14, fuel tank filler; 15, oil bath air cleaner; 16, distributor; 17, fuel pump; 18, carburettor; 19, generator; 20, battery; 21, rear door. (Author's collection, courtesy Volkswagen)

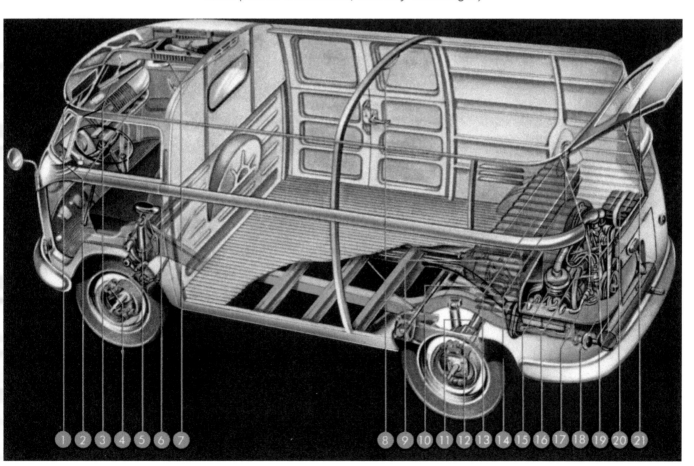

for deliveries within Wolfsburg, and one, thought to be chassis no 10, was saved from destruction and, having undergone complete restoration, was displayed at the Wolfsburg Museum.

The Ben Pon Volkswagen dealership was among the first to receive examples of the Transporter, and the agency was responsible for exporting two early production vehicles to the USA.

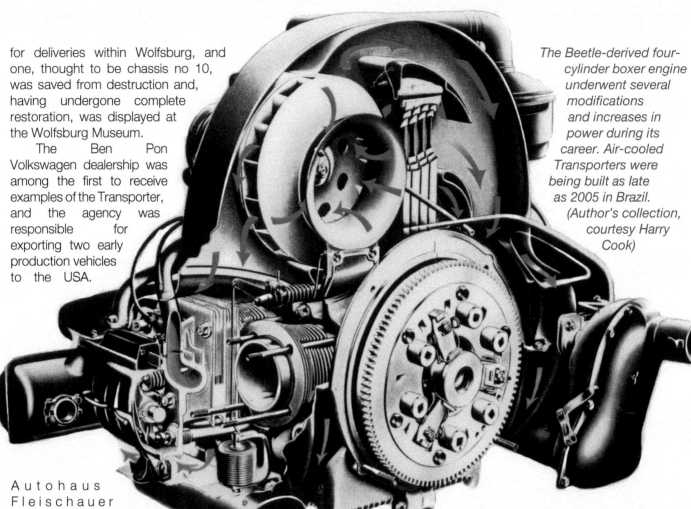

The Beetle-derived four-cylinder boxer engine underwent several modifications and increases in power during its career. Air-cooled Transporters were being built as late as 2005 in Brazil. (Author's collection, courtesy Harry Cook)

Autohaus Fleischauer of Cologne also received examples from the initial production run, the dealer selling a vehicle to the 4711 Perfume company which, incidentally, had the vehicle decorated with the firm's corporate logo and colour, thus setting a popular trend. At the end of 1950, Volkswagen's order books had swollen to 10,000 vehicles, sufficient to satisfy the 1951 production quota.

It was not until April 1951, a year after deliveries had begun, that Volkswagen's Type 2, the Transporter's official designation, was given a rear window, a modification that was universally welcomed. Before then, vehicles were adorned with a large VW emblem on the upper section of the rear panel. With 100,000 Beetles having been sold at the time

of the Transporter's introduction, and with reassuring demand for the Bulli, potential customers were secure in the knowledge that it was designed and built using proven technology. Even the familiar sound of the Transporter's air-cooled flat-four engine prompted confidence and trust, and there wasn't a garage in the whole of Germany that was not fully acquainted with Volkswagen engineering.

It was the Transporter's construction, with its integral chassis built in unit with the body, that was the outstanding feature, technology at the time, whilst not uncommon in motorcar practice was all the more exceptional in

respect of commercial vehicle design. This explains why Volkswagen likened the Transporter's construction to the principles of the aero industry: at the time of the vehicle's introduction, anything having a lightweight structure was so compared.

Beetle technology influenced the Transporter's independent front and rear suspension which conformed to classic Porsche engineering. Contemporary publicity material stressed that the suspension, which had been perfected as a result of having been tested on the Kübelwagen, was maintenance-free. Trailing arms were bolted to the leading hubs and were attached to transversely-mounted torsion bars encased in two cylindrical tubes placed one on top of the other. At the rear, the torsion bars were again fitted transversely, but within a single case, and were attached to trailing arms positioned ahead of the gearbox. In both instances, shock absorbers were fitted as an integral part of the suspension system, and were fitted as part of the axle assembly. The design of the Transporter's rear swing-axle system could be said to induce the dreaded characteristic that would allow difficult handling whilst cornering at high speed – a trait known as 'wheel tuck-under' – but this is a feature few Transporter owners have experienced unless driving with too much verve!

The steering mechanism followed Beetle practice by comprising a transverse link and unequal length track rods with the steering box, of the worm and nut type, attached firmly to the tube encasing the upper torsion bars. King and link pins connected the steering gear to the front hubs.

All-round Lockheed hydraulic braking was utilised from the outset of production, whereas the Beetle saloon had to wait until the spring of 1950 for what was, essentially, a modification from the original cable-operated brakes (and even then hydraulic braking was only applied to cabriolets and export models). The Transporter's 9.06in (230mm) drum brakes were single circuit, and conventionally operated, with two leading shoes on the front wheels, and a leading and trailing shoe on each of the rear wheels. The mechanical parking brake was also of a straightforward design, the long, floor-mounted lever operating the rear drums.

The engine and transmission were pure Beetle in their design, the 1131cc air-cooled flat-four developing 25bhp at 3300rpm. Its success was derived from a fundamental aim towards longevity, and, as such, the engine was designed to be under-stressed. The two-piece magnesium-alloy crankcase, as well as featuring cast-iron cylinders that were finned on the outside to aid cooling and reduce weight, also benefited from Mahle aluminium flat-topped pistons and forged connecting rods, while the 4-bearing, forged-steel crankshaft,

In addition to cooling air being ducted through vents in the roof, the front windows of a Bulli open to allow for greater ventilation. Opening windscreens often featured on cars of the 1930s and the immediate postwar era.
(Courtesy Ken Cservenka)

with the camshaft driven directly from it, operated entirely within the crankcase.

In common with many air-cooled engines, that of the Transporter incorporated an oil-cooler. This took the form of a large, vertically-mounted fan bolted to the top of the crankcase and driven by the dynamo, itself belt driven via a pulley on the crankshaft, which forced air around the unit through metal ducting. Cooling air was drawn in through the louvres on either side of the Transporter at the rear.

Air which was forced over the engine to cool it, was also used to heat the cabin area, but like all other air-cooled Volkswagens, the system only worked efficiently while the engine remained clean and well-maintained. Any contamination from oil build-up around the engine would almost certainly result in fumes permeating the cabin. To allow the passage of warm air into the cabin, a control knob was positioned within the cab, adjacent to the floor-mounted choke button; when not required, the air was expelled into the atmosphere, there being a safety mechanism to obviate hot air re-entering the engine compartment and being the cause of overheating. To ventilate the cabin, cool air was channelled through a roof-mounted duct, the Transporter at the time being the only vehicle to employ such a system. Needless to say, integral heating and ventilation was a luxury in an era when only the most prestigious cars, and certainly not commercial vehicles, employed such desirable features.

There was considered no need for the engine to have a separate oil filter, as the means of filtration for its 4.5 pint (2.56 litres) oil capacity was a rudimentary removable gauze filter. Neither was there a separate sump, the oil being contained at the base of the crankcase. The oil pump was camshaft driven and positioned at the rear of the crankcase, the lubricant being dispersed throughout the engine via apertures drilled in the crankshaft.

The design of air filtration was exclusive to the Transporter, and was mounted alongside the engine, unlike the Beetle which had its air filter installed above the engine. The same arrangement was adopted for the Karmann Ghia coupé and convertible models when they were introduced in 1955.

The faithful 'crash' type 4-speed gearbox was also derived from the

Early Transporters relied upon six-volt electrics and, for the first ten years, were fitted with semaphore signalling. The owner of this vehicle has fitted amber flashers for safety reasons and has discreetly placed them within the headlamp cowlings. Note also the alloy wheels.
(Author's collection)

Beetle and comprised a two-piece light alloy unit with the starter motor positioned on the top of the right-hand side. The cable-operated, single dry-plate clutch was common to the Beetle, and the final drive was through a spiral-bevel gear to swinging half-axles and secondary spur reduction gear in the rear hubs. Given the long linkage from the forward control position to the gearbox, gear changing was unexpectedly smooth, positive, and rapid, characteristics that were noted in early road test reports.

The 6-volt electrical system was in keeping with European vehicle design at the time. Six volts rather than twelve did have its disadvantages, especially for the headlamps which often emitted no more light than a glow-worm, and when there was much demand on the battery. An identifying feature of early Transporters is the absence of flashing direction indicators which did not become available until 1960. For the first ten years, therefore, semaphores located in the pillars aft of the cab doors were fitted, and, while such a device was commonplace on many other vehicles they, nevertheless, presented a potential hazard as they were often not easily discernible.

The early Transporters were provided with the most basic of instrumentation, comprising a speedometer calibrated to a maximum of 50mph (80kph) and warning indicators for oil pressure, dynamo output, main headlamp beam, and direction semaphores. A fuel gauge wasn't even considered necessary, but in the event of a low fuel situation it was possible to release the reserve 5 litres (1.1 gallon) of petrol into the 8.75 gallon (40 litres) tank. The cab

The Transporter range was expanded in May 1950 by the introduction of the Kombi, an early example of which is pictured here.
(Courtesy Ken Cservenka)

interior was starkly utilitarian, there being no covering trim on the bare metal other than compressed paper material up to window height and rubber matting covering the floor. There were compensations, however: electrical lighting was fitted to the cab and cargo areas, and, together with fresh air ventilation circulated via roof ducts, swivelling quarter lights and sliding cab windows, added to the level of comfort.

As might be expected of a vehicle the size of the Transporter, performance from the 1131cc engine was anything but spirited. When fully laden it would take at least 15-16 seconds to reach 30mph (48kph) from standing, and double the time to achieve 50mph (80kph). Such lethargy was academic when traversing difficult terrain which called for great tenacity: the vehicle made little fuss when starting on steep hills fully laden, though a penalty was increased fuel consumption, often no better than 20mpg (14 litres/100km).

Fuel consumption under normal driving conditions was more respectable, it being possible to achieve between 25-30mpg (11.5-10 litres/100km) fully laden. When British Volkswagen agent C&H Blundell undertook to drive the length and breadth of the country in

a mere 3½ days travelling 2118 miles (3389km), petrol consumption of the Microbus employed for the purpose averaged 27mpg (10.5 litres/100km). This was particularly remarkable since the vehicle carried eight people and their luggage and the engine was only turned off once – for no more than 10 minutes – apart from refuelling and scheduled stops. The trial, despite its success in proving the Bulli's mechanical reliability, was not without its drawbacks: passengers seated at the rear of the bus found the heat from the engine uncomfortable, and while those seated at the front enjoyed a more temperate climate, with sufficient ventilation, those in the middle were denied both warmth and ventilation!

Expanding the model range
The introduction of the Kombi in May 1950 and the Microbus a month later broadened the Transporter model range. The Kombi, which in effect was a panel van with three rectangular windows on each side, brought a new appearance to the Transporter, making it look more like a station wagon than a commercial vehicle. Its arrival won universal appeal for its dual role capability; from freight mover to people carrier. The interior design of the Kombi facilitated the

The Microbus appeared a month after the Kombi to further extend the Transporter catalogue. Such vehicles were used for school transport, airport services and private hire. (Courtesy Ken Cservenka)

conversion, allowing seating in the central area of the vehicle to be fitted or removed almost instantly, thus it was possible to accommodate three people in the cab with a further three at the rear whilst leaving sufficient space for a vast amount of freight or baggage. The Kombi's rear seating was essentially austere insomuch that the tubular steel frames were simply furnished with somewhat uninviting vinyl material, each seat being secured to the floor with butterfly type fasteners to allow for quick and effortless removal and installation.

Next to appear was the Samba Bus, a more elaborate, better equipped and more comfortable vehicle than the standard Microbus,

The Samba Bus was introduced in April 1951 to become the flagship Transporter. This Volkswagen publicity image depicts just one of the many roles undertaken by Samba Buses. (Courtesy Volkswagen)

which was introduced at the Frankfurt International Automobile Exhibition in April 1951. Such was the sophistication of the Samba Bus, with its vast glazed area, that it was marketed as the Transporter flagship. Eighteen months later, the Pick-up made its debut in the autumn of 1952, this appealing to tradesmen, builders, horticulturists and forestry workers whose prime need was for a highly practical utility vehicle rather than one offering comfort. These and other variants underwent a variety of modifications, which are discussed in greater depth in the next chapter.

Production changes

Styling modifications, including the addition of a rear window in April 1951, and a rear bumper in March 1953, were among the first specification changes to be applied to the Transporter. The latter date coincided with initial modifications to the vehicle's mechanical specification when criticisms surrounding the 'crash' gearbox led Vokswagen to introduce synchromesh on second, third and top ratios. There had been nothing wrong with the earlier gearbox itself, which, incidentally, was fitted to the Porsche 356 until 1952, the problem being that many drivers found it difficult to successfully master the art of double-declutching.

A larger and more powerful engine was introduced at the end of 1953 in readiness for the 1954 model year, by which time vehicles were being built with right-hand drive, those models enjoying instant success when made available in the UK. The superb pulling power of the 25bhp 1131cc engine meant that owners had a tendency to overload their vehicles, often by significant margins, and therefore the arrival of a 30bhp engine was met with enthusiasm, if not relief.

Whilst hardly significant, the additional 5bhp and 61cc, achieved by raising the compression ratio

A landmark in Transporter history. Heinz Nordhoff presents the 100,000th vehicle to company employees on 9th October 1954. (Courtesy Volkswagen)

from 5.8:1 to 6.1:1, increasing valve diameter from 28.6mm to 30mm, widening the bore size from 75mm to 77mm and fitment of a distributor with vacuum advance mechanism, afforded better acceleration and improved overall performance. The result of the modest gain in power was a top speed of 60mph (96kph) compared to 56mph (90kph) though it took 75 seconds to get there. The main advantages were to be found at the lower end of the speed range, it taking 9.6 seconds to make 30mph (48kph) from standing, and under 17 seconds to reach 40mph (64kph).

The first road test of a right-hand drive Transporter appeared in the 2nd April 1954 edition of *Commercial Motor*. In presenting a highly favourable report, journalist and vehicle tester Laurence J Cotton was clearly impressed by the Transporter's performance when he subjected the vehicle (registration OLD 45) loaned by VW Motors of London to a series of tests carried out over one day and accounting to more than 200 miles. Cotton chose routes that afforded a wide range of driving conditions,

from the congestion of Central London and the City to the rural byways of Surrey. Throughout the tests the fully laden Transporter showed a readiness to easily cope with every situation, including a willingness (albeit with some clutch abuse) to stop and start on the 1 in 4.3 gradient of Succombs Hill, a favourite venue and proving ground for motoring journalists keen to put all types of motor vehicles to the severest of tests.

Further modifications throughout 1954 included an improvement to cab seating and the effectiveness of the heater, and, in the interest of easier operation, a combined ignition and starter switch replaced separate controls. The most significant event of 1954, however, was the construction of the 100,000th Transporter which left Wolfsburg on 9th October. The auspicious occasion was seized upon by Heinz Nordhoff who presided over a ceremony which saw the vehicle, suitably decorated with a garland of flowers, leave the assembly line accompanied by cheering of factory personnel.

Significant styling and mechanical modifications were introduced in the spring of 1955. One of the changes was to adopt a peak above the split windscreen to conceal twin grilles for improved ventilation. This illustration, which appeared on the cover of the 1955 catalogue, depicts the Transporter's frontal styling in the fashion of artwork attributed to Reuters, the artist responsible for much of Volkswagen's publicity material. (Author's collection)

Major styling and mechanical changes were implemented in March 1955, a date that is significant insomuch that fundamental design revisions at Volkswagen previously coincided with the factory's annual end-of-summer shutdown. Now a rarity, pre-1955 Transporters are identified by their cab roof design which is smooth in appearance and without the familiar peak above the windscreen. The restyling which brought about the distinctive overhang above the split windscreen enabled the concealment of twin grilles beneath the peak that were instrumental in providing for a

much improved heating and ventilation system. The modification allowed the intake of fresh air through the vents to be directed to a distribution box located at the underside of the cab roof panel, from which the rate of airflow could be mechanically controlled. At the same time, but not quite so obvious, were important alterations to the vehicle's rear styling which resulted in the engine compartment hatch being made noticeably smaller, and above it an opening tailgate to give access to the Transporter's interior. Both the latter modifications meant that the Transporter became more representative of a

station wagon, thus making it an even more useful vehicle.

Provision of a tailgate was made possible through experience in the design and development of two previously introduced variants of the Transporter: the Samba Bus and the Pick-up. Developing the Pick-up had meant adoption of a lower platform line to facilitate easier loading and unloading of freight, without inhibiting engine access for maintenance purposes, and in achieving this Volkswagen engineers allowed for an under-deck cargo hold, and relocation of the fuel tank above the gearbox, and the spare wheel behind

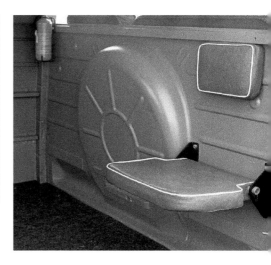

Other modifications introduced in 1955 concerned the Transporter's rear styling. By making the engine compartment hatch smaller it was possible to devise an opening tailgate, as depicted in this brochure illustration. Note the outward-facing cooling louvres. (Author's collection)

For 1955 the spare wheel was moved from the engine compartment to behind the driver's seat, as seen on this Panel Van. (Courtesy Ken Cservenka)

A new design of facia was adopted post-1955. Now a full-width affair, it more resembled that fitted to the Samba Bus. The styling changes are depicted in these brochure illustrations. (Author's collection)

vehicle's specification; additionally the petrol filler tube was repositioned to the right-hand side of the vehicle due to the relocation of the fuel tank, provision of the external flap obviating the need to open the engine compartment when refuelling. Measures to enhance the

vehicle's handling and ride resulted in the fitting of hydraulic shock absorbers, and at the same time smaller diameter wheels, 15 inch size (381mm), replaced the original 16 inch (406mm) type. Not least, the austere dashboard gave way to an altogether more attractive and full-width design that was similar to that fitted to the Samba Bus, and generally the vehicle interior was given

the driver's seat. The Samba Bus also featured a tailgate, a welcome facility when loading passengers' luggage onto the deck above the engine compartment.

The design changes to post-March 1955 Transporters also included strengthening the chassis, a requirement owing to ongoing improvements to the

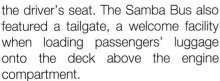

The revised facia as seen on a post-1955 vehicle. (Author's collection)

a make-over so as to be all the more aesthetically pleasing and comfortable.

A new factory

The rise in popularity of Volkswagens gave the motoring Press much to speculate on during the early to mid-1950s. The phenomenal increase in sales of the German vehicle was noted in 1952 when an editorial in *The Autocar* debated the state of the British motor industry compared to what was happening overseas. A sense of alarm prevailed, especially as many British car makers were unable to maintain intended production levels as a consequence of shortages in the supply of steel. Volkswagen, nevertheless, was exporting a third of all production, and vehicles were sold in 28 countries. In excess of a million Volkswagens had been built by the end of 1955, and,

incredibly, a quarter of the total output was produced in that year alone. News of Volkswagen's success contradicted Laurence Pomeroy's prediction of 1939 when *The Motor's* technical editor wrote of the German firm "so far as the British market is concerned, our manufacturers may, I think, sleep quietly in their beds!"

Though Wolfsburg had a capacity to construct more than a quarter of a million vehicles annually, which in time it did, there was evidence of some strain caused by Volkswagen's overwhelming success. With output of the Transporter running at between 40,000 and 50,000 units annually by the mid-1950s, and which was anticipated to rise significantly, the decision was taken to transfer production to a purpose-built plant before serious overloading of the factory occurred.

At Heinz Nordhoff's instigation, the new factory, which was equipped with the latest technology and production methods the motor industry could offer, was built at Stöcken on the outskirts of Hanover, some 75 kilometres from Wolfsburg. Designed and constructed by way of diversifying vehicle production, the factory was operational in just 14 months from the time Nordhoff approved its construction. Achievement of such a tight schedule was the responsibility of Otto Hoehne who was appointed Heinz Nordhoff's personal assistant in 1954. Hoehne was experienced when it came to establishing efficient working practices since it had been his task to operate Volkswagen's 'slave' factory at Brunswick, close to Wolfsburg, from its creation in 1938, its purpose being to serve the main works with its day-to-day requirements and materials.

Owing to over-capacity at Wolfsburg, Transporter production moved to a purpose-built factory at Hanover. Production of Transporters took place in a modern environment. (Courtesy Brian Screaton/Volkswagen)

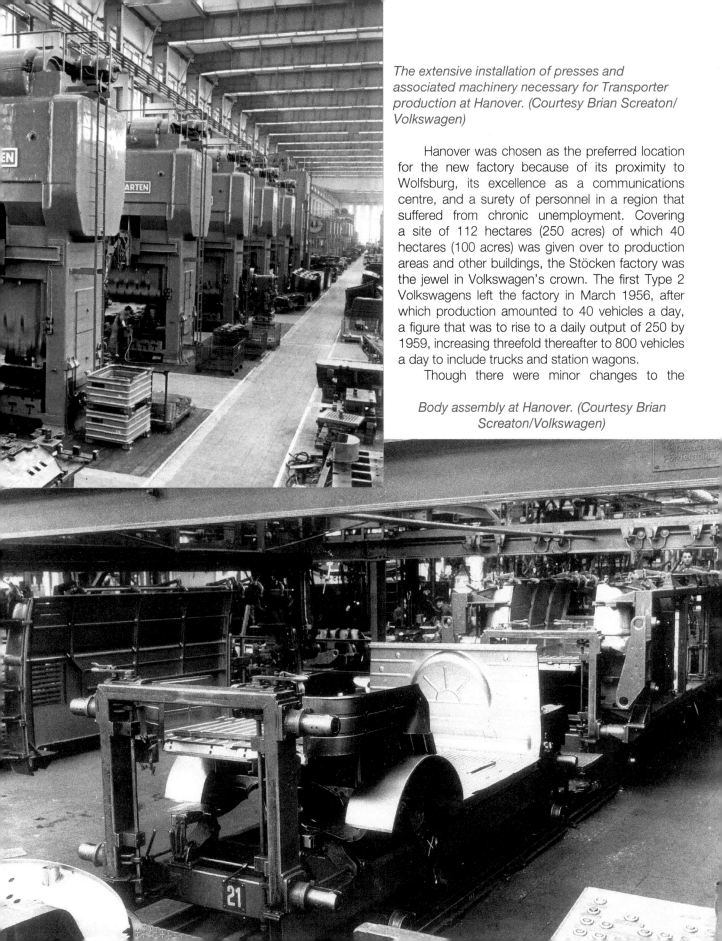

The extensive installation of presses and associated machinery necessary for Transporter production at Hanover. (Courtesy Brian Screaton/ Volkswagen)

Hanover was chosen as the preferred location for the new factory because of its proximity to Wolfsburg, its excellence as a communications centre, and a surety of personnel in a region that suffered from chronic unemployment. Covering a site of 112 hectares (250 acres) of which 40 hectares (100 acres) was given over to production areas and other buildings, the Stöcken factory was the jewel in Volkswagen's crown. The first Type 2 Volkswagens left the factory in March 1956, after which production amounted to 40 vehicles a day, a figure that was to rise to a daily output of 250 by 1959, increasing threefold thereafter to 800 vehicles a day to include trucks and station wagons.

Though there were minor changes to the

Body assembly at Hanover. (Courtesy Brian Screaton/Volkswagen)

Surface treatment of a bare body within the Hanover works. (Courtesy Brian Screaton/ Volkswagen)

Modern manufacturing techniques installed at Hanover included automatic spray painting; this picture shows the primer being applied. (Courtesy Brian Screaton/Volkswagen)

Transporter's specification, including some cosmetic revisions, it was not until May 1959 that further significant modifications were introduced. Vehicles destined to the United States were fitted with redesigned bumpers that incorporated taller overriders, together with an upper bar running almost the width of the main blade, features that were shared with the Beetle Cabriolet and the Karmann Ghia variants. Vehicles intended for other markets also received modified bumpers which were of a heavy duty type and larger overall.

American specification bumpers have become a desirable add-on feature with British and European Transporter enthusiasts. Another modification was the incorporation of brake or stop lamps to the rear light assemblies, thus, for safety reasons, making obsolete the single stop lamp in the centre of rear panel.

The most important modification concerned the engine and transmission:

replacing the 30bhp engine, an entirely new 34bhp unit allowed for better acceleration, though the top speed of the vehicle remained essentially the same as before. The capacity of the engine was unaltered at 1192cc, although there were design changes which affected parts interchangeability. In addition to revising the compression ratio, changes were made to the crankshaft and dynamo pulleys by

In May 1959, vehicles destined for the USA were fitted with modified bumpers, as shown on this high roof Panel Van dating from 1963. This type of bumper design was also employed on American specification Beetle Cabriolets, and has since become a fashion accessory for Volkswagen enthusiasts. (Courtesy Ken Cservenka)

reducing the size of the former and increasing that of the latter, the effect being a reduction in the cooling fan speed and making the unit less noisy.

The construction of the engine was different to that which it replaced. The crankcase was made stronger with the fitment of more rugged studs and bolts, and a redesigned crankshaft with larger bearings proved more durable. Improved cooling was achieved by increasing the amount of space between the cylinders, and the cylinder heads were fitted with wedge-shaped combustion chambers that incorporated valve gear positioned at an angle. Tappet clearances were altered from 0.004in to 0.008in, a detachable dynamo pedestal replaced one that was cast into the crankcase, and a fuel pump with a modified drive mechanism was fitted. The new engine was installed in the Transporter ahead of it being universally fitted to the Beetle saloon and other variants from July 1960.

The gearbox was also replaced with one having synchromesh on all forward ratios and an entirely new casing – a single piece unit instead of two separate halves – so that it was more representative of the design fitted to the Porsche 356. A feature of the new gearbox was that it was easier to maintain than the type it replaced: detachable side plates facilitated changing driveshafts without the need to dismantle the whole assembly, which meant benefits to garage personnel in respect of time employed, and to the customer regarding lower labour charges.

A new decade

The success and popularity of the Transporter can be judged by sales amounting to well in excess of half a million vehicles by 1960. By far the most popular vehicle in the range was the Panel Van, which accounted for some 243,000 examples. This was followed by the Kombi, of which more than 150,000 were delivered, and the Bus version, which was almost as popular at a little under 150,000 units. During the ten year period of production, slightly fewer than 130,000 Pick-ups were sold, representing approximately 19 per cent of the Transporter market. Out of a total of some 678,000 Transporters, a small quantity, approximately 6000 (1 per cent), accounted for specially adapted models such as ambulances, fire tenders and police vehicles.

Despite the modifications that had been continually introduced, the Transporter nevertheless displayed a measure of antiquity. Semaphore signals reigned over flashing indicators, tail lamps were arguably ineffective owing to their limited glow, and the electrics remained reliant on the 6-volt system. Semaphores were abandoned in 1960, their place taken by small, bullet-shaped flashing indicators at the front, neatly positioned above the headlamps, and combined stop and direction lamps at the rear. In common with many vehicles at the time, the rear flashers were combined with the stop indicators and, therefore, not equipped with amber lenses, a feature not introduced until 1962. Other improvements were to

August 1961, 300,000 Transporters left the Stöcken factory. It was also within that time that the millionth Transporter was constructed, an event that coincided with Volkswagen building its 5 millionth vehicle. Heinz Nordhoff again seized upon these landmark occasions, which placed Volkswagen as the world's third largest producer of motor vehicles after General Motors and Ford, and as Germany's leading industrial manufacturer, for publicity purposes.

More power from a new engine

The Transporter's performance was enhanced in 1963 when a larger and more powerful air-cooled, flat-four

include the adoption of sealed beam headlamps and the provision of a fuel gauge, the latter being a long awaited feature. Safety measures included padding to facia surfaces, and the fitting of grab handles.

During the period between the beginning of 1960 and the end of

This Volkswagen publicity photograph shows the flashing indicators. It was 1962 before separate rear flashers were fitted; before then they were incorporated within the brake light assembly. (Courtesy Volkswagen)

Cooling louvres were modified so that from 1963 they faced inwards instead of outwards, for safety reasons, as depicted on this pristine Panel Van. (Courtesy Ken Cservenka)

From 1963, the bullet-shape front indicators were replaced by larger disc (fish-eye) lenses, as seen on this Panel Van. Whilst the modification was adopted for safety reasons, not all enthusiasts approved of the styling. (Courtesy Ken Cservenka)

engine, with a capacity of 1493cc and
output of 42bhp, was introduced (not
across the range but as an option to the
existing type). The engine itself was not
entirely new as it had been introduced
two years earlier to power an all-new
saloon, the Type 3, which had at one
time been intended to supersede the
Beetle. As it happened the Type 3
saloon's life expectancy proved not to
be as long as anticipated, and it was
the Beetle, with its classic shape, that
demonstrated itself as being all the
more popular and durable.

For many customers the option of

*A wider tailgate was fitted from
1963, as shown on this Kombi. To
facilitate opening the heavier door,
self-supporting torsional struts were
fitted. (Courtesy Ken Cservenka)*

A late modification to the Splittie was the option of sliding doors instead of the side-hinged type which could prove hazardous when operated with heavy traffic around. (Volkswagen publicity material, author's collection)

the larger engine was welcomed: not only did it afford a higher maximum speed, its increased torque made for improved overall performance. The smaller 1200cc engine remained available to those customers less inclined towards the benefits the larger 1500cc engine presented, but only for two years, by which time demand for the lesser powered vehicle had almost completely evaporated.

The 1500 engine displayed a number of design modifications. Because it had been engineered for the Type 3 saloon, with its low-profile body styling and 'notch-back' engine compartment, the engine was of a flatter shape, and incorporated a redesigned cooling fan that was smaller in diameter to the previous type, and which was fitted to the rear of the

crankcase. Despite the fan's reduced diameter it, nevertheless, succeeded in providing for increased airflow. The height of the engine, a mere 16 inches (407mm), was a masterpiece of design, and had been achieved by constructing it around an entirely new 4-bearing crankshaft. There had been no need to redesign the crankcase as such, merely to modify the existing 1200 unit. In addition to being specified for the Bulli, the new engine was also fitted to the Karmann Ghia models.

Though benefiting from an extra 8bhp, the performance of the Transporter was not transformed to a miraculous degree. The larger engine did, however, allow the Bulli to be designated as having a one-ton payload, whereas the 1200 remained as a three-quarter ton payload model,

and, moreover, the additional power was sufficient to warrant the fitting of a governing device to restrict top and cruising speed to 65mph (104kph) after the vehicle's maximum speed was discovered to be around 75mph (120kph). Volkswagen engineers had specified the speed restriction for two reasons: to prevent over-revving of the engine; and to ensure against loss of stability when cornering. Experience has shown that many owners decided to remove the governing device despite the manufacturer's concern regarding the vehicle's 9.4 inches (239mm) ground clearance, its 76.4 inches (1941mm) overall height, and ample top speed.

Extra power meant that the one-ton Transporter was equipped with larger and more efficient braking, the lining area being increased by 22 per cent compared with the 1200 three-quarter ton model. There were other specification modifications: final drive ratio was altered from 5.73:1 to 5.21:1, top gear being essentially an overdrive was 0.82:1 while final drive was actually accomplished by the spur reduction gears on the rear wheels. There was a need to uprate the suspension, making it stiffer in order to achieve improved handling and a more compliant ride.

Other specification changes introduced during 1963 included adoption of even smaller wheels, reduced in diameter from 15 inches (381mm) to 14 inches (356mm), fitment of less expensive painted steel hubcaps on all models except for the more prestigious types, for example, the Microbus, which continued to receive chromium plated designs. In what can only be deemed as penny-pinching tactics, hubcaps no longer had the VW emblem painted in a contrasting colour. Mechanical changes to specification consisted of the oil bath type air filter relocated from the left- to the right-hand side of the engine compartment, and, in May 1964, fitment of a new type of Solex carburettor complete with improved automatic choke.

A series of safety measures were introduced so that after 1963 engine cooling louvres faced inwards rather than outwards, supposedly to prevent injury or damage in the event of an accident, and, likewise, door handles were changed from the pull-type to push-button design. Direction indicators were redesigned so that amber flashers showed at the front of the vehicle, and at the same time the bullet-shaped housings were abandoned in favour of larger and more visible disc type lenses (also referred to as fish eye lenses).

Styling issues were also paramount insomuch that the rear window was enlarged in size to afford better rearward visibility, a move coinciding with the fitment of a wider tailgate. The increased weight of the tailgate meant that its sliding stays were replaced by self-supporting torsional struts, and the familiar T-handle was superseded by a push-button device which, within two years, was modified to incorporate a protective finger shield as a means of aiding its operation, a modification that was applied to cab doors at the end of 1963. The side-hinged cargo doors, always a menace when opening and closing when there was heavy traffic, were at last viewed as being hazardous and were substituted by sliding doors. A whole variety of door arrangements could be specified to cater for differing usage and body styles but, generally, right-hand drive vehicles were fitted with doors on the left-hand side (pavement) and vice-versa; though it was possible, of course, to specify sliding doors on both sides. There were changes to the cab interior: the driver's seat was now adjustable, and the passenger bench seat could be folded forward to allow for additional cargo capacity.

More changes, and demise

During the four years between the introduction of the one-ton 1500cc Transporter and its demise in 1967 to coincide with the announcement of a heavily redesigned vehicle, a number of important modifications were initiated. The 1200cc three-quarter ton model was dropped from the catalogue in 1965, a move that reflected the 1500's popularity, in as far as it was almost exclusively the larger engined variant that had been exported to America since 1963.

Performance of the 1493cc engine received a boost in 1965 when a further 2bhp at 4000rpm became available, courtesy of redesigned valve gear, and, in August 1966, 12-volt electrics gave rise to improved illumination and the benefit of specifying a wider range of electrical accessories. Few customers were sorry to see an end to the vagaries

By late summer 1967, nearly two million Transporters had been sold. Produced in several body configurations, Bullis saw service in a multitude of applications, including vending hot dogs. (Courtesy Ken Cservenka)

After seventeen years of production the Transporter had become a familiar sight on roads around the world. More than forty years after it was built, this Splittie was still performing excellent service when photographed on Easter Sunday 2006. (Author's collection)

of 6-volt electrics, which included dismally poor headlamp illumination and equally wretched rear lighting, not to mention the strain on battery power when long, cold winters prevailed. The arrival of a 12-volt system heralding two-speed windscreen wipers and a headlamp dipping system that employed finger-tip control instead of being foot-operated was, for many, a bonus, yet some opposition remained, and there continued to be a market for 6-volt vehicles in terms of vehicle cost. Other changes to vehicle specification included improved interior appointment and provision of seat belts to comply with advancing safety regulations.

The autumn of 1967 saw the seventeenth year of production, a period in which 1.8 million Transporters had been sold. The Bulli had achieved legendary status: not only was it available in several body styles, but it could be specified in as many as 80 different body arrangements. Examples served as travelling shops, tipper trucks, moveable service towers and mobile offices, many of its uses being standard factory options. Additionally, vehicles could be built to special order by coachbuilders and specialist firms approved by Volkswagen.

Having achieved worldwide status, the Transporter nearly became a victim of its own success when the concept of the multi-purpose vehicle was taken up by other manufacturers keen to profit from a growing market. Despite the split-screen Transporter with its unique appearance having become a friendly and familiar sight on roads around the world, Volkswagen nevertheless decided the time was right to revamp the model's image by making it more up-to-date, in keeping with increasing demands made upon it by an ever more discerning clientele.

Chapter 4

Technology and evolution – the Bay Window years

Volkswagen made a brave move introducing a completely new Transporter in 1967 to replace the cosy and friendly looking split-screen vehicle, which, during its seventeen year career, achieved cult status. In addition to it being seen as a mild-mannered and efficient all-purpose vehicle that appealed to families and business users alike, it was also perceived as a tool for certain social and political persuasions. Increasingly, the 'Splittie' was being marginalized as a uniform for the militant left and hippie brigade. Despite such connotations there was, nevertheless, a deeply-felt regard for this go-anywhere vehicle which, like the Citroën 2CV, Fiat 500, Mini and the Morris Minor, had the ability to bridge social barriers.

To enable Volkswagen to maintain its phenomenal lead in what had emerged as a niche market freight-mover-cum-people-carrier-cum-camper-van, the need had arisen to modernise the Transporter's concept before rival manufacturers were able to devise comparable vehicles. Apart from the recognisable VW roundel on its blunt and flatter profile front panel,

and the essence of a design resembling that of its predecessor, there was an obvious difference between the split-screen Transporter and the model superseding it.

After seventeen years of production, the Splittie had achieved cult status. The new model, when introduced in 1967, arguably lost some of its predecessor's charm, but, nevertheless, was more modern in appearance, slightly larger in size, and had a more accommodating cab. Shown in this introductory press photograph is the Panel Van and Pick-up. (Courtesy Brian Screaton)

The MkII's immediate identifying feature was its large and curved one-piece windscreen that was 27 per cent greater in area (2 inches/50.8mm deeper, and 9 inches/230mm wider)

Characteristics of the new model Transporter included a flat frontal profile and large, curved, one-piece windscreen, the latter giving rise to its Bay Window appellation. (Author's collection)

than previously, thus giving rise to the 'Bay Window' appellation. The vehicle's appearance, too, suggested a much more commodious body, though the overall length was only extended by 5 inches (125mm), and width and height by an inch (25mm). The abandonment of the distinctive frontal styling, with its split windscreen, vee-line and characteristic offset headlamps, was a precursor to a significant number of design modifications.

The 1968 model year MkII Transporter featured grilles relocated from their discreet position above the windscreens to prominently below the bay window, thus giving a clue as to the vehicle's improved heating, ventilation and windscreen demisting. Direction indicators, now rectangular instead of circular, were placed beneath the headlights, but well above the bumpers, and styled so as to be seen from the

Two generations of Transporter: the Bay Window model is a late example and has received a measure of customisation.
(Courtesy Ken Cservenka)

Right top: Other characteristics of the Bay Window model were ventilation grilles below the windscreen, turn indicators positioned immediately above the bumper, and sliding side doors. (Volkswagen publicity material/author's collection)

Right middle: Detail of the second generation Transporter's styling showing the ventilation grilles, turn indicators, and the exposed step to the cab. (Author's collection)

Right bottom: The extremities of the bumper were formed to provide a step into the cab. A Volkswagen publicity image, the photograph also illustrates the sliding door arrangement. (Author's collection)

side. The bumpers were shaped to be wrap-around in style, and were stronger and of larger section than previously to afford greater protection. An added feature of the bumpers was the flat, rubber-covered side members which acted as steps to facilitate cab entry and exit.

The once exposed door hinges were concealed for aesthetic as well as safety and maintenance reasons; windscreen wipers were designed to be more efficient, while improved screen washers were pneumatically operated and benefited from a larger capacity reservoir. The cab windows, previously of the sliding type, were changed to winding types to universal appreciation, and engine cooling louvres were rearranged from below the waistline to a high level position on the rear quarters. The latter proved to be a welcome modification as there was less likelihood of road dust entering the engine compartment. In the case of the Pick-up, the engine cooling louvres necessarily remained at low level and were configured in three banks of three above the rear wheelarches.

Winding cab windows were fitted to Bay Window models and engine cooling louvres were placed aft of the rear side windows. (Author's collection)

The positioning of the cooling louvres was a welcome modification as it was less likely that road dust would enter the engine compartment. (Author's collection)

The MkII was introduced as a complete model range comprising Panel Van in standard and high roof formats, Kombi, Pick-up with single or double cab, and Microbus. An addition to the model configurations was the Clipper, which in the MkI era had previously had been marketed as the Samba Bus. Immediately noticeable about the latter was its larger side windows, three instead of four or five smaller windows, depending upon the model.

Safety measures introduced on the MkI were incorporated in the design of the new model as standard, such as inclusion of sliding doors, a 41.7in (1059mm) opening replacing the double door. Wider cab doors, lengthened by 2½ inches (6.25cm), facilitated access and exit to and from the Transporter, while inside the vehicle access from the cab to the body of the cargo area was much improved by the inclusion of individual seats rather than a bench; seatbelts and grab handles were provided for all passengers, and backrest locks were incorporated into the front seats. A complete redesign of the cab interior allowed for padding to cover the dashboard surfaces, visors, armrests, seat capping and parking brake lever. Soft material was applied to all controls including window winders and ventilation quarterlight catches, the rear-view mirror was encased in plastic, and all other surfaces were made non-reflective. For extra security, the steering wheel was deeply dished and padded, while the hooded instrument panel contained instruments that were recessed and clearly labelled. All variants were supplied with two large rectangular external mirrors that folded on impact.

Attention to safety meant relocating the spare wheel on the Panel Van and other models to a well at the back of the

MkII Panel Vans were available in high roof format, as shown in this Volkswagen publicity illustration. Note also that the position of the turn indicators allowed them to be seen from the side. (Author's collection)

The interior of a high roof Panel Van. A full-width cab dividing wall was available at extra cost. (Volkswagen publicity material/author's collection)

Sliding doors fitted to both sides of Bay Window Panel Vans proved a popular option. (Volkswagen publicity material/author's collection)

vehicle so that it was mounted upright, while on the Pick-up it remained behind the seats. In the interest of gaining as much interior space as possible, it was not unusual for owners to move the spare wheel so that it fastened externally to the cab nose.

Structurally, the MkII was similar to the split-screen model in that it featured sturdy integral construction, the longitudinals running the length of the chassis frame, and crossmembers and outriggers providing for suitable bracing and support for the coachwork. Modifications to the engine mounting arrangement had been made so that it no longer utilised the transmission as anchorage but had its own dedicated mountings upon a crossmember, with a third mounting at the front forming a triangle section to improve engine

Panel Van interior showing tailgate, spare wheel located in a well above the engine compartment, and walk-through cab. (Volkswagen publicity material/author's collection)

The cab interior of the MkII Transporter showing the dished steering wheel, instrument console, and seating. (Volkswagen publicity material/author's collection)

Bay Window Panel Van cab interior. (Courtesy Ken Cservenka)

It was not unusual for owners of Bay Window Transporters to carry the spare wheel on the nose of the vehicle in order to achieve as much interior space as possible. (Courtesy Ken Cservenka)

Bay Window Panel Van driving position, showing instrument console. (Courtesy Ken Cservenka)

support and eradicate a lot of vibration and torque reaction. Mechanically, MkII Transporters benefited from more efficient headlamps and separate brakelights. The braking system, too, came in for overhaul, and with it provision for dual circuitry. For ease of maintenance, the translucent plastic brake fluid reservoir was mounted on the left-hand side of the dashboard, and, reassuringly, an indicator warning lamp positioned on the facia warned of braking system faults or leaks on depressing the brake pedal. Steering was lightened by the alteration of the steering ratio, and the fitting of ball joints to the steering mechanism in place of king pins avoided much greasing, and made for easier routine servicing. There was revision to the front and rear tracking, but more fundamental was the abandonment of reduction gears in the rear hubs in favour of revised gearbox ratios.

The transmission underwent significant alteration, especially the double-jointed rear axles. These incorporated the constant velocity joints which were capable of absorbing a degree of axial play and which replaced swing axles that were at the mercy of severe changes in wheel camber. The move to double-jointed rear axles at last satisfied owners who for long had been worried about experiencing the dreaded 'wheel tuck-in' characteristic whilst corning at speed. At last, a negative rear wheel camber could be achieved, regardless of vehicle load weight or body lean.

The MkII demonstrated a much improved ride over that of its predecessor thanks to changes to the suspension layout. *Popular Imported Cars* magazine, in putting the vehicle through its paces, discovered a car-like

ride, and handling "that had to be tried to be believed". Furthermore, the road test report revealed that "so smooth was the Transporter's ride qualities that even substantial bumps in the road could be taken at speed". Something also characteristic about the MkII was its handling in crosswinds owing to the vehicle's slab-sided bulk, the effects of which were compensated for by its good-natured roadholding.

The arrival of the MkII also saw another increase in power, the Beetle's 1500 engine having been enlarged to 1584cc, thus designated the 1600, to produce 47bhp at 4000rpm. The extra output had been achieved by utilising the existing crankshaft but increasing the cylinder bore to 85.5mm, and fitting the Solex PIOCT-2 carburettor, a series of measures that were needed if only to compensate for the additional vehicle weight of approximately 180lb (81kg) according to model specification, as well as a requirement to keep abreast with constantly changing traffic conditions in respect of acceleration ability. Despite the power increase the vehicle's maximum speed of around 65mph (104kph) remained the same

Clear instrument layout. Easy-to-read instruments. Plastic control knobs marked with symbols. Heating and ventilation controls.

Controls and instrument layout of the MkII Transporter. (Volkswagen publicity material/author's collection)

as its predecessor, though Volkswagen engineers had deemed it appropriate to discard the engine governing device. Fuel consumption was also as before, at between 23 and 27mpg (12-11 litres/100km), but an increase in the fuel tank capacity, from 10.6 to 15.8 gallons (48 to 72 litres), allowed for an average cruising range of 300 miles (480km) between refuelling.

At the wheel of the Bay Window model there was an element of spaciousness not apparent with the split-screen Bulli. Visibility was dramatically improved, courtesy of the large one-piece curved windscreen, and for driver convenience the instrument and facia layout was something of a revelation. Seats were well upholstered and the degree of adjustment provided for greater comfort. Three large dials were incorporated in the instrument binnacle: on the left, a fuel gauge

together with warning lights for oil pressure, generator, turn indicators and headlamp main beam; the speedometer was centrally located, and on the right, a clock was fitted, depending on model specification. Heating controls were situated on the right- or left-hand side of the instrument panel, according to whether the vehicle was left- or right-hand drive, respectively, and the radio controls were housed in the centre of the facia. In front of the passenger seats there was a capacious and padded glovebox. The parking brake, with its umbrella type handle, was located beneath the facia, and the ignition lock was positioned on the opposite side of the steering column to the turn indicator stalk.

Early improvements
Not quite so evident, but no less important, a number of revisions

were made to the MkII's specification during the early years of production. Soundproofing was improved, which made for more relaxed travel; the steering column was designed to collapse in the event of impact, and the doors were strengthened and the body given greater rigidity in accordance with ongoing safety demands. Wider section tyres, radials at that, were specified from August 1970, and, at the same time, the braking system was uprated to include discs at the front and a pressure limiter at the rear, along with new and more durable driveshafts. Arguably the specification of radial tyres was late in arriving, though it should be mentioned they were fitted to the Microbus from the commencement of MkII production.

Coinciding with the production of the 3 millionth Transporter in 1970 there was yet another increase in power

For the 1973 model year, cab front styling was modified to allow the turn indicators to be positioned above the headlamps and at the extremities of the ventilation grille.
(Courtesy Ken Cservenka)

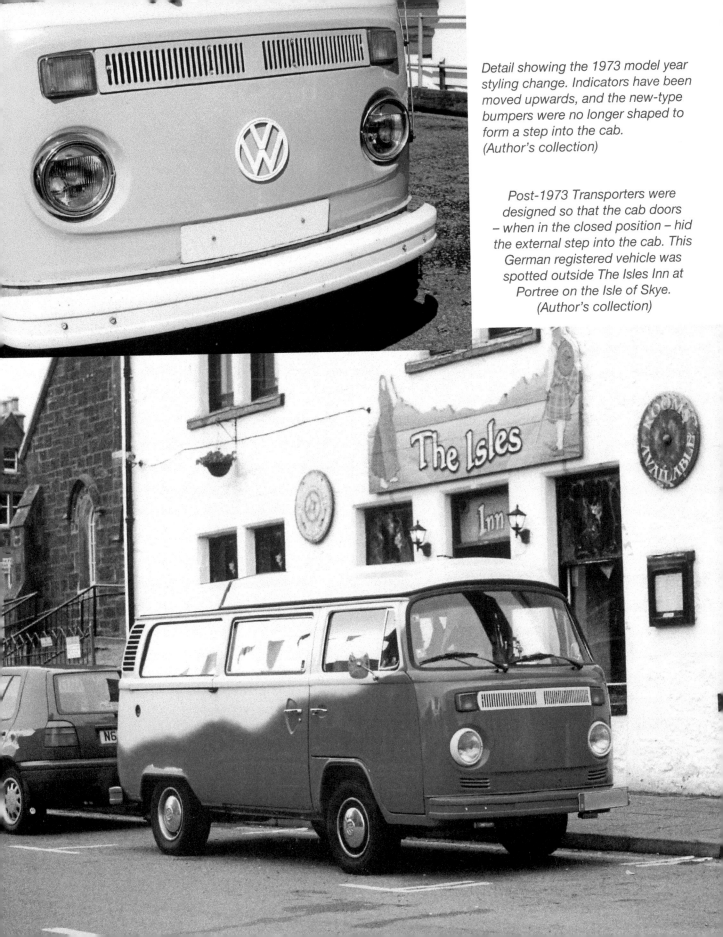

Detail showing the 1973 model year styling change. Indicators have been moved upwards, and the new-type bumpers were no longer shaped to form a step into the cab.
(Author's collection)

Post-1973 Transporters were designed so that the cab doors – when in the closed position – hid the external step into the cab. This German registered vehicle was spotted outside The Isles Inn at Portree on the Isle of Skye.
(Author's collection)

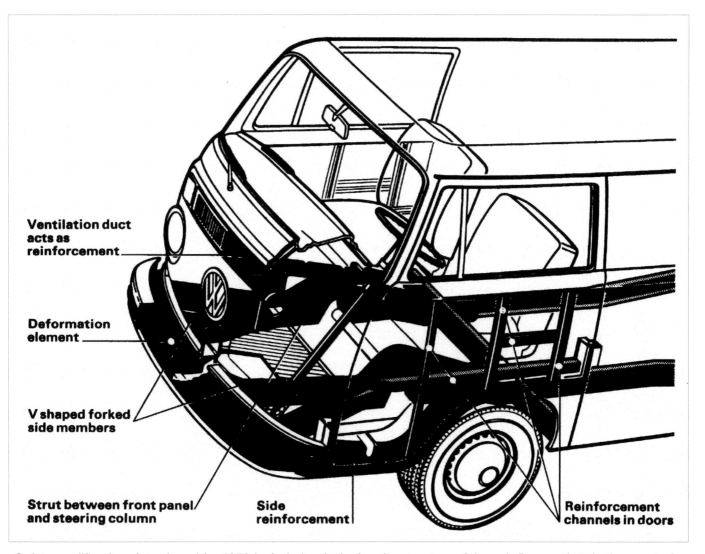

Ventilation duct
acts as
reinforcement

Deformation
element

V shaped forked
side members

Strut between front panel
and steering column

Side
reinforcement

Reinforcement
channels in doors

Safety modifications introduced for 1973 included redesigning the structure of the cab floor so that, in the event of a frontal impact, it deformed. The deformation element and other safety details are clearly illustrated in this Volkswagen publicity item. (Author's collection)

from the 1584cc engine to 50bhp at 4000rpm thanks to the adoption of dual port cylinder heads. This was something of a stop-gap though, for the following year the option of the 1.7-litre engine was announced to address criticisms from some quarters that the Transporter's performance was still lacking. Output dramatically increased from 50 to 66bhp to give a top speed of nearly 80mph (129kph).

The 1679cc engine had been designed for use in the stylish Type

4 variants (411 and 412) when they were introduced to Europe in 1968 but delayed until 1971 for debut in America. When fitted to the Type 4 cars, the engines were modified to run on regular grade fuel, hence the compression ratio being reduced from 7.8:1 to 7.3:1. Despite this, the engine offered around 23 per cent more power than the 1600 unit, and, because of space being at a premium when fitted to the 411, the engine's cooling fan was fitted to the end of the crankshaft

instead of the more usual upright position. When fitted to the Transporter, the 1.7-litre engine proved smooth and responsive in operation as well as being easily accessible for servicing and maintenance.

When fitted to the 411 and 412 variants for the American market the 1.7-litre engine was given fuel injection to conform to that country's emission regulations. Carburettors, though, were specified for the Transporter, and owners praised the performance of the high-revving engine, the ideal speeds for gear changing being 22mph (35kph) from 1st to 2nd, 37 (59) from 2nd to 3rd, 60 (96) from 3rd to top. Not for the first time, therefore, Volkswagen engineers decided on the fitment of a speed limiting device.

For safety reasons larger rear lights were fitted for the 1971 model year, and, at the same time, the fuel filler was relocated rearwards so as not to hinder refuelling when the sliding doors were open. Additional soundproofing and padding was fitted to the body interior for greater comfort, but the most important of modifications was to the design of the cab front for the 1973 model year. Outwardly, the cab styling was little changed except for the relocation of the direction indicators, which were moved from immediately above the bumpers to above the headlamps either side of the grille. The construction of the front of the vehicle was, however, substantially modified so that in the event of collision it became a crunch-zone with a deformable area around the cab thanks to the design of the cab floor. Further mechanical changes implemented for the 1973 model year included provision of larger brake disc pads, a new steering box, and redesigned steering column. The external step up to the cab was redesigned to be hidden when the doors were closed.

A feature of particular interest was the adoption of a three-speed automatic gearbox as an on-cost option on all models except the Pick-up. The gearbox, like the 1.7-litre engine to which it was mated, was also derived from the 411 series of variants, and when installed in the Transporter offered brisk performance. The transmission was conventional enough, with its torque converter installed in the gearbox bellhousing, though it should be stressed that the

A number of technical modifications were introduced for the 1974 model year, including the fitting of an alternator on 1.6-litre engines, and increasing the size of the 1.7-litre engine to 1.8-litres. In the autumn of 1975, the 1.8-litre engine was replaced by a 2.0-litre unit, though, by this time, the oil crisis was having an on-going effect on motoring, and Volkswagen, in common with other manufacturers, was devising new and more efficient engines. Pictured on a stormy afternoon in the height of summer, this 1975/76 vehicle, complete with nose-mounted spare wheel, shows to good effect the 1973 model year styling changes. (Author's collection)

design had no similarity to the semi-automatic transmission systems seen on the Beetle and Porsche 911. There was some loss in horsepower at the rear wheels, but this was compensated for by the fact that the automatic transmission made the most of the engine's torque.

Contemporary road tests show the automatic Transporter as being a well-mannered vehicle in its handling, especially insomuch that the familiar noisy and jolting characteristics experienced with this type of transmission was pleasantly absent. British motorists were (and still are) largely suspicious of automatic gearboxes, other than when fitted to the most prestigious cars, fearful of not having complete control of the vehicle. European drivers quickly discovered the advantages of not having to physically operate the clutch, especially in city and urban environments, and as for American motorists the thought of having to manually change gear was considered quaint. Those British drivers who did opt for the automatic Transporter found the transmission to be very smooth and accommodating.

Specification changes for the 1974 model year included an automatic lock fitted to the sliding doors for safety and security purposes, and a lockable filler cap on the fuel tank rather than a mere filler flap (an indication as to the preciousness of petrol at the time of a global oil crisis). With increasing reliance on electrical accessories, an alternator replaced the dynamo on 1.6-litre Transporters, and for 1.7-litre models an engine modification increased the capacity to 1.8-litres. This brought with it an increase in fuel consumption, to 22mpg (13litres/ 100km), a figure commensurate with the 1.7-litre automatic variant, and significantly worse than those for the 1.6-litre Transporter (25mpg/11.5 litres/ 100km).

The increase in power and subsequent rise in running costs arrived at a most unfortunate time, the oil crisis bringing with it fuel rationing

When the 2.0-litre engine was introduced it improved the Transporter's performance without compromising fuel economy. With a top speed of just under 80mph (129kph) and a claimed average fuel consumption of 24mpg (12 litres/100km) the Transporter, like the example pictured here at Grasmere in the English Lake District, promised effortless touring. (Author's collection)

as well as being the cause of a severe and worldwide depression in the motor industry. However grave the oil crisis was at the time, the events that led to panic measures in order to conserve fuel supplies did have a more positive effect, in that vehicle manufacturers were encouraged to develop more economical and efficient engines. Volkswagen was not alone in devising new power units and, in the autumn of 1975 for the 1976 model year, replaced the 1.8-litre engine with one of 2-litres. Though of greater capacity than the engine it superseded, the 2-litre unit improved upon performance without compromising running costs, and for those customers who were not inspired by performance alone, there remained the option of the faithful 1.6-litre Transporter with its modest 68mph (109kph) maximum speed.

With the bore and stroke of the 1800 engine increased to 94 and 71mm, respectively, the 1970cc 2-litre engine promised a commanding 70bhp at 4200rpm to afford a top speed of 79mph (126kph) and claimed average fuel consumption of 24mpg (12litres/100km). These figures were marginally compromised when mated to the optionally available automatic transmission, affording 76mph (122kph) maximum speed and 22mpg (19lts/100kph) fuel consumption.

VW bus enthusiasts agree that the 2-litre engine, which was borrowed from the VW-Porsche 912 and 914, is the ultimate power unit, and one which, when suitably run-in, can provide a much higher top speed than Volkswagen would admit to. Some owners are confident their vehicles can approach 95-100mph (152-160kph) under ideal conditions. At the time of the 2-litre engine's introduction, rumours emanating from Volkswagen indicated that a 2.2-litre engine was proposed for the Transporter, but this failed to materialise.

The ultimate box-on-wheels

By uprating engine capacity to 2-litres, Volkswagen engineers additionally increased the Transporter's versatility by strengthening the chassis and stiffening the suspension in order to provide a higher payload, raising it from 1 to 1.2 tons. Thus the greater payload Transporter was described in Volkswagen publicity literature as being the "ultimate box-on-wheels" and was marketed alongside the existing 1-ton model. Volkswagen in the mid-seventies, therefore, was able to market a formidable range of commercials, station wagons and microbuses. At least nine versions of vehicle were offered in a variety of engine sizes and wheelbase lengths: thus the Panel Van in 1 or 1.2 ton payloads became available, with or without a high roof; the Pick-up could be specified with either a single or double cab and with a choice of standard or enlarged platforms, and there was the Kombi, Microbus and Microbus L. A number of anomalies existed, however; for example, the Panel Van was not available in the heavier payload with automatic transmission, high roof or second sliding door, and the Pick-up could be specified with either size engine rather than just the 1.6-litre as previously.

Concerns about pollution, especially in America, and particularly California, led Volkswagen to specify Bosch fuel injection rather than carburettors in respect of certain markets. During the 1970s, the 1.8-litre and 2-litre Transporters were fitted with fuel injection when exported to the United States, and for vehicles destined for California it became necessary to additionally specify a catalytic converter. In order to meet the strict demands imposed on manufacturers exporting vehicles to America it was necessary for Bosch to devise a computer (the renowned 'black box') which metered an exact amount of fuel in response to volume of air and engine speed. Notwithstanding the complexities of the fuel injection system, Transporters so fitted were noted for their performance, reliability, and longevity, and whilst maintenance was hardly a do-it-yourself operation, there was simplicity in that help was at hand via electronic analysis installed at Volkswagen dealerships and other garages.

The 2.0-litre Transporter was claimed by Volkswagen to be the ultimate box-on-wheels. (Volkswagen publicity material/author's collection)

Right top: The 2.0-litre was marketed as a willing workhorse, this Pick-up pictured alongside a ship and unloading its cargo of vegetables. (Volkswagen publicity material/author's collection)

Right middle: In addition to the single cab Pick-up, the Double cab Pick-up was a favourite with construction industry clientele. (Volkswagen publicity material/author's collection)

Right bottom: Increasing the Transporter's payload to 1.2 tons, which meant strengthening the chassis and stiffening the suspension, the vehicle's versatility, as depicted with this Kombi, was assured. (Volkswagen publicity material/author's collection)

The 2-litre Transporter was the swan song of the Bay Window model, and after its introduction for 1976 modifications to the vehicle range were kept to a minimum. On-going developments within Volkswagen witnessed the manifestation of several projects, not least was the proposal to market a four-wheel drive version of the MkII, another project that failed to come to fruition. The fact that an all-wheel drive version of the MkII Transporter did not materialise is something of a mystery since it would have made the ideal off-roader given its adeptness for long-distance journeying, often over the most demanding terrain.

Revisions to post 1976 MkII Transporters were mainly of a superficial nature, thus changes to trim and furnishings were mostly evident. There were also large-scale anomalies when it came to overseas production, hence vehicles constructed in South America and South Africa had differences to those produced in Germany. Examples of derivation are seen in the body configuration of South African MkII

The 2.0 litre Bay Window range included the Microbus, as seen here serving as airport transport. (Volkswagen publicity material/ author's collection)

Kombis which had five side windows instead of three, and models of Microbus had wrap-around rear windows, a feature of the German-built split-screen Samba Bus and which was abandoned with the arrival of the Clipper.

Production of the MkII Transporter was scaled down in readiness for the debut of a completely new model, the MkIII, in August 1979. Thirty years separated the appearance of the Bulli in 1949 with the arrival of the new model, a period which had seen many changes to that of the original specification. With production of 2.4 million Bay Window examples, it materialised as being a considerably different vehicle to the original split-screen Panel Van. Though the last of the MkII vehicles were highly practical and built for hard work, they were, nevertheless, far more sophisticated than the original Bulli: the finish and furnishings of the cab were far improved, instrumentation was more comprehensive, and there were distinct upgradings which made the interior appointment more car-like,

Bay Window production was scaled down in 1979 in advance of the introduction of a new model in August that year. This late model Kombi has the optional extras of rubber bumper inserts in addition to chrome badge and hubcaps. (Courtesy Ken Cservenka)

while safety features, impressive as they were, complied with international regulations.

Despite the MkII Transporter's comfortable image the need for change had arisen, if only for Volkswagen to maintain its enviable share of the all-purpose vehicle market. Marketing strategies on behalf of the motor industry had raised demand for something known as the Sports Utility vehicle ...

Though and end to Bay Window production had arrived in Europe, the vehicle remained available in Mexico for two decades and is still being produced in Brazil, although the air-cooled engine was replaced by a 'Total Flex' 1.4-litre water-cooled unit in 2005. According to Volkswagen, the new engine, which can run on alcohol, is of more modern design, is quieter running, and uses less fuel than its predecessor.

Chapter 5

Technology and evolution – third generation and beyond

For some time before production of the MkII Transporter ceased, rumours were rife about development of a new model which would be an entirely new concept. Furthermore, because of the Transporter's thirty year production run, predictions were that the Bay Window replacement was likely to be of radical design. Owing to Volkswagen having embarked upon a strategy whereby the emphasis for car production was on water-cooled engines and front-wheel drive rather than the rear-mounted, air-cooled boxer, there was every reason to believe that the Transporter would adopt similar principles and, therefore, share a kinship with the K70 of 1970, the Passat of 1973, and the Golf and Scirocco that followed.

There was some relief on the part of traditional Volkswagen owners – though a number of potential customers anticipating the MkII's successor to espouse front-wheel drive might have been disappointed – that the new model remained faithful to the Beetle-based drivetrain. Only a few vehicles, which included Volkswagen's Mexican and Brazilian constructed products, Porsche, Skoda and the Polish-built

The styling of the third generation Transporter led it to being dubbed the Wedge model. Also called the T3 or T25, it was known in America as the Vanagon. Styling characteristics of the first series of vehicles are depicted here on an example employed by the emergency services. (Courtesy Ken Cservenka)

baby Fiats continued to follow the rear-positioned engine layout, and even fewer demonstrated allegiance to air-cooling and the horizontally-opposed cylinder configuration. Even Renault, which postwar had adopted the rear-engine format for some of its models, gave way to front-wheel drive apart from its Alpine models, the last of which entered service in 1985 under the guise of the V6GTA.

The MkIII Transporter, when

introduced in August 1979, faced great rivalry in a highly competitive market. Not only was there a surfeit of European models ready to vie with the Volkswagen, growing competition from Japan was evident with the emergence of Toyota's Hi-Ace, Nissan's Ekonowagon, and Mitsubishi's Canter. Elsewhere, Bedford's CA and CF series of light commercials of the 1950s and '60s, and Ford's Transit were eating into the market sector once exclusive to the Bulli. Compared to the original Split-Screen Transporter, equivalent commercial vehicles had evolved to become larger and more versatile, while adopting an impressive array of body styles to suit every purpose.

When announced, the MkIII Transporter was seen to inherit a fundamental identity from its forebears, though styling was more modern. Immediately obvious about the vehicle was its size, and, whilst sharing the same height as the MkII it was considerably wider, by 5 inches (127mm), and 2½ inches (63.5mm) longer. Though still essentially a box-on-wheels, the vehicle's styling reflected a contemporary trend, with its curved front panel and a deeply raked windscreen which was 21 per cent larger than that of the MkII to afford vastly improved visibility. Access to the cab interior was made easier by virtue of longer doors, and the roof was noticeably flatter, thus providing for greater overall headroom

The Wedge, though the same height as the Bay Window model, is 5 inches (127mm) wider and 2½ inches (63.5mm) longer. The windscreen, too, is larger (by 21 per cent) and the cab doors are longer to afford easy access. Note the circular headlamps incorporated into the grille, and that the VW emblem is smaller than on previous models. Depicted here is an Auto Sleeper conversion. (Courtesy Ken Cservenka)

and allowing fitment of wider and taller doors to facilitate conveyance of more commodious consignments. The frontal design had been conceived not only as a means of giving the Transporter an up-to-date appearance, but also with regard to aerodynamics and some measure of fuel efficiency, the latter being somewhat academic and largely dependant on vehicle use. These features, therefore, helped to give the MkIII its distinctive appearance which marque enthusiasts dubbed 'wedge' shaped.

In America, where the MkIII Transporter was known as the Vanagon, the Wedge was greeted with more than mild enthusiasm. *Road and Track* magazine reported that Volkswagen engineers had to choose from twelve possible engine-drive configurations, their selection narrowing to just three rear-engine options, and finally deciding not to change the existing layout. On the road the vehicle performed impeccably enough for the journal's road-tester to state it to be a marked improvement over the Bay Window model. *Pickup, Van & 4WD* magazine was equally generous in its praise for the vehicle, claiming it to be "in most aspects simply light years away from even last year's model in terms of driveablity, comfort, utility and handling".

Other styling features of the Wedge included a prominent grille into which circular headlamps and the VW emblem, smaller than before, were incorporated. Beneath the grille rectangular direction indicators were positioned in such a way that they were visible from ahead and sideways, and below them a massive impact-absorbing bumper complied with then current safety regulations. The large grille could have suggested the Transporter be fitted with a forward-positioned engine, that is until the cooling louvres at the rear, only slightly modified from those fitted to the MkII, confirmed otherwise.

At the rear, the Transporter was restyled to provide for a full-length top-hinged tailgate to give much improved access to the vehicle interior, and which removed the need for a separate external engine compartment cover. The window built into the tailgate was huge by comparison to previous models, and, with the tailgate open, access to the engine for maintenance purposes was via a removable panel on the floor of the luggage compartment, itself lowered by 5½ inches (142mm) to provide for useful additional space. Further restyling concerned the rear lamp clusters, to incorporate both reversing and fog lights, and there was some reshaping of the cooling louvres to make them less obtrusive.

The vehicle interior was given a facelift, described by some commentators as being functional rather than aesthetic. The simple facia made extensive use of plastic material, its pod-like structure containing two

dials: one housing the speedometer, odometer and trip recorder; the other a clock and fuel gauge, warning indicators taking the place of all other instrumentation. There was space to fit a radio, still an optional extra, and ample stowage for small items. The well-padded cab offered much in the way of spaciousness and comfort, although the Panel van had rubber floor matting whereas bus versions were carpeted throughout. Despite its shape and bulk, which gave the MkIII a more van-like look than its predecessors, the Vanagon had more the feel of a car about its driving position. The seats were fitted with safety belts, and were comfortable, demonstrating good ergonomics and lateral support. Increased cabin space gave rise to improved pedal layout that was all the more accommodating as a result.

Handling characteristics were a different matter, the third generation Transporter being just as vulnerable to crosswinds as its predecessors. Although engine noise was hardly obtrusive, drivers were always alert to the hard-working boxer unit in the tail.

In developing the MkIII, Volkswagen engineers had considered various

Third generation Transporters were designed to eventually accept water-cooled engines. The air-cooled boxer was at its limit of development, and moreover, the use of diesel engines for vehicles the size of the Transporter was a practical proposition. The give-away styling feature on water-cooled models is the additional (lower) grille, as shown on this example, which bears all the characteristics of having endured a considerable mileage. (Author's collection)

options, including abandonment of air-cooling in favour of water, substituting a diesel engine in place of the petrol flat-four, and provision of four-wheel drive, five prototypes of the latter having been extensively tested. Ultimately, the conventional Transporter layout was chosen simply because it was efficient and presented the least development costs in respect of tooling despite there being suitable 1.6 and 2-litre water-cooled engines available and already in use with other models.

Lifting the engine inspection cover revealed either the well-proven 50bhp 1.6 or 70bhp 2-litre air-cooled boxer units which happily ran on low octane petrol. To enable the engine to be accommodated within its modified compartment, it had been necessary to minimise its bulk by bolting the cooling

fan to the nose of the crankshaft and relocating ancillary equipment, such as air filter, alternator, coil, distributor and fuel pump, to the sides of the power unit. Standard transmission was courtesy of a four-speed manual gearbox, though a three-speed automatic box could be specified with the 2-litre engine.

Considering the Wedge's increased weight compared to the MkII – a difference of some 300kg (661lb) – the 1600 engine proved to be underpowered. Customers discovered driving the vehicle to be an almost irksome experience, with a constant need to change gear, especially over hilly terrain or along winding roads. The 2-litre engine was, therefore, a recommended alternative, and though affording more relaxed driving, it was, nevertheless, hardly fuel efficient.

A departure from earlier practice was the choice of suspension, the familiar torsion bar technology giving way to coil springs with double wishbones at the front, and semi-trailing arms incorporating rubber buffers at the rear. In addition to telescopic shock absorbers all round, the front suspension was aided by an anti-roll bar. The steering, too, was modified, the worm and roller type yielding to rack and pinion, a consequence being a welcome reduction in the turning circle, something which benefited manoeuvring in confined spaces. As a security measure, the MkIII's steering column was a two-piece affair joined by a safety coupling, which in the event of frontal impact was designed to break.

Vehicles specified with the 1600 engine were fitted with a cable-operated clutch, while on 2-litre models this was hydraulically activated. Automatic transmission versions of the Wedge were of similar arrangement to their MkII predecessors and employed a torque converter rather than a conventional clutch. Unlike European customers who were largely indifferent towards automatic transmission, American clients had few worries in this respect, mainly preferring automatic gear selection to manual shift.

The additional weight of the Vanagon called for the vehicle's stopping power to be uprated, hence adoption of disc brakes at the front but retaining rear drums, servo units being fitted to 2-litre models. A dual-circuit braking layout was standardised, as had been the case with the MkII Transporter, the primary circuit acting on the front brakes, the secondary on the rear, to prevent rear wheels locking under extreme braking pressure.

Torsion bar suspension, which Professor Porsche had patented in 1931, was abandoned on grounds of cost. Whilst extremely durable and affording a comfortable ride, the system used on previous models of Transporter was expensive to manufacture and took up an inordinate amount of space. Payload wise, the Vanagon fulfilled all requirements courtesy of a construction arrangement that resulted in surprisingly little wastage: doors and walls were as slim as they could be, and the vehicle's floor structure, owing to the latest computer aided design, was four inches thinner than previously, and without any loss of strength.

The dawn of a new era

The Wedge's 2-litre engine with its capacity to propel the Transporter to a maximum of between 80 and 90mph (129-145kph) and return an average of 21mpg (13.5 litres/100km) was, in reality, little match for the fuel economy promised by the contemporary diesel engine. Oil engines were enjoying increasing popularity with European customers, though American motorists equated their use to large trucks. Moreover, fuel economy was hardly relevant to American motorists. In truth, the Volkswagen air-cooled boxer engine was at the limit of its development; to design a more modern and more powerful unit would have been impractical.

Increased popularity of the diesel engine did not, therefore, bode well for the future of the petrol-driven, horizontally-opposed air-cooled motor. Increasingly stringent demands for cleaner engines, especially in California, also signalled the demise of the air-cooled boxer, particularly because the technology required to comply with emission controls was responsible for massively dissipating vital power.

The fate of the familiar air-cooled Volkswagen engine was sealed when, in 1980, a diesel-engined version of the Wedge was introduced. Volkswagen engineers had for some time been looking towards developing the Transporter theme beyond air-cooled principles, and introduction of the diesel-powered vehicle only a year after the Vanagon's debut signalled a gradual adoption of water-cooling and front-wheel drive.

No one could truthfully argue that the design of the third generation Transporter did not clearly suggest

Water-cooled Wedges were introduced in 1980 with a diesel-engined model. Note the auxiliary grille at the front of the vehicle, behind which is located the radiator. (Courtesy Ken Cservenka)

Though the radiator of the VW Golf diesel-engined model was fitted at the front of the vehicle, the rear-mounted cooling louvres remained to allow adequate ventilation to the engine compartment. In order for the engine to fit into the space usually occupied by the air-cooled boxer, the diesel engine was installed at an angle of 50 degrees to the vertical. (Author's collection)

that Volkswagen engineers intended installing a water-cooled engine at some time, probably sooner rather than later. A mere glance at the front of the vehicle was surely sufficient to acknowledge there to be space enough in which to fit a radiator unit. A clue as to the change in technology arrived with models sporting a discreet additional horizontal grille below the usual affair. It came as some surprise, however, to discover the diesel engine used to power the VW Golf or Rabbit (according to market), turned to an angle of 50 degrees to the vertical, appearing rather detached, and sitting in the tail of the Vanagon, taking the place of the air-cooled flat-four petrol unit. Had the 1588cc 50bhp diesel engine been fitted in its usual upright position it would have taken up more space than the naturally-aspirated petrol affair, so, in order to overcome this problem, Volkswagen's engineers simply laid it on its side. The main

modification that was necessary to lay the engine sideways was to the sump, the cast aluminium device bolting to both the crankcase and bellhousing to offer two distinct advantages: increased rigidity to the drive unit; while the aluminium alloy aided cooling.

The diesel engine fitted to the Transporter had maximum power and torque figures that were identical to those relating to the 1584cc petrol engine. A benefit, however, was high torque over a wide speed range to improve flexibility. To make the diesel engine suitable for use in the Transporter, a larger flywheel and heavy duty clutch were specified;

Diesel-engined Transporters were popular because performance was on a par with the 1600 air-cooled model and additionally offered good fuel economy, which was good news for commercial users. (Courtesy Ken Cservenka)

Wedge models were offered in all the usual body configurations including the Double-cab Pick-up. Diesel engined models were fitted with larger flywheels, a heavy-duty clutch, and an oil cooler. (Courtesy Ken Cservenka)

Cooling air for the water-cooled Transporter is drawn onto the front-positioned radiator; the coolant is then directed to the rear of the vehicle along protected pipework. Air drawn into the engine compartment through vents adjacent to the rear wheelarches on this Double-cab Pick-up aids the cooling process. (Courtesy Ken Cservenka)

additionally, in order to cope with heavy load conditions, fitment of an oil-cooler ensured that engine temperature was regulated; and to compensate for the greater starting loads associated with a diesel engine, both starter motor and battery were of increased output.

The cooling arrangement, by virtue of the radiator being completely detached from the engine and located at the front of the vehicle, was convoluted. Water-cooled Transporters were easy to identify, thanks to the aforementioned additional grille positioned immediately above the front bumper. Cooling air, drawn into the system was directed to the radiator in the usual manner but aided by provision of two thermostatically-controlled electric fans, the coolant then being circulated to the rear-positioned engine via pipework protected by the vehicle's underframe.

In terms of performance, the diesel-engined Transporter was on a par with its 1600 air-cooled counterpart, the lethargic acceleration and unremarkable top speed reminiscent of the early split-screen Bullis. The essential difference was in the diesel's smoothness, along with its excellent torque which minimised the effect of the model's 220lb (100kg) weight penalty over the air-cooled petrol vehicle. Designed for economy, the diesel-engined Transporter delighted the business user despite a slightly higher purchase price – a situation that was more acute in mainland Europe than in Britain owing to many European countries' taxation policies which gave diesel a big price advantage.

For those customers loyal to the air-cooled layout, the traditional design of Transporter remained – but not for long as, by the end of July 1982, the last 2-litre vehicle had left the factory. The 1.6-litre Transporter continued in production for a few months more but, by the end of the year it, too, was deleted from the catalogue. These events, concluding

33 years of continuous production, signalled the end of an era in which nearly 5 million Transporters had taken to the world's roads.

A water-cooled flat-four

For 1983, and following a three-year development period, the Transporter was offered with a water-cooled boxer engine of 1915cc capacity. The new engine was not just a re-working of the old air-cooled unit; it was a completely new design, though at first glance the two units could be considered as having similar appearance. Water-cooling was chosen as it offered the best route towards increasing power coupled with better fuel economy and reducing noise.

Design-wise, the new engine was shorter than its predecessor because the cylinders were closer together; the crankshaft had a shorter stroke (69 compared to 71mm) and the crankcase was fitted with an integral water jacket that occupied the space once filled by finned cylinder barrels. Thus the new barrels became cylinder liners within the hollow water jacket, there being metal O-rings top and bottom, to prevent coolant permeating into the crankcase or combustion chamber. Cylinder heads resembled those fitted to air-cooled engines but differed by having dedicated water jackets with cooling apertures at either end. Larger valve gear and reshaped intake and exhaust passages were designed to afford improved flow, while pistons, combustion chambers and spark-plug location were so arranged to provide for the most efficient performance and an 8.6 against 7.3:1 compression ratio.

The Wasserboxer's camshaft was designed with lift and profile that gave increased power at low and mid-range engine speeds. The fuel-injection system, a modification of the Bosch L-Jetronic known as Digi-jet because it used digital rather than analogue

European production of air-cooled Transporters ceased in July 1982. Water-cooled boxer engines – known as Wasserboxers – were developed over a three-year period and were considered to provide improved fuel economy and quieter performance. This Holdsworth conversion with a four-headlamp arrangement was pictured in the summer of 2006. (Author's collection)

technology and was somewhat more simplified, limited engine speed to 5400rpm by shutting off the fuel pump, the sensing device being incorporated within the transistorised ignition control unit.

Cooling for the Wasserboxer followed the same principle as with the diesel-powered Transporter, the radiator being front positioned and a two-speed electric fan operating to reduce the temperature of the coolant which fed back to the engine via two steel tubes located beneath the body. Under normal conditions the coolant remained in a closed loop, flowing only through the cylinder jacket and heads: as the temperature increased the thermostat opened to allow the coolant to pass through the radiator, and, if appropriate, the under-dashboard heater (and on Microbus and Kombi

models, an auxiliary heat exchanger positioned beneath the rear seat).

Overall, adopting the Wasserboxer accounted for a 22 per cent increase in horsepower (82bhp compared to the air-cooled engine's 67, the reason for reducing the 0-60mph/0-97kph time from 21.2 second to 18.3), a 19 per cent improvement in fuel economy (19mpg against 16 in city or urban conditions) and 50 per cent noise reduction.

Modified, too, was the transmission, the gearbox receiving reinforced housings along with the pinion and main shafts. Gear selection was simplified; the number of mounting points being reduced from five to three, so that two supported the gearbox and one the engine. Owing to the engine being shorter than was the case with the air-cooled unit, it sat farther back in the chassis, and the transaxle was moved proportionately forward to reduce the driveshaft angle to zero, thus placing less strain on the inboard CV joints and extending their lifespan.

For European markets, the Wasserboxer was available with a choice of 4- or 5-speed manual transmission or a 3-speed automatic gearbox. American customers were given less choice – 4-speed manual or the automatic. When testing the water-cooled Vanagon, *Road & Track* magazine found the 4-speed manual transmission favourable over the 3-speed automatic, the main reason being that the shift points detracted from optimum performance by being set too low.

More power and all-wheel drive

With growing popularity for the multi-function vehicle – otherwise known as the Sports Utility Vehicle, SUV for short, Volkswagen widened the appeal of its Transporter by offering a 2.1-litre water-cooled flat-four model with four-wheel drive, together with the option of a catalytic converter on both the 2.1 and 1.9-litre derivatives. For customers seeking better performance from their vehicle than that available from a normal diesel engine there was the option of a turbo-diesel model, albeit with slight loss in fuel economy.

The 70bhp 1.6-litre turbo-diesel engine was introduced in the spring of 1985 and at the same time as the 2.1-litre water-cooled unit. The former model found favour with European customers used to diesel-powered cars, but in America there was considerably less enthusiasm for it. The latter model, marketed as the Syncro, could be identified by its rectangular headlamps, another styling feature intended to keep abreast with modernity, but it was the performance that really mattered, the 2109cc engine promising 95bhp at 4800rpm.

When introduced in 1985, the Syncro, with its 'part-time' four-wheel drive arrangement, offered truly all-terrain traction. A viscous coupling device replaced the more usual central differential as found on most other 4x4s. Note the circular headlamps fitted to this vehicle rather than the more usual rectangular type. (Courtesy Ken Cservenka)

The Syncro was introduced to compete with the growing number of Transporter-type vehicles that were being sold by American and Japanese manufacturers. With its four-wheel drive arrangement developed in conjunction with Steyr-Daimler-Puch in Austria over a period of ten years, Volkswagen effectively entered a whole new marketing territory.

The design of the Syncro's all-wheel drive was based around a viscous coupling device that replaced the central differential usually found on other 4x4s. The technology behind this arrangement allowed for a final drive that benefited from ideal weight distribution to allow a certain amount of wheel slip at very slight differences between drive and output. The system meant that should the rear wheels spin owing to a loose or slippery surface, the viscous coupling would transmit the majority or all of the power to the front wheels. With traction restored and the vehicle moving to a dry surface, power would be transferred to the rear wheels; likewise, should the vehicle be subjected to a completely slippery surface, the traction would be split automatically between the front and rear wheels according to the degree of

slip, and without effort on behalf of the driver.

A further characteristic of the Syncro was its ability for off-roading, and in this case called for driver action to select a pneumatically-operated locking system activated via the instrument console. For even finer control when negotiating steep inclines, a crawler gear, 60 per cent more effective than first gear, could also be selected. Such technology should have set this very different breed of Transporter apart from any likely rivals, and in particular vehicles such as the Jeep and Land Rover.

The Syncro was offered initially with the 1.9-litre 78bhp water-cooled boxer engine; other planned derivatives included a 1.6-litre 70bhp turbo-diesel, while elite models, marketed as Caravelles, were promised the 2.1-litre fuel-injected boxer engine producing 112bhp at 4800rpm. A Caravelle Carat

The Syncro's all-wheel drive technology was developed over a ten-year period in conjunction with Steyr-Daimler-Puch and addressed the proliferation of four-wheel drive vehicles produced by a growing number of Japanese and American manufacturers. Syncros, with their 2.1-litre, water-cooled engines, were available throughout the Transporter range, as shown by this Double-cab Pick-up. (Courtesy Ken Cservenka)

Syncro Pick-up at work on rough terrain: for off-road work the driver can lock all four wheels for optimum traction, as well as selecting a crawler gear to negotiate steep inclines. (Courtesy Ken Cservenka)

Left top: Syncro technology meant that, should the rear wheels lose traction, the viscous coupling arrangement automatically directed power to all four wheels. This Scandinavian registered Syncro Minibus has a high roof and has been fitted with frontal protectors. (Courtesy Ken Cservenka)

Top of the T3 Transporter range was the Carat Microbus. (Courtesy Ken Cservenka)

was also anticipated, this having a catalytic converter, the output reduced to 95bhp at 4800rpm.

When *Autocar* undertook testing of the Caravelle model in the early part of 1985, the road test personnel found some disappointment, possibly having expected the vehicle to live up to the expectations of its off-road abilities as suggested in Volkswagen's publicity

material. Certainly there were no criticisms about the Syncro's smooth performance on tarmac roads: once off Austria's autobahnen and onto ice and snow covered mountain roads it was a different story. Though there was an impressive amount of grip and traction on steep ice-covered roads when moving from handbrake starts, in such instances the driver being unaware of traction being centred on the front-wheels, neither petrol nor diesel engines provided the amount of

Carat Microbus interior showing the luxury seating. (Courtesy Ken Cservenka)

Cab interior of the Carat Microbus. Note the padded steering wheel and the finely upholstered door panels. (Courtesy Ken Cservenka)

vehicles that were sold during that year were, in effect, left-overs from the previous year, and it was not until 1993 that a replacement became available.

Volkswagen's Eurovan had arrived. Known as the T4, it looked modern and adopted styling trends familiar with other marques. The Transporter was no longer appreciably different to any other vehicle, and to positively identify it as being a Volkswagen one had to look for the V over W badge.

Under the skin there were few features that linked the new Transporter with the old: a new engine range included two petrol engines, one of 2.0-litres (1968cc) commanding 84bhp at 4300rpm and another of 2.5-litres

torque at low engine speeds to afford true off-roading performance.

Possibly an indicator as to the vehicle's realistic level of performance was the fact that Volkswagen had purposely denied motoring journalists the opportunity to attempt an off-road section for test purposes. Notwithstanding the comments made in the Press following the Syncro's media launch, the vehicle was an impressive performer under normal circumstances, and that included taking roads known to be seriously affected by severe wintry conditions.

Eurovan – the fourth generation

For the 1990s and beyond, the technology that produced the new generation Transporters finally abandoned the rear-drive layout that had been the lifeblood of the familiar and faithful Bulli for forty years. Production of the Wedge-cum-Vanagon came to an end in 1991, after which the new models were an entirely new breed of vehicle, having a front-mounted, water-cooled transverse engine and front-wheel drive. For the American market there wasn't a 1992 model, those

(2461cc) with maximum power of 114bhp at 4500rpm. Three diesel-engined vehicles were offered: a 1.9-litre turbo-diesel of 1896cc capacity and maximum power of 68bhp at 3700rpm, 2.4-litre five-cylinder non-turbo of 2370cc and 78bhp at 3700rpm, and a 2.5-litre Tdi of 2459cc and 102bhp at 3500rpm.

Below: The Wedge models were replaced by the fourth generation Transporter in 1991, the new model having water-cooled engines and front-wheel drive. The Eurovan, as the T4 was called, is seen here along with its smaller sibling.
(Courtesy Volkswagen)

The T4 was built in a range of payloads, body configurations, and two wheelbase lengths. This is the long wheelbase TDI with sliding doors on both sides of the vehicle, the double opening rear doors made possible by the vehicle employing front-wheel drive.
(Courtesy Volkswagen)

In promoting the T4 Volkswagen set about devising vehicles with features that would rival other marques: attractive interiors with car-like dashboards, height-adjustable seats, in-vehicle entertainment and, for business purposes, a range of payloads: 800, 1000 and 1200kg. Two wheelbases were offered, 2920 and 3320mm, as well as a choice of roof heights; standard features included a sliding door on the nearside and twin hinged doors at the rear, though some models offered a second sliding door on the offside. A range of body styles were available to include vans, pick-ups, chassis cabs, double cabs and, not least, a Syncro four-wheel drive option matched to a five-speed gearbox.

Though the T4 proved to be an attractive proposition and, dare it be

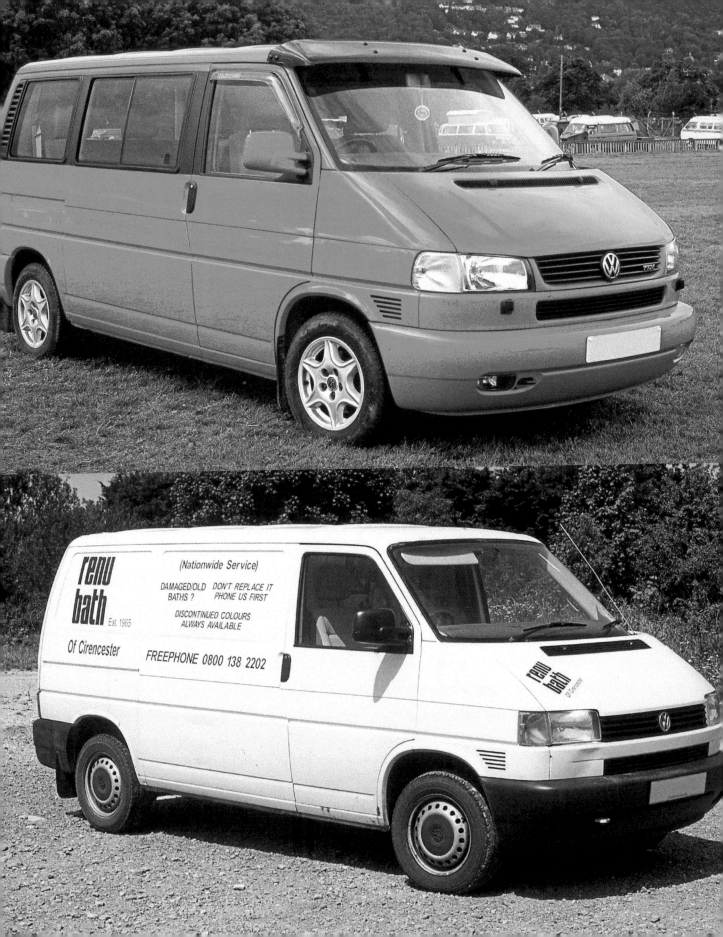

renu
bath
Est. 1965

(Nationwide Service)

DAMAGED/OLD   DON'T REPLACE IT
BATHS ?   PHONE US FIRST

DISCONTINUED COLOURS
ALWAYS AVAILABLE

Of Cirencester   FREEPHONE 0800 138 2202

renu
bath
Of Cirencester

Left top: The T4 was the choice of both commercial and domestic users and rivalled the likes of Mercedes, Ford, Renault, Peugeot and Toyota. The Caravelle shown here proved popular with minibus and taxi operators. (Courtesy Ken Cservenka)

Left bottom: The T4 proved itself in respect of load capacity and driveability. As well as the choice of fleet users, it was also specified by individual business clientele. (Courtesy Ken Cservenka)

said, brought the Transporter design up-to-date in terms of engine design, it failed to capture the character, charisma and sheer driving enjoyment of either the Splittie or Bay Window models.

T5 – A vehicle for the new millennium

There's no doubt that the T4, when introduced, emerged to become a popular choice for business users and motorhome converters. There was no reason, therefore, for Volkswagen to compromise the T5's popularity when the new model was launched for the 2003 model year, and from the vehicle's styling alone it's easy to appreciate that a family resemblance had been continued. For all that, though, there were significant differences between the T5 and its predecessor: it was longer, wider and taller, by 183mm, 64mm and 29mm, respectively (7.2, 2.5 and 1.14in), and the design team had given the styling a mild makeover so that the vehicle appeared all the more purposeful.

In order that the T5 should appeal to as wide a range of clientele as possible, the vehicle came in payloads spanning 795 and 1245kg, together with a choice of three roof heights and two lengths of wheelbase, all of which added up to there being available a loading capacity of between 5.9 and 8.4 cubic metres.

Of course, Volkswagen relied solely on diesel power for the T5, the choice being a 1.9-litre engine or a 2.5-litre TDI, each with two power outputs, 85 or 104PS and 130 or 174PS, respectively, to afford completely adequate torque and pull. Whereas the 1.9-litre engine had a five-speed gearbox as standard equipment, the 2.5TDI could be specified with six-speed manual or tiptronic-style semi-automatic transmission.

As far as body configurations go, there was a choice between panel vans and pick-ups, chassis cabs and double cabs, special purpose options, such

Introduced for 2003, the T5 (seen here in service with Anglian Home Improvements) upheld its predecessors' qualities, but in a more modern style. (Courtesy Ken Cservenka)

Utilities such as Thames Water also favoured the T5. Panel vans are available in two wheelbase lengths and three roof heights to provide a maximum of 8.4 cubic metres load capacity and 1245kg payload. (Courtesy Ken Cservenka)

as tipper trucks, as well as the Shuttle people carrier. Top of the range was the Caravelle, a well-equipped vehicle which in camper mode offered stylish accommodation.

The T5 was introduced with remote control central locking, height and reach adjustable steering wheel, driver's seat with height and lumbar support adjustment, airbag and ABS braking. The facia, with its sensibly laid out instruments and controls, was driver friendly, and there was even a dash-mounted gear lever that was a feature on a production car in 1934 and which has recently found favour with a number of manufacturers. As for the ride quality, that, like the build quality, was exemplary. But who would have expected anything less from a Transporter?

Chapter 6

The variants

The basic design of the Transporter had many attributes which stemmed from the uncomplicated design of what was little more than a box-on-wheels. At the front was the driver and at the rear the drive train; in between came a vast cargo area; thus the vehicle adapted itself easily to many roles. Heinz Nordhoff decreed that all variants, Pick-up, Kombi and Microbus, be developed and tested, proving beyond all doubt the Bulli's versatility as an all-purpose vehicle. It was car-like to drive and more accommodating than most other utility vehicles. Furthermore, it was reasonably priced and cost little more than the Beetle saloon. The Transporter, therefore, presented itself as being the ideal investment for the business user who wanted more in the way of comfort and adaptability than a mere van: it was, essentially, the ultimate workhorse.

The Pick-up

When it was launched in September 1952 the Pick-up became the essential commercial vehicle for the trader who demanded practicality, reliability and the means of carrying large

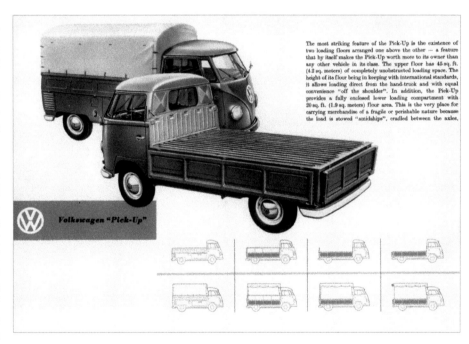

The Pick-up was introduced in 1952 and immediately appealed to a broad clientele, not least builders and the construction industry. This brochure illustration, in addition to depicting the vehicle, illustrates its various configurations, including use of the load area protection and the under-compartment locker. (Volkswagen publicity material/author's collection)

quantities of materials. Customers also appreciated the usefulness and security of the weather-tight stowage compartment of ample proportions concealed beneath the load platform, access to which was via a top-hinged panel. To illustrate the Pick-up's resourcefulness, Volkswagen's publicity

95

sheltered from dust and moisture, and locked for extra security. Both side-panels and tailboard, due to their quick-release retainers, can be lowered in no time, enabling the goods to be loaded from the most convenient side.

The vehicle is of all-steel construction, sturdy and rigid in every detail. Its upper loading floor, protected from wear by hardwood skid runners, easily stands up to rigorous loading. The Pick-Up cab offers the same degree of comfort and interior appointments -- above all the roof-mounted ventilation -- as the other Volkswagen Transporter models. Quick and manoeuvrable, easy to load, it will complete its delivery rounds much earlier than might be expected.

Increased comfort for the driver! For he is the one keeping the goods in trust and having to account for them; driving must become a pleasure to him if he is to move with speed and safety on the road. The new Volkswagen cab helps to make work easier for him; his driving position is undersupported by the density spring, softly shaped cushion and backrest -- comfortable, safe, without fatigue. In use movement he can adjust the temperature or fresh air supply to suit his own requirements and add to his comfort. His view is unobstructed all round. Windows are of safety glass, the one directly in front of him is fitted with a clearvision area to give a wider margin of safety. In front of the handy two-spoke steering wheel is the central multi-purpose instrument, right before the eyes of the driver. Fingertip steering, switches and pedals are extremely easy to operate. Underneath the attractively styled dashboard is a full-width parcel tray to hold smaller items that need be kept close to hand.

The side panels afford plenty of space for effective advertising. Inscription of the firm's name etc.

Hardwood skid runners protect the body floor and make loading of heavy goods easier.

No matter what the circumstances, the body floor at loading platform level greatly facilitates loading and unloading, whatever the method of loading may be.

Any items of a fragile or perishable nature requiring special protection are stowed in the "Treasure Compartment" located between the axles, the best sprung part of the vehicle. There it is unaffected by dust and dirt and safe from pilferage.

This early Pick-up was photographed at an enthusiasts' event and has the load area cover in place. Note the sign written side panels, a feature which Volkswagen advocated as an ideal means of advertising. The bullet-shaped indicators were adopted for European market vehicles in 1960, having been fitted to American market models since 1955. (Courtesy Ken Cservenka)

The Pick-up's flat cargo area was achieved as a result of redesigning the Transporter's drivetrain. These publicity pictures, released on the Pick-up's introduction, portray the cab, under-locker and cargo deck. (Volkswagen publicity material/ author's collection)

material promoted its qualities by an artist's impression of an imaginary load, one that comprised a perfectly and neatly packed consignment of cartons and toolboxes, which, for marketing purposes, was excellent but hardly realistic!

Particularly outstanding in terms of a pick-up type vehicle was the degree of comfort the cab afforded, especially the roominess, which was unusual with a utility vehicle. The Pick-up's design was the result of redesigning the basic Transporter chassis layout, a process which, owing to its complexity and expense, had been deferred until finances and engineering resources

The Pick-up's cab was comfortable and inviting, features not often found on the majority of contemporary utility vehicles. (Courtesy Ken Cservenka)

problem could not have been more difficult. The process entailed reshaping the fuel tank to make it flatter, and relocating it from the right-hand side of the engine compartment to above the rear axle and gearbox. The spare wheel was moved to behind the cab seats, though it was later positioned within the concealed locker.

The design changes allowed for the Pick-up's load platform to be at a height of 38.2 inches (970mm), and the absence of wheel housing intrusion or awkward corners afforded an impressive floor space of 45sq/ft (4.2sq/m). The surface of the load platform incorporated hardwood skid runners to allow for both strength and manoeuvrability, while easily fastened drop sides and tail facilitated loading and unloading. Cradled beneath the load platform between the front and rear axles, the 20sq/ft (1.9sq/m) secure under-locker was referred to in early publicity brochures as being the "treasure compartment", no doubt as a result of literal translation from the German when describing the closet's use in keeping valuable tools and equipment out of sight.

For those customers requiring increased carrying capacity Volkswagen offered, in the autumn of 1958, a Pick-up with a larger platform, which, in addition to giving an extra 13.5 inches (340mm) width also allowed the under-platform compartment to be accessed from both sides of the vehicle. The 55sq/ft (5.1sq/m) load space made this model a favourite with builders and horticulturists, and was afforded similar optional equipment as the standard platform vehicle, comprising a tarpaulin cover (which doubled as a useful advertising medium), along with bows and ties for fastening purposes. At reduced cost, the Pick-up could also be specified without tail or sideboards.

The Pick-up was originally offered as an 800kg (1764lb) payload vehicle increasing to 940kg (2073lb) with

allowed such work to be undertaken. For its intended purpose the Panel van's load platform would have been too high, therefore creating difficulties in respect of loading and unloading. A means of lowering the platform to a convenient working height, and extending it rearwards was, therefore, the prime necessity, yet finding a solution to the

The Pick-up's load platform allowed 45sq.ft (4.2sq.m) load space: generous by any standard. (Courtesy Ken Cservenka)

Fitted with its tarpaulin and ties, this 1961 Pick-up has been carefully restored. Note the outward facing engine cooling louvres and under-locker ventilation grille. (Courtesy Ken Cservenka)

The under-locker was referred to in Volkswagen publicity material as the 'treasure compartment', a phrase that possibly has suffered as a result of literal translation. The drop tail and sides of the Pick-up proved extremely easy to manhandle, much to the relief of vehicle owners and drivers. (Courtesy Ken Cservenka)

the introduction of the 1500 model and to 1090kg (2402lb) on versions fitted with the 1600 engine. With the arrival of even more powerful engines the payload increased accordingly to around a tonne.

The Pick-up evolves
The range of Pick-ups evolved to include a Double-Cab model capable of accommodating six people. Also known as the Crew-Cab, the six-seater was primarily aimed at the construction industry though it was widely sought for a plethora of uses. The origins of the Crew-Cab stem from a conversion that was undertaken by the coachbuilding firm of Binz around 1953, and it was that firm's efforts that eventually led to Volkswagen undertaking production of the variant at Hanover.

Production vehicles were produced by taking the rear section from the standard model, shortening and mating it with a specially designed and constructed cab, a process calling for expensive tooling, particularly as it was necessary to devise an extended

Right top: A popular derivative of Pick-up was the Double-Cab, which was sometimes known as the Crew-Cab. Favoured by the construction industry, it could transport up to five people along with a generous amount of materials and equipment. (Volkswagen publicity material, courtesy Harry Cook)

Right: The Double-Cab Pick-up evolved from a conversion undertaken in 1953 by the Binz coachbuilding company. The build process of this type of vehicle called for some expensive tooling since the roof section had to be specially fabricated, and new doors and panels supplied. (Courtesy Ken Cservenka)

VW Pick-up with double cabin Goods *and* people —
if this is your transport problem,
this double cabin Pick-up will solve it.

3 people
plus 430 lbs. load in rear cabin

6 people

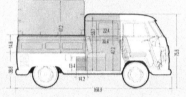

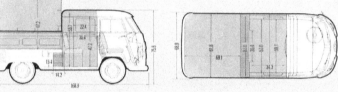

Body design and styling is shown to good effect in this photograph taken at a VW Bus event. Note the outward-facing cooling vents and the open engine hatch. A casualty of the early Double-Cab conversions was the absence of an under-deck hold. (Courtesy Ken Cservenka)

roof section and supply new doors and panels. The result was a highly functional utility vehicle with a 30sq/ft (2.75sq/m) cargo platform capable of transporting gangs of workers and their equipment.

A casualty of the Double-Cab design was loss of the standard Pick-up's under-platform locker, though there was sufficient space below the rear bench seat in which to fit a modest amount of equipment. Furthermore, removal of the rear bench seat when not required allowed for increased capacity. For ease of access Double-Cab models were designed with three doors, two on one side of the vehicle, and a single on the other. Further variations on the Pick-up theme included a long-wheelbase model to provide a platform length

of 12ft (3.66m): designed for long, lightweight loads, the vehicle could be supplied with either a standard or double-cab, and a further feature, on the standard cab variant, was a double-length underfloor compartment.

The long-wheelbase Pick-up was developed in response to the needs of a Dutch biscuit manufacturer whose requirement was for a larger capacity vehicle than was then currently available. Weight was not the main criteria but rather the volume of the packing boxes, which persuaded Volkswagen to recruit the Dutch coachbuilder Kemperink to devise a suitable vehicle based on the Transporter chassis. Kemperink's offering was such a success that Volkswagen was besieged with enquiries and orders for similar

conversions, a situation that led to the coachbuilder being awarded official approval to construct vehicles carrying full manufacturing warranty.

The Kemperink conversion process involved cutting a Pick-up in two and

Right top: Volkswagen marketed a range of special purpose vehicles, including a tipper truck as depicted here. Note the engine cooling louvre configuration as applied to later vehicles. (Courtesy Ken Cservenka)

Right: This tipper truck was converted in Italy at Verona. The lifting mechanism is hydraulically operated via a drive taken from the engine. (Courtesy Ken Cservenka/ Jochen Brauer)

Other special purpose vehicles included those equipped with swivelling towers. (Courtesy Ken Cservenka)

inserting a middle section, thus stretching the overall length by 90cm (35.43in) to 5.34m (17.5ft). Additionally, it was necessary to substitute throttle and clutch cables with longer types and to replace brake lines.

A range of special arrangement Pick-ups was marketed by Volkswagen to cater for a wide number of uses to include tipper devices with hydraulic lifts, height adjustable towers, extending and swivelling ladders, and articulated trailers. Hydraulic tipper truck conversions were supplied through the Lenerich coachbuilding firm of Promotor GmbH, the weight of the tipper mechanisation limiting the vehicle's payload to 860kg. Ladder trucks, and those vehicles with height adjustable towers, were converted by various Volkswagen approved coachbuilders, among the first of these to offer such vehicles was the Westfalian firm of Meyer.

The uses to which the Pick-up could be applied were seemingly endless, there being special models

This extending ladder conversion was pictured at a VW Bus event. Vehicles such as this were originally constructed by the coachbuilding firm Meyer. (Courtesy Ken Cservenka)

A limited range of special purpose vehicles are depicted in this Volkswagen publicity item. (Author's collection)

Enterprising customers lost no time in improvising vehicles to meet their own particular requirements. The huge variety of applications the Pick-up was made to serve included the transportation of animals; farmers, for example, adapted their vehicles as mobile milking machines, especially in locations that were distant from the milking parlour. For dairy work Pick-ups served as ideal milk delivery vehicles, the bonus being they offered a greater range than could a battery-electric milk float. In Bermuda examples were found to be ideal for stevedoring purposes at docks, and elsewhere fire brigades were known to specially convert Double-Cab models for fire fighting use. Many well-known companies, such as AEG, Gervais, Heinkel, and Nestlé, as well as service providers at airports and docks, opted for the sturdiness and reliability offered by the Transporter Pick-up, and each one that took to the road was a good advertisement for Volkswagen.

Pick-ups were pretty much mechanically identical to the other Transporter models except for their chassis layout and platform height. The modified design was eventually adopted throughout the entire Transporter range from 1955, and resulted in a larger and more user-friendly rear loading hatch being fitted, and, accordingly, specification of a notably smaller engine compartment cover.

Modification of the chassis layout meant reconfiguring the engine cooling grilles on Pick-up models, and, owing to the lower profile body arrangement, they were relocated downwards and further aft on the bodywork. On Bay Window models the grilles were further modified by being repositioned in three banks of three louvres, each extending along the length of the rear panels above the wheelarches. There was a further modification in that the fuel filler flap, owing to relocation of the petrol tank, was repositioned lower and

designed to cater for all trades. Special vehicles, or those specially adapted, were available through Volkswagen dealerships and carried a catalogue reference SO to indicate their uniqueness. In all cases, special models were sold with full Volkswagen warranty. The Volkswagen catalogue carried some thirteen special models based on the Pick-up: these included vehicles fitted with an adjustable tail lift to facilitate loading heavy items onto the load platform; pane glass carriers; low loader; adaptations for transporting long sections of pipework; turntable ladder vehicles, and those with hydraulic lifting platforms for high level maintenance, such as street lighting.

When the Bay Window Pick-up was introduced it featured a modified design of engine cooling louvres, hence the three banks of three ventilation grilles. (Courtesy Richard Copping/Ken Cservenka)

further forward on the body, between the lower compartment lid and the leading edge of the louvres.

The utilitarian nature of the Pick-up meant that the level of trim was more spartan than was otherwise the case with Transporter models. Bumpers were plain and merely painted, while the cab trim, though sufficiently comfortable, could only be described – at best – as being adequate.

Being a utility vehicle the Bay Window Pick-up was fitted with plain painted bumpers. Note the ventilation grilles at the rear of the cab. The modern-type wheels on this vehicle are a recent fitment. (Courtesy Ken Cservenka)

When introduced, the Wedge-type Pick-up was offered with a choice of single- or double-cab, the latter having four-wheel drive shown here. (Courtesy Ken Cservenka)

The Pick-up sold in large numbers throughout all stages of model development, and, when the Wedge models arrived in 1979, it retained all its historical body style variations. The lockable lower compartment continued as a feature on single-cab models and, in the case of the double-cab, Volkswagen engineers were at last able to offer this facility, albeit the capacity was reduced owing to chassis layout.

Photographed in the summer of 2006 in west London, this Type 25 Double-cab Pick-up continues to provide excellent service. Note the under-platform locker, a feature not apparent on early Double-cab models. (Courtesy Andrew Minney)

The Syncro, with its four-wheel drive, was popular with fire brigades and other emergency services. (Courtesy Ken Cservenka)

Increases in power afforded to the Transporter range meant that the Pick-up was all the more attractive when compared to many other makes of vehicle, and introduction of the 2-litre 70bhp engine ensured an adequate top speed, even when carrying heavy loads.

A wide range of applications became available with the introduction of the T4 in 1991. With the drivetrain incorporated within the cab area, the effectiveness of the tipper truck can be appreciated. (Volkswagen publicity material/author's collection)

New format

With the appearance of the T4 in 1991 the Pick-up remained as an important and popular vehicle in the Transporter range. Available as a single- or double-cab, all major running components, engine, gearbox, final drive and fuel tank, were incorporated within the vehicle's cab area, thus leaving the rear section to support a wide range of applications, such as dropsides, tipper and more specialised uses. In addition to vehicles fitted with ribbed steel dropside bodies, those with alloy bodies were optionally available. Double-cab variants were able to accommodate six people, and modest amounts of luggage could be stored in the box beneath the rear seat cushion. Unlike their predecessors, neither the single-cab nor the double-cab models offered an under-platform storage facility.

The T4 Pick-ups were available as a chassis cab or as a Pick-up, with a choice of 2.4-litre diesel or 2.5-litre turbo diesel engines, and with a single wheelbase of 3320mm (131in) and overall length of 5136mm (202in) for the chassis cab, and 5271mm (207.5in) for the Pick-up. Specification of the Syncro four-wheel drive Pick-up allowed for a 2.4-litre diesel engine only, a wading depth of 250mm (10in) and climbing ability of 36.7 per cent.

More than a van

Owing to the body configuration of the Panel van and Pick-up, the majority of variants that appeared were based on these models, and, according to Volkswagen publicity material, as many as 80 different conversions were available. This number does not include the Kombi, Microbus, and the many versions of Camper that were to emerge, nor does it include those vehicles that were customised to special order by independent coachbuilders.

While some of the official conversions merely reflected which

The high-roof Panel Van was introduced in 1962 and was popular with traders, especially those in the clothing industry who welcomed the additional height when transporting racks of clothes. (Courtesy Ken Cservenka)

side of the vehicle loading doors were fitted, others were representative of a comprehensive range of models serving a wide scope of applications, some of which were highly unusual. Transporters could usually be adapted to meet any need, whether snow ploughs or fire engines, mobile shops or market stalls, ambulances, mini fuel tankers and mobile exhibition or display vehicles. Bullis were used extensively by the police, and performed a wealth of duties, including mobile police stations, surveillance operations, radio control centres, radar speed units, and even fully-equipped forensic laboratories. The interiors of these vehicles often called

for a high degree of versatility and, not least, fittings designed to meet special requirements, these being addressed through specialist coachbuilders, such as Westfalia.

One of the more popular special-bodied models was the high roof van, which provided an interior height of 5ft 5in (1651mm). Introduced in 1962, this was a particularly sought after conversion, especially by the clothing industry to transport garment racks to shops and exhibitions. Volkswagen anticipated the clothing industry as being a niche market and carefully arranged for it to be graphically represented in Transporter publicity

The usefulness of the high roof model is shown here with a Bay Window Transporter that is converted to vend ice cream.
(Courtesy Ken Cservenka)

The Bulli was a popular choice with the ambulance service. Before Volkswagen offered a standard factory model, the Bonn coachbuilding firm of Miesen was offering specialist conversions.
(Courtesy Ken Cservenka)

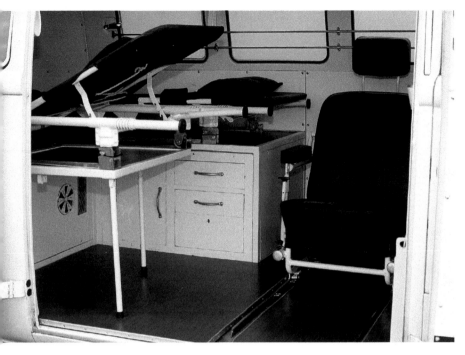

Ambulance interior showing stretcher and other special equipment.
(Courtesy Ken Cservenka)

material. In addition to its high roof, a further advantage was the presence of double wing doors which made loading and unloading easier than was the case with the standard model. Sliding doors, which were a chargeable extra, afforded even greater convenience and, moreover, provided increased safety.

To illustrate the effectiveness and expediency of the high roof model, Volkswagen took a somewhat cavalier approach in publicising the vehicle, claiming it was possible for a person to stand upright inside the load compartment. For anyone of even average height the assertion could be deemed as being optimistic ...

There was glibness about Volkswagen's attitude towards marketing the high roof van and its cost-effectiveness. It was reckoned that the larger surface area of the vehicle's sides was commercially lucrative in respect of advertising, the message from the ad men being: "just pay the sign writer and the vehicle will advertise for you wherever it goes at no further expense". How prospective customers viewed the statement that cost-conscious businessmen had estimated that to rent an equal sized advertising space would cost as much in a year as the purchase price of the vehicle itself, can only be guessed!

The Transporter appeared in many guises and was favoured by companies, institutions and business users everywhere vehicles were sold. They were ubiquitously seen at sports events and other locations serving as mobile hamburger and hot-dog stalls, selling fish and chips, or dispensing ice cream. As refrigeration units embodying dedicated compressor units, they ensured perishable goods were kept in optimum condition, and when specially insulated or equipped, the vehicle was ideally suited for transportation of fragile materials and medical supplies, including blood and plasma.

Amongst the most specialist of all applications was that of ambulance, with or without an emergency trailer, and this, like many of the other variants, was modelled on the Kombi and Bus models. The Transporter's compact dimensions were useful when negotiating busy city centres, and compared favourably with estate car conversions used by some ambulance operators. The first conversions were constructed by Miesen of Bonn, a coachbuilding firm specialising in ambulances, and appeared within weeks of the Kombi going on sale, thus pre-dating Volkswagen's standard factory model. Miesen's offering included roof vents to draw fresh air into the body of the vehicle, but getting the patient-bearing stretcher in and out of the ambulance must have proved difficult since access was via the side loading doors.

Volkswagen's standard factory model, designated Type 27, was introduced in December 1951. The vehicle was developed in conjunction with the Red Cross and the German Ambulance Service, and also met the requirements of other operators. The conversion incorporated a specially designed bottom-hinged rear hatch to facilitate stretcher loading and unloading; for privacy, rear quarter-windows were frosted, while others were furnished with curtains, and a roof fan provided fresh air to the vehicle interior. Other standard features included a searchlight and illuminated roof sign, interior cabinet for medical instruments, plastic interior trim panels of a washable type, and dimmed lighting in the patient area. A sliding window and blind was fitted between the cab and rear section; there were two chairs – one portable and the other folding, an attendant's seat, two stretchers complete with mattresses and pillows, along with fitting and fixings to allow them to be slid easily in and out of the vehicle and to be securely held whilst the ambulance was in motion.

Volkswagen fire tenders were employed by fire brigades as well as by private operators. With ladders attached to the roof and pump equipment being manoeuvred, the vehicle appears ready for action. (Courtesy Ken Cservenka)

Fire tender conversions were prepared by a number of specialist coachbuilders, in addition to there being a standard Volkswagen special-purpose model. The hoses, stored inside the load area of this fish-eye Splittie, can be seen. (Courtesy Ken Cservenka)

A high roof version was also offered, not as a standard Volkswagen option but one supplied by the Hanover firm of Clinomobil. Ambulance crews favoured the last-mentioned because it facilitated patients being easily lifted into the body of the vehicle via a rear split hatch arrangement.

Another role in which the Transporter excelled was that of a fire tender, for official fire brigade service and for private operating purposes within companies and industrial complexes. Examples were supplied by specialist converters, as well as there being a standard Volkswagen model, such conversions being undertaken by Bachert, Branbridge, Magirus Deutz, and Meyer-Hagen. Conversions were constructed using Panel vans and Kombis, as well as Pick-ups, the latter both single- and double-cab types. Special equipment fitted to fire

Fire-fighting equipment, including hoses and pump assembly, is shown loaded aboard this Splittie fire tender. (Courtesy Ken Cservenka)

Bullis made ideal hearses. Note the modified rear hatch.
(Courtesy Rod Grainger)

service vehicles included swivel and extension ladders, provision for dry foam, and heavy duty water pumps. Special vehicles, often constructed as long wheelbase types, were sometimes commissioned for military use and for rescue and civil defence purposes, the latter being popularly referred to in Germany as 'catastrophe vans', which were used in the event of emergency, such as flooding, land slides and, in fact, any major accident or disaster.

There were few applications to which the Transporter could not be lent: examples were seen performing a myriad of roles, from airport support vehicles to hearses designed to carry two coffins.

The Samba Bus

When it was introduced at the Frankfurt Automobile Exhibition in the spring of 1951, the Samba Bus effectively launched the class of vehicle now known as people carriers. Perceived as being the Transporter flagship, with its stylish and tasteful appointment, both externally and internally, the vehicle set a trend and standard by which others would be judged, though at the time there was simply no other vehicle quite like it.

Known as the De Luxe Microbus in some markets, the Samba was the third passenger carrying variant of the Transporter to appear, the first being the Kombi in March 1950, the

second being the Microbus which was introduced two months later. The Kombi was immediately regarded for its versatility as a people carrier, there being two removable bench seats within the body of the vehicle, or as a capacious freight mover – with the bench seats removed – while a third

The Samba Bus was introduced in the spring of 1951; this early example is finished in an original colour scheme of Chestnut Brown over Sealing Wax Red. (Courtesy Ken Cservenka)

option was to carry passengers and freight, such was the adaptability of the seating arrangement. As well as being functional, the Kombi successfully combined comfort with good mannered handling characteristics, tenacious roadholding and reliability.

The Microbus was offered as a 7, 8 or 9 seater and, by nature of its design, was austerely trimmed. Vehicles served a variety of uses, mainly as school buses, business transport, service buses for rural area, taxis and leisure vehicles.

The Samba was immediately identifiable from the standard Microbus by its exterior styling which included two-tone colour schemes, additional brightwork (the VW roundel and hub caps were chromed) and, more strikingly, by the window arrangement.

Samba Microbus interior showing stylish appointment. (Courtesy Ken Cservenka)

Kombi interior showing a utilitarian style of seating compared with that of the Samba Bus.
(Courtesy Ken Cservenka)

Pictured from the rear, the tailgate through which passengers' luggage can be loaded is evident. The roof level windows provided for a light and airy vehicle interior, while the opening roof was designed to take full advantage of warm and sunny weather. (Courtesy Ken Cservenka)

The glass area was substantially increased by there being four square windows along each side of the vehicle behind the cab doors instead of the standard Microbus' three rectangular type, and, additionally by a wrap-around Plexiglass window on each rear quarter. A particular feature of the Samba was the four narrow Plexiglass roof lights along each side of the bus to give it a Pullman-type appearance, along with a Golde full-length easy opening sunroof. Further characteristics were double doors, rather than the usual sliding type, which made access easier, and provision of a top hinged rear door through which passenger luggage could be loaded onto the platform above the engine compartment.

By virtue of the expansive glass area, the interior of the Samba was

Samba Buses can be identified by their two-tone paintwork and degree of brightwork. Note also the high level windows and opening roof. (Courtesy Ken Cservenka)

bright and airy; piped and fluted seats were indicative of luxury, as were carpeted floors, a headlined roof, chromed fittings, and a clock within the passenger area. A number of optional extras afforded even greater luxury, such as a radio, white wall tyres, and a roof-mounted luggage rack. For increased privacy it was possible to specify a glass division behind the cab, itself luxurious compared to other models of Transporter: featuring more comfortable seating than the standard Microbus, controls and a full-width facia were finished in light colours, the latter comprising comprehensive instrumentation.

By today's standards, Volkswagen's publicity material of the 'fifties, with its elegant Reuters artwork, could be accused of contravening political correctness, especially the suggestion that that double doors suited 'corpulent passengers'. There was some journalistic licence in claiming that roof-mounted ventilation, sliding cab windows and opening rear quarterlights amounted to air-conditioning. Mention of the Samba having two rearview mirrors actually meant a single external mirror fitted to the driver's door, the other being an internal mirror which, in fact, would not have afforded very much in respect of rear visibility. The claim that Volkswagen buses hardly needed any repairs, even after 60,000 miles (96,000km) or more, and that operators had no need to worry that a vehicle would not return safely from its journey owing to the ease and safety with which it moved, even in the densest traffic, had surely to be viewed with some scepticism.

The Samba offered luxury courtesy and transfer services between airports, docks, and hotels, and were used at all the favourite holiday resorts in Europe and elsewhere. Their rugged construction made them ideal for operating in areas of notoriously poor

Why won't your wife let you buy this wagon?

"It looks like a bus."
"I wouldn't be caught dead in it."
Do these sound familiar? Your wife is not alone. It is hard to convince some women what sense the VW Station Wagon makes.
Its chunky shape, for instance, allows it to hold more than the biggest conventional wagon. (Yet it is a good four feet shorter, and a lot less exasperating to park.)
She might like the easy way it loads. The side doors give her almost 16 sq. ft. for big supermarket bags, a baby carriage, etc.

The Volkswagen Station Wagon does not have to take anything lying down. She can cart home an antique chest, standing up. Or delicate trees from the nursery. (Wide things, too. It will hold an open playpen.)
She can comfortably pack in eight or more Scouts, with all their cook-out gear.
She can give the family some extra sun on the way to the beach. (Why no other station wagon has a sun-roof is a mystery.)
Even if the traffic is bumper to bumper on hot days, she will not have to worry about

the radiator boiling over. There is no radiator, no water. (The Volkswagen engine is air cooled.)
She may get a kick out of beeping to the other women who drive VW Station Wagons. (They have a kind of private club.)
Or maybe she likes to see where she is going. (The VW wagon has incredible visibility on hills and curves.)
If these facts don't convince her, why not give up gracefully.
(For this year, anyway.)

This Volkswagen of America publicity item shows the Samba Bus to good effect. Marketed as the Station Wagon in the USA, the vehicle shown has the American specification bumpers. (Author's collection)

roads and where mountain conditions dictated use of smaller vehicles rather than larger, less manoeuvrable coaches.

New generation variants
When the Bay Window models were introduced, the Microbus and Samba were redesignated the Clipper and Clipper L, respectively. Both models were identical in appearance to the Kombi, though the Clipper L could be specified with two-tone paint finish, the roof being white without exception,

Bay Window Transporters continued the Microbus theme, the vehicle pictured is a standard model. (Courtesy Ken Cservenka)

The De Luxe Microbus was originally known as the Clipper, until BOAC complained that it had use of the name for its Clipper service between London and the USA, Volkswagen was infringing the airline's patent. (Courtesy Ken Cservenka)

The last edition of the Microbus De Luxe is represented here. Note the brightwork along the body sides. The auxiliary driving lamps were not a standard feature. (Courtesy Ken Cservenka)

at no extra charge. The differences between the two models were minimal, the Clipper L having a steel sunroof as standard, a greater unladen weight, by 55lb (25kg), and a correspondingly lower payload. The Clipper L was luxuriously furnished with soft upholstery, ashtrays, seatbelt anchorages, armrests, grab handles and coat hooks. The Clipper, while also being well appointed, had vinyl upholstery and a more modest level of trim to attract a slightly lower price.

The Clipper models had only been in production for a few months when British Overseas Airways Corporation (BOAC) disputed use of the Clipper name on grounds that the airline had for some time been operating its Clipper service between the United Kingdom and America. Volkswagen accordingly

The Carat Microbus was the top-of-the-range model on T25 Wedge derivatives. These vehicles offered the utmost comfort for passengers and driver alike. (Courtesy Ken Cservenka)

discontinued use of the Clipper appellation, renaming its models the Microbus and Microbus L.

The Microbus theme was continued with arrival of the Wedge models, and vehicles benefited by having a lower loading platform than before, a wider and full-height tailgate to facilitate packing and unpacking of luggage, and wide opening sliding side doors. MkIII models, with their taller side windows and increased size windscreen and rear window, provided for lighter interiors, and the roof, being flatter than before, offered an increase in overall headroom. Standard Microbus models had vinyl trimmed seats, and floors were covered with rubber matting, while de luxe versions had soft, but hard-wearing, corduroy material and carpeted flooring.

Mechanically, the Microbus followed the pattern of other Transporter models, and, in the case of the Vanagon, refinements to the driving position and seating ergonomics added to overall comfort and handling characteristics. The ultimate MkIII was the Caravelle, which was offered in four levels of finish, the 12-seat Carat affording truly refined travel.

With the advent of the T4, and more recently the T5, the Transporter has encountered growing rivalry from vehicle manufacturers like Mercedes, Ford, Nissan, Renault, Toyota, and General Motors. The T5, which is specified with a 1.9-litre diesel or 2.5-litre turbo diesel engine, might appear virtually identical to its predecessor but is 183mm (7.20in) longer, 64mm (2.52in) wider and 29mm (1.14in) higher in short-wheelbase and standard roof format. The wide range of vehicle types is made possible by there being three roof height options, along with provision of a long-wheelbase variant. While the plush Caravelle Minibus remains in the catalogue, the T5 Shuttle offers a budget alternative.

Chapter

Home from home

With the Transporter, Volkswagen was able to promote a "home on wheels that was planned to the last detail for independent touring". The first official conversion, by Westfalia, appeared in 1953 but, by then, a number of specially commissioned vehicles had been prepared for customers wanting a compact motorhome.
(Volkswagen publicity material/author's collection)

Campers, caravanettes, motorhomes, call them what you will, are now an established sight on roads throughout the world. The growth in popularity of the ubiquitous camper began in the early postwar years, and it is Volkswagen's Type 2 Transporter which has to take much responsibility for what has emerged as a huge global industry. From humble beginnings when the Transporter helped kick-start the camper van experience, the UK market alone supported sales of more than 11,000 type B camper van conversions in 2005.

The Bulli did not start the camper phenomenon, but rather made the concept of the motorhome all the more practical and affordable. The origins of the motorhome are to be found in the depths of the 20th Century when travellers devised innovative ways of converting their motorcars to what, in effect, were motorised tents; thus the camping-car was conceived. Though a small number of purpose-built motorhomes materialised before the Second World War, they were usually vast machines that were constructed on lorry or bus chassis, and, therefore, were unwieldy to drive around. Eventually, it was more affordable and easier to handle contraptions that established a trend: camper conversions appeared on Model T Fords and other popular makes of car, and there were some makeshift offerings, such as that on a Simca Cinq, cousin to the diminutive Fiat 500, exhibited at the 1936 Paris Motor Show.

Once the preserve of the more affluent members of society, caravans and caravanning enjoyed popular interest at Earls Court in 1948, venue of the first postwar London Motor Show. Shortages in materials as well as the after-affects of war meant that the caravan industry faced unprecedented change: not only did the advent of small and low-powered popular cars dictate

there being a downsizing of caravans generally, there began a demand for folding caravans and trailer tents. All this combined with a desire for cheaper holidaying, greater freedom to roam, or just getting away for the weekend.

The arrival of the Transporter satisfied mounting demand for what became known as the multi-purpose vehicle: not only did it provide for everyday commercial or multipurpose transport, it offered easy conversion to a camping car. With its forward driving position, compact rear drivetrain, and inherently useful central space, the Volkswagen had potential to carry all that was required for a camping holiday, even washing facilities and the kitchen sink! Not only were running costs favourable compared to towing a caravan, the irritating tasks of negotiating traffic and difficult roads, especially at peak holiday time, finding suitably level sites, reversing, hitching and unhitching, often after dark or in bad weather, were eliminated.

The Westfalia story

The first official camper conversion appeared in 1953 when German coachbuilder Westfalia unveiled its Camping Box, though it is known that at least one other professionally converted vehicle predated it by some months. Another early camping conversion based on the Transporter appeared between 1951 and 1952 when a Dresden garage supplied a Bulli to a local coachbuilder to be fitted out to special order. Having been delivered to the coachbuilder minus interior fittings, the vehicle was furnished with cushioned box units, formed from solid oak, to contain storage units as well as housing cooking and washing utensils. In fact, the conversion offered everything that was required for a camping holiday, including the facility to easily convert the seating arrangement into comfortable bedding.

Likewise, caravan manufacturer Westfalia began converting Transporters in 1951 with a one-off commission to transform a Bulli into a camper van for a serving US army officer stationed in Germany. This led to further orders being received, and to Westfalia displaying a converted Transporter, finished in the brown, yellow and beige colour scheme that would be become distinctive to the product, at the 1952 Frankfurt Motor Show. Westfalia converted around 50 Transporters to individual order before embarking on a modular production system marketed as the Camping Box. An example of the former was purchased by Erna and Helmut Blenck and taken on a year-long tour of Southern Africa, their adventures being recorded in a book published in 1954 and entitled *South Africa Today*.

Westfalia was established in 1844 as a manufacturer of agricultural equipment and diversified into caravan and trailer construction in the 1920s and '30s. Though Westfalia's factory suffered extensive war damage, the firm was able to resume limited production in peacetime, and in 1948 displayed a steel-plated caravan at the 1948 Hanover Motor Fair. The popularity of the Camping Box meant that, by 1957, Westfalia had produced its one-thousandth Kombi-based camper conversion, a figure that would rise substantially so that by the early 1970s, 30,000 units a year were leaving Westfalia's production line, the majority (75%) of which were destined for the USA.

The Camping Box, available in standard and export formats, was an ingenious space-saving design comprising three purpose-built sections: that at the front fitted against the vehicle bulkhead to provide seating, storage and cooking facilities; the centre was given over to a table and seating-cum-bedding, while at the rear there was

Marketed as the Camping Box, Westfalia's conversion was based on the modular system comprising three purpose-designed sections. Seating was provided at the front, the centre living quarters converted to a bed, and the rear served as a roomy storage area. The vehicle pictured is complete with the side awning to make outdoor living all the more practical and comfortable. (Courtesy Ken Cservenka)

a commodious storage cupboard for linen and clothing. Tea cloths and towels could be accommodated on the leading loading door, and built into the rear loading door was an enamel washing bowl and hinged mirror. An optional feature of the standard conversion was a hinged roof hatch which could be opened for ventilation purposes when the vehicle was stationary. On export models the roof hatch was a standard fitment, along with deluxe interior fittings to include curtains and birch ply panelling, and an awning to promote the camping effect as well as affording additional recreational space.

Westfalia's designs evolved to set a standard by which other camper conversions would be judged. The Deluxe Camping Equipment Model introduced in 1956 offered interior roof and side panels made from birch ply, and cabinets that were crafted in light oak to give a rich effect. Accompanying the usual roof hatch and luggage rack, an awning tent provided for additional spaciousness and comfort, while the vehicle's interior furnishings served for daytime or sleeping use. Space utilisation meant provision of a single burner cooker, coolbox or gas refrigerator, washing facilities, and sufficient cupboard space in which to house linen, crockery and everything needed for a holiday on the move.

A number of interior layouts offered the Westfalia customer a choice of accommodation style. Providing a degree of flexibility, each arrangement made optimum use of the Kombi's interior space, some having dinette style interiors that converted to sleeping areas, others having pull-out folding beds. The familiar roof hatch was replaced by Westfalia's pop-up type roof; alternatively it was possible to specify Dormobile's full-length concertina-style roof, marketed by British coachbuilder Martin Walter of Folkestone in Kent.

Contemporary Westfalia brochures depict vehicles furnished with a wide range of luxury fittings, including discreet interior lighting, running water, built-in crockery, cocktail and storage cabinets, cab seats with backs that flipped forwards to provide additional

The 1978 VW Campmobile...

The Westfalia was marketed as the Campmobile in Canada and the USA, this Volkswagen publicity item illustrating the second series Bay Window Transporter. Features of the model shown included an icebox or refrigerator, kitchenette console with water tank, and utensil cabinet. The cab passenger seat swivelled to form a dining room and living room chair. Note the repeater indicators fitted to the cab door's rear quarters.
(Volkswagen publicity material/author's collection)

living area seating, fitted coolbox, door-fitted cooking and washing utensils, awning and toilet tents, the latter supplied complete with a wooden-seated toilet bucket.

Westfalia conversions, commonly known in America as Campmobiles, perpetuated throughout the Bay Window, Wedge and T4 models. Most apparent about the Bay Window vehicles were the three styles of elevating roofs available, ranging from the simple pop-up type to those that were front-hinged, to give maximum

headroom in the camper's living quarters, and others which were side-hinged, the latter designed to afford maximum spaciousness in the central living area. A popular conversion aimed at providing as much interior space as possible was to remove the spare wheel from inside the vehicle and attach it externally to the cab nose. Westfalia offered the Transporter with as many as seven styles of interior layout, each of which catered for particular budgets, equipment specification, choice of furnishings,

and number of berths. One of the most popular models based on the Wedge was the Joker which could be specified with a fixed raised roof, or a rear-hinged elevating type.

The Joker theme was retained for the T4, though models produced on the new generation chassis were marketed as the California. The California Event, launched in 2001, was a variant chosen to acknowledge fifty years of Volkswagen camper conversions. A luxury model built on a long wheelbase and with a high roof, the special edition

A popular model produced by Westfalia based on the T4 Wedge model was the Joker. Available in two editions, Joker 1 had four berths and Joker 2 had five. (Courtesy Ken Cservenka)

even featured a bathroom with a fitted toilet and hinged washing basin.

Introduction of the T5 meant an end to Westfalia's long association with Volkswagen. Though Westfalia had been acquired by the Daimler/Chrysler/Mercedes Benz group sometime previously, Volkswagen allowed the converter to continue production of its T4 models, a policy that was not acceptable with the arrival of the T5. Camper conversions built on the T5 chassis retained the California appellation on the standard model, while the more expensive type was known as the Comfortline: both were Volkswagen factory-produced vehicles, the first to appear.

Westfalia was among a select number of official Volkswagen converters, though conversions were undertaken by a myriad of companies, with varying degrees of success. Whilst official conversions carried the full Volkswagen warranty, others were supplied with nothing more than the converter's guarantee. In selecting specific converters, Volkswagen reasoned that any conversion should meet all necessary requirements for retaining vehicle strength, and those firms chosen had declared to maintain the criteria stipulated.

There was a measure of contention between Volkswagen and non-approved converters, much of which concerned the installation of elevating roofs. Designed to provide for increased spaciousness within the vehicle, as well as providing for additional berths, elevating roof conversions, unless designed and engineered to Volkswagen's precise standards, were said to compromise vehicle rigidity and, therefore, safety. Whilst official conversions employed roofs that maintained roof strength, others featured lightweight and full-length affairs that could arguably contravene Volkswagen's stringent specification.

It was not only coachbuilders and specialist converters who readily transformed the Transporter into the ideal motorhome: individual owners with a keen DIY aptitude were known to convert their vehicles, their designs often innovative but not always in accordance with official approval. As far as specialist converters were concerned, the Transporter's shape

Westfalia's long association with Volkswagen ended in 2004 when Daimler/Chrysler/Mercedes Benz acquired the coachbuilder. Thereafter, for the first time Volkswagen produced a dedicated, factory-built camper conversion, having previously contracted its camper activities to specialist converters. The vehicle illustrated is the California, which is built on the T5 platform. (Courtesy Ken Cservenka)

and size meant that, whilst virtually endless detail permutations were possible, some uniformity in layout and interior design was inevitable. Though it is rare to discover absolutely identical conversions, even from the same converter, a basic formula prevailed: seats used during the daytime to allow adults and children to sit around a collapsible table unfolded at night to provide a double and single bed, the latter usually located above the engine compartment. The cab, furnished with curtains, converted into a child's bed.

Camper vans – American style
With the greater proportion of Westfalia's output exported to the USA, it comes as no surprise to find American-based converters using the Transporter to offer

a wide range of camping cars. Though the onset of WW2 was responsible for a hiatus in highway construction, with which arrived a short-lived downturn in auto sales, the late 1940s and early '50s witnessed soaring car production. Motorists travelling interstate were soon used to driving along a system of highways covering some 40,000 miles (64,000km) connecting cities and states from the Atlantic to the Pacific. Increasing leisure time, growing prosperity and the advent of lightweight materials gave rise to interest in trailer caravans and motorhomes. Not everyone wanted the like of an Airsteam to be towed behind a car: for many, a compact motorhome was far more accommodating, and the Bulli fitted the bill.

A converter of note was

Sportsmobile, which offered a Transporter conversion from the early 1960s, and which received official Volkswagen approval. Marketed as the 'Family Wagon Camper', the Sportsmobile had a 110V electricity mains hook-up, along with various options, such as a pop-up roof, mosquito screens, and an elaborate awning arrangement which served as a tent or sun room. The vehicle's interior specification included a heater, cab hammock bunk, and even a chemical toilet built into a seat located behind the cab. A later development was the Penthouse Top, a full-length elevating roof of Sportsmobile design which, in addition to providing interior space, incorporated a slide-out bed suitable for two children.

Sportsmobile
THE "FAMILY WAGON" CAMPER

AMILY WAGON · CAMPER · UTILITY WAGON

witch from one to the other in less than a minute—arrange fur-
shings to fit your activities. Luxurious styling, highest quality
aterial and craftsmanship assure maintenance-free year-round
ijoyment. Optional Pop Top snaps up in a second to catch the
ghtest breeze. Free-standing canopy and side walls accessories
d a room in minutes, to hold your campsite or to enjoy at home.
anopy top may be left off for a private sunroom or solarium. Side-
alls have sewn in nylon floor.

American converter Sportsmobile won Volkswagen approval for its vehicles, which were fully equipped to include mains electricity hook-up, mosquito screens, elevating roof, and an awning which doubled as a sun room. (Author's collection)

Sportsmobile's conversions were available for specialist fitting by Volkswagen dealers; likewise, they were obtainable for DIY installation and, in both events, afforded a degree of flexibility to customer requirement. Standard specification included a pull-out bed, wardrobe bag, LPG cooker, coolbox and washbasin with water pumped from a container built into a storage unit. Such was the flexibility of the Sportsmobile system, it could be removed in its entirety within a short space of time (the manufacturer's claim that 'everything snaps out in a minute' might be considered as being rather optimistic) to allow the Transporter to be used as a multipurpose vehicle or freight carrier. Sportsmobile conversions continued to be available with the introduction of Bay Window, Vanagon and T4 models, the accent being on luxury in the American idiom.

The growing demand for camper vans in North America led to the appearance of a number of Transporter conversions from existing converters as well as those newly established. Many of the designs were modelled on the proven Westfalia format to feature functional interiors with a host of optional extras to include elevating roofs and awning tents. The

Californian firm E-Z Campers (as in 'easy') promised camping fun for the whole family with its five-berth El Viajero model that sported an attractive wood panelled interior, and featured a two-burner cooker as well as the usual requirements, such as coolbox, washing facilities and pumped water supply. Kamper Kits, another Californian converter, emerged in the early 1960s to supply a luxury conversion complete with ash panelled interior, fine upholstery and a fashionable awning of striped and fringed design. "For an outdoor holiday with the comfort you like" was Kamper Kits' marketing message.

Distinctive with its picture window along one side of the vehicle was the Riviera produced by Riviera Motors of Oregon. Highly regarded for its quality finish and colour-matched interiors, Riviera conversions usually featured pull-out beds with under storage that were wider than the norm owing to a unique wardrobe design; common also were awning tents that, when erected, provided for additional space. With the arrival of Bay Window models, Riviera conversions featured glass fibre high tops to incorporate Penthouse Top elevated roofs and a variety of interior layouts as well as luxury accessories, including air-conditioning. Luxury was

Sportsmobile conversions offered a penthouse roof which is shown in the elevated position in this brochure illustration. That the vehicle depicted has two louvred windows indicates this is a Kombi conversion rather than a Panel Van which would have had three louvred windows. (Courtesy Richard Copping and Ken Cservenka)

In common with usual practice, Volkswagen of America and Volkswagen Canada did not provide a factory-built camper conversion. They did, however, make available through dealer networks, DIY conversion kits, those in America being known as Campmobile, the Canadian equivalent being Canadiana. (Courtesy Ken Cservenka)

also the hallmark of the Safaré, another California conversion, its high roof with built-in sliding windows allowing in excess of six feet standing room height inside the vehicle. As well as air-conditioning, the Bay Window Safaré featured mains electricity and water hook-up, waste water tank and built-in chemical toilet.

Whilst Volkswagen refrained from supplying a factory model camper until 2004-5, Volkswagen of America and Volkswagen Canada did manufacture camping conversion components that could be sold and fitted through Volkswagen dealerships or for DIY installation. The US version was known as the Campmobile, and its Canadian counterpart the Canadiana. The kits, for fitment to Kombi and Microbus, displayed a Westfalia influence, and were regarded for both quality and finish, the Canadiana being of a more basic design compared to the Campmobile.

Campmobiles were available in six options to cater for customer choice and level of equipment, each comprising ceiling and side-wall birch panelling, seats that folded to form a double bed, vinyl floor covering, folding table with extension leaf, side door shelves, clothes closet with mirror, wall-mounted lighting, food storage compartment, curtains, and three floor-level storage cabinets. Extras included an icebox, water storage with pump, two-burner gas stove, chemical toilet, awning tent, elevated roof, and shower unit with enclosure. In full camping mode, Campmobiles could be specified with a hammock bed for the cab area, sun deck and access ladder, and roof-mounted sleeping quarters complete with mosquito net.

British influence
Britons, too, came to recognise the importance of the camper van and the freedom and independence such vehicles promised. Throughout Britain there emerged a number of respected

Dormobile was known for its conversions on the Bedford chassis before the official Volkswagen Dormobile appeared in 1961. This is the brochure rear cover illustration appropriate to the vehicle's introduction. (Author's collection)

converters, some having diversified from bespoke coachbuilding prewar in order to stay in business, and discovered a young, thriving and lucrative market. In the mid- to late-1950s, there were 23 motorhome constructors, 6 of which based their designs on the Transporter. Of those coachbuilders, none are as famous as Martin Walter of Folkestone in Kent, saddlemakers who turned to motorcycles in 1910 and coachbuilding in 1916.

Noted for coachwork on a variety of chassis, including Daimler, Hillman Lanchester, Talbot and Vauxhall, Martin Walter sold out to Abbey coachworks in 1937 and, after the war, in 1954,

produced the Dormobile motor caravan using Bedford's CA chassis. Legend has it that the Dormobile concept came about when a Martin Walter director saw people sleeping in their cars whilst waiting to board cross channel ferries, thus giving him the impetus to devise what was to become the ubiquitous motorhome. By the time the Volkswagen Dormobile appeared in 1961 at the London Motor Show, Domobile had become synonymous with motor caravans in much the same way as Biro and Hoover were associated with the ball point pen and vacuum cleaner, respectively.

At the time of its introduction, the

Dormobile was one of two conversions that carried full Volkswagen approval (Devon was the other) and vehicles were available through VW Motors of St. John's Wood in London. Whether the vehicle represented good value for money at £915 – no purchase tax was payable – can be judged by the price of Martin Walter's other vehicles, the Commer costing £894, Thames £801 and the Land Rover at £1158, this at a time when a similar sum of money (inclusive of purchase tax) bought a Ford Zephyr or Vauxhall Velox. A feature of the Dormobile was its side-hinged elevating roof complete with windows and opening ventilators, for long a

The Dormobile cost £915 on introduction (compared to the firm's Commer conversion at £894 and the Thames at £801), and came complete with the Martin Walter side-hinged elevating roof and renowned 'Dormatic' seating, both evident in this publicity photograph. (Author's collection)

Martin Walter patent, and fitted as standard on a Volkswagen conversion for the first time. The roof opened out like a canopy to allow standing within the vehicle, as well as permitting two adults or children to sleep in fold-away roof level bunks. A light fitted to the cab facia flashed to warn against moving off with the roof raised.

An essential feature of the Dormobile was its patented 'Dormatic' seating arrangement, an ingenious but simple design that made it easy to convert the seats to a variety of positions. The vehicle's interior could be effortlessly transformed from that of a people carrier to dinette; to either

a double or two single beds, or, to provide an unrestricted floor space, the seats, trimmed in hard wearing Duracour could be folded against the body sides. The Dormobile's standard specification comprised curtains on all windows, fluorescent interior lighting, two-burner Calor gas cooker, 7 gallon (32 litre) water container together with an electric pump which delivered the contents to the sink. There was ample cupboard space, and even a wardrobe, but interestingly, the metal cabinets initially specified gave way within a few months to plastic covered furniture.

Later generation Dormobiles were as innovative in interior layout as

their predecessors, the Bay Window model having the Calor gas cooker relocated from the living area to the cab and incorporated within the front passenger seat. To access the cooker meant tipping the seat forward, thus revealing the fold-out appliance. When a completely new version of the motorhome appeared in 1970, the accent was on luxury, especially with fitment as standard of a refrigerator, gold coloured carpeting with matching curtains, and woven upholstery.

Devon – the ideal holiday home

Devon was the other Volkswagen

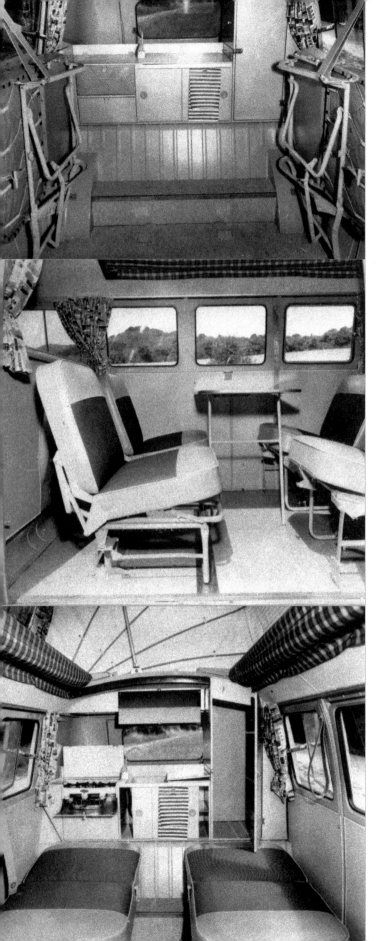

Above: Standard Dormobile specification included with this fish-eye Splittie would have been two-tone paintwork, elevating roof with windows, curtains to all windows, 'Duracour' upholstery, and built-in two-burner Calor gas cooker with adjoining sink and draining board. (Courtesy Ken Cservenka)

Far right: Bay Window Dormobiles were luxuriously appointed, and included woven upholstery, gold coloured carpeting and curtains. (Courtesy Ken Cservenka)

Right: The Bay Window Dormobile. (Courtesy Ken Cservenka)

Left: Dormobile's 'Dormatic' seating arrangement is shown stowed away for cargo carrying purposes (top left), in dinette position (middle left), and converted to form two beds (lower left). (Author's collection)

approved conversion that appeared in the 1950s, predating the Dormobile by four years. The Devon, marketed as the Caravette, materialised as a result of an association between Volkswagen dealer Lisburne Garage of Babbacombe Road Torquay, and Sidmouth cabinet maker J.P. White. Responsibility for fitting out the camper van fell to J.P. White, while Lisburne Garage undertook marketing, sales and distribution, and after-sales service. Two versions of the Caravette were available when the Devon went on sale in January 1958, the standard model costing £897.10s, and the deluxe version £1092.10s. For those customers already in possession of a Transporter and wishing to convert it to a motorhome, Lisburne Garage would undertake the work – as long as the vehicle was structurally suitable – for a cost of £200.

In its basic form the Caravette accommodated two adults, the dinette arrangement in the centre of the vehicle transforming into a double bed when unfolded. Two Formica covered tables were supplied, one forming the centre base of the double bed, the other folding away out of sight when not in use. Interior appointment was superbly finished in hand polished light oak, seating was covered in washable fabric, while curtains and a chequered floor pattern complimented the overall effect. A cooker was housed into the top of a corner unit, and there was provision for a limited amount of storage space, although the specification lacked a washbasin, which was optional and at additional cost.

The deluxe edition, a four-berth model marketed as the MkII Caravette, offered more in the way of comfort and facilities so that the space above the engine compartment doubled as a child's bed, while a second child could be accommodated within the cab. Along with a washbasin (still an optional extra) that could be hinged out of the

way when not in use and housed within the leading side door, a Calor gas stove was built into the rearward double side door. Rearrangement of the vehicle interior not only provided increased space but also allowed for a wardrobe, albeit of limited capacity.

Reviewing the Caravette, *The Motor* heralded the vehicle as being "A holiday caravan conversion" and further proclaimed that "the cult of the motor caravan is growing". *The Motor* decided that the Caravette, and therefore presumably its contemporaries, offered deluxe camping rather than complete caravanning, and, in consequence, whilst there was no provision for increasing interior headroom, a number of tent extensions were available, prices ranging from a little under £19 to in excess of £36 according to size and specification. In order to make optimum use of the vehicle interior it was possible to specify a roof rack, the cost of which was £18.

As well as the standard and deluxe model Caravettes, an intermediate model, the Mark III, was introduced at the price of £910. Rather than being marketed as a family tourer, the Mark III was aimed at a completely different clientele – that of the 'Gentleman of the Road', in other words the commercial traveller or businessman who preferred their independent lodgings rather than relying on bed and breakfast or hotel accommodation. Of different layout to the camping versions, the Mark III was arranged to afford daytime working space as well as somewhere to conduct business. The working day over, the interior converted to sleeping accommodation. The advantage of the vehicle, according to contemporary publicity material, was that it doubled as a family camper at weekends and for holidays. Interior features included a filing cabinet and storage system, along with a cooker and pumped water supply, but a coolbox and door-

The Devon marque of motorhome materialised as a result of Lisburne Garage of Torquay and Sidmouth cabinet maker JP White combining resources to produce what was to become one of the best known Volkswagen campers. The MkIII, a brochure cover of which is reproduced here, was marketed for the 'Gentleman of the Road' – in other words, the travelling salesman. (Author's collection)

mounted storage units were absent. Whilst such a model seemed a good idea at the time of its introduction, the evidence is that few were sold, and within two years it was deleted from the Devon catalogue.

During 1960, the Caravette range was reduced to a single model, this no doubt being due to JP White undertaking conversion of the Austin 152 and Morris J2, both of which, along with

Here is the Devon CARAVETTE

MOTORISED CARAVAN ON
THE VOLKSWAGEN MICRO-BUS

the ideal holiday home . . . complete and ready for YOU!

Sleekly Elegant   *Finished to Perfection*

THE FINEST DUAL PURPOSE VEHICLE YOU CAN BUY

The Devon Caravette in post-1960 form showing the Transporter in full camping mode and as an all-purpose vehicle. (Author's collection)

the Volkswagen, were displayed at that year's London Motor Show. Combining the best features of all previous variants, the new Caravette was available as a Kombi or Microbus, both of which were similarly equipped and accommodated two adults and two children. The lounge-cum-dining room converted to a double berth at night, single bunks being located in the cab and above the engine compartment. With its water supply built-in beneath the front bench seat, a fitted washbasin, coolbox and cooker, this Caravette really was home from home, especially when equipped with optional awning or tent.

Aware that the motorhome market could sustain a budget model, Devon introduced the Devonette for 1962. Priced £150 lower than the Caravette, the Devonette's emphasis was on increased interior space and basic camping, hence it lacked some of the furnishings and features of the more expensive model. The same year saw the Caravette equipped with an awning as standard, and both this and the Devonette could be fitted with Devon's Gentlux elevating roof at a cost of £65 to provide for 6ft 6in (2m) interior height.

Over subsequent years Devon made revisions and improvements to its range of vehicles. The Torvette was specified for 1966 to replace the Devonette, and a year later arrived the Spaceway modification which allowed both Torvette and Caravette models to have a walk-through facility from the cab into the living quarters. A rearrangement of vehicle interiors was necessary to provide for the Spaceway effect, now a standard feature on most motorhomes.

With the arrival of the Bay Window Transporter, Devon responded to the vehicle's greater dimensions to produce more flexible layouts. The quality of workmanship and Devon's well-appointed, imaginative and practical interiors were instrumental in there being an enthusiastic following for the vehicles. Caravette and Torvette models remained available with the Bay Window format and were joined at the top of the range by the Eurovette with its quality design and level of equipment, all of which were fitted with Devon's own elevating roof.

For 1971, the Caravette and Eurovette were replaced by the Moonraker which combined the best features of the two models. Another new model, the Sunlander, replaced the Torvette for 1971, but within months the name reverted to Devonette to recall a past era. The Moonraker was tastefully furnished with rich carpet

Top: Devon Caravette Spaceway with roof in elevated position to show lights and ventilators. (Courtesy Ken Cservenka)

Above: Caravette Spaceway interior showing the cooking arrangement in position for outdoor use. The folding table can also be seen. (Courtesy Ken Cservenka)

trim to window level and patterned vinyl floor covering. Interiors were fully equipped and easy conversion of the seating arrangement provided sleeping accommodation for three, increasing to five with the elevated roof model. A feature of the upper berth was its two solid base foam mattress sections which, when joined together, formed a comfortable double bed. Such was the Moonraker's quality appointment that it lived up to the claim of being "the ultimate in luxury".

Introduced at the same time as the Moonraker, the Sunlander was a budget model aimed at a clientele whose preference was for only occasional camping use, and for more general purposes at other times. With additional interior seating than was otherwise the case, the Sunlander's equipment level was relatively meagre, with provision of a basic cooker and absence of washing facilities; instead of a coolbox, food storage comprised nothing more than plastic lined compartments contained either end of the rear seat locker. Renamed Devonette, the vehicle retained its basic appointment and, according to publicity material, somewhat mimicked a proper motor caravan by being essentially an estate car but having cooking, dining and sleeping facilities. In common with its more expensive sibling, the Devonette could be optionally equipped with a pop-top elevating roof and Devon's freestanding Motent.

The early 1970s saw Devon negotiate with Volkswagen a scheme whereby the Caravette – known officially as the Devon VW Caravette – was available through Volkswagen dealerships, and being licensed by Volkswagen carried full manufacture

Left: When the Torvette replaced the Devonette in 1966, the new model sported a walk-through interior. (Courtesy Ken Cservenka)

The last of the Bay Window Devon campers adopted the Moonraker name, as used on earlier models. Seen with its roof elevated, the Moonraker is highly regarded for its exclusive interior. (Courtesy Ken Cservenka)

warranty. To the uninformed, therefore, it would seem that the manufacturer was marketing its own design of motorhome, and to emphasise the point, nowhere in Volkswagen's advertising was there anything to suggest otherwise.

The Devon VW Caravette could be adapted as a people carrier with eight forward facing seats; in a trice the interior became dinette style and, with little effort doubled as a comfortable and superbly equipped family camper complete with fitted cooker with washbasin alongside. For 1974, Devon again offered the Eurovette, now suitably updated and marketed as the firm's top of the range camper and selling alongside the VW Caravette. The Eurovette's remarkable specification featured a sophisticated cooker that was designed for interior or exterior use, for the latter it would swing through 90 degrees. An electric

Devon sold its business in the late 1980s to Devon Conversions, which continued trading in Devon's factory producing models on the T25 chassis. The vehicle illustrated is a Moonraker complete with high roof. Note the auxiliary driving lamps fitted to the lower grille. (Courtesy Ken Cservenka)

water pump, fluorescent lighting, large coolbox, increased capacity sink and storage units were all features welcomed by prospective customers.

To celebrate Devon's twenty-first year of business in 1978, the firm made available 50 special edition Eurovettes, all of which were sumptuously furnished, generously equipped, and painted Oceanic Blue and White.

The last of the Bay Window models were introduced in 1978, with Devon recalling the Moonraker appellation for its top of the range vehicle, and

introducing the Sundowner for the entry level camper. Instead of using either the Kombi or Clipper microbus as a base vehicle for the Sundowner, for the first time Devon constructed the vehicle on the Panel Van, hence its unusual side window arrangement. Rather than the solid wood fittings applied to earlier models, those of the Moonraker and Sundowner were formed from chipboard and covered with Melamine, no doubt as a means of keeping costs and weight to a minimum. The new models were, nevertheless,

supplied with ample storage facilities, furnishings, and a range of equipment that made these the best appointed vehicles Devon had then produced.

In retaining its proven and well-liked style of layout for the third generation Transporter, Devon also chose to preserve the Moonraker and Sundowner names, though in 1982 introduced a new top of the range model, the Sunrise. With its new type of full-length elevating roof, the front of which was higher than the rear and designed to incorporate a ventilation panel protected by a fly screen, the Sunrise featured the highest quality furnishings and fittings. Buoyant sales as well as increasing demand for motorhomes generally encouraged Devon to introduce two additional models to its Volkswagen range in 1986. For clients wanting a top quality two-berth vehicle with every conceivable luxury, that included central heating, clothes drying cabinet, full plumbing, refrigerator, and even a microwave oven that was additional to a conventional cooker, Devon reintroduced the Eurovette name. The Caravette also made its return, still as a people-carrier-cum-family camper, but designed to be more accommodating than the existing Sundowner.

By the late 1980s the competitiveness of the motorhome market was such that increasing numbers of converters were offering conversions on a wide range of vehicle chassis. Devon decided to retire from the motor caravan trade entirely by selling its business and concentrate on welfare vehicles and minibuses. Acquiring Devon's motorhome business, Devon Conversions continued to operate in what had been Devon's factory before moving production to County Durham in 1992 where the Eurovette and Moonraker models continued to be built. When the T4 chassis was introduced Devon Conversions announced two new models, one continuing the Moonraker name, the other marketed as the Aurora. Featuring different layout styles, both were comprehensively equipped and furnished. Staying in County Durham, Devon Conversions moved to new premises at Ferryhill in 1996 where, on introduction of the T5 chassis, production concentrated on a new model of motorhome, the award-winning Moonraker V.

Danbury Multicar

When the Chelmsford, Essex, firm of Danbury Conversions unveiled its motor caravan in 1964, it was evident that the vehicle was, foremost, a multi-purpose affair and, secondly, a dedicated motorhome. The Danbury was less extensively furnished than the Dormobile or Devon, the emphasis on layout being of a modular nature that could be adapted at will. To provide a double bed meant rearranging seating in the vehicle's central area, and utilising the cab and space above the engine compartment for children. Noting that the Danbury lacked an elevating roof with which to afford additional interior space, it is, therefore, surprising to discover that optional high level bunks were available which, supposedly, offered somewhat confined sleeping facilities for up to seven people, three of them adults.

Danbury's early models were constructed on Panel Vans, which meant the converter having to fit its own windows, and, should the customer so specify, fit doors to both sides of the vehicle. Later versions were designed around the Kombi, and aspects of Danbury's style of layout that were particularly attractive included the design of table and cooker, both of which could be used inside or outside the vehicle. Accessories such as awnings also became a popular fitment, as did more luxury items that included a larger awning, longer bunks to suit taller occupants, better-equipped cooker, a built-in radio and clock.

When *Motor* published its caravan test feature in 1967 to publicise the Danbury it was the double doors on both sides of the vehicle that endeared the evaluating journalist. Novel features, such as the under seat storage box lids that doubled as trays, were also liked, and there was much to praise in the way the interior seating adjusted to specific requirements.

In accordance with other suppliers, Danbury adopted interior layouts to provide for walk-through cabs, and, to release more internal space, the spare wheel could be carried on the vehicle's nose. Other features to appear on the Danbury were awning tents, mains hook-up, a Webster elevating roof which, when raised, allowed some 6ft 6in (2m) standing space, a refrigerator and side bunks. Washing facilities were improved and interior storage was enhanced with the fitting of wall and roof pockets. Final words after an in-depth trial of the Danbury were: "We started off feeling rather cramped in the Multicar, but as we got the hang of the moveable units, it turned out to be quite spacious, even under bad weather conditions. In fine weather, with the canopy over the double doors at one side, it was a very pleasant way to live."

Danbury received official Volkswagen recognition in the late 1960s and, similarly to Dormobile and Devon, was able to market the motorhome with full manufacturer's warranty. Though Volkswagen approval was lost in 1972 owing to Devon negotiating an exclusive contract with the manufacturer, it was restored in 1977.

With arrival of the Bay Window Transporter, Danbury established revised layouts for its models that were based on the Kombi and Microbus variants. Both types reflected a multi-purpose design that provided, according to Danbury publicity material, all the amenities of a luxury caravan combined with the practicalities and economy of a vehicle designed for everyday use. It was typical Danbury interior design, with its moveable seating, that made conversion of people carrier or load mover to comfortable motorhome an effortless task. Innovation meant that, for travelling purposes, the interior seats faced forwards, and were easily repositioned to form a dinette arrangement, there being such novelties as a 'pop-up' cooker that was otherwise

Bay Window Danbury conversions are much more common than Splittie types, of which there are only two known survivors. Selling points of the Danbury (according to the sales brochure) were its forward-facing seats (to prevent travel sickness), and ease of clearing away after a meal using the Danbury full-size sink. (Courtesy Ken Cservenka)

Danbury interior. Features included an L-shape day settee and a fold-away cooker and grill. (Courtesy Ken Cservenka)

stored in the seat base behind the front passenger seat. Accessories included an elevated roof, awning, and child's cab bunk.

In 1977, Danbury entered the luxury market with the Danbury Volkswagen Deluxe, a motorhome featuring an elevating roof complete with twin bunks, a built-in two-hob cooker, teak

furnishing and fittings, heat-resistant table and worktops, pumped water, coolbox, a full set of stainless steel cutlery, and Melamine crockery.

Danbury survived the Bay Window and Wedge eras, remaining in business until the end of the 1980s. Although the marque disappeared before the advent of the T4 Volkswagen, it, nevertheless, made a comeback in 2002 in respect of Brazilian-built campers, details of which are to be found at the end of this chapter.

Unsung conversions

The fact that the ubiquitous Volkswagen camper was free of purchase tax and could be driven at similar speeds to that of private motor vehicles is largely thanks to Peter Pitt who was instrumental in expanding the United Kingdom motor caravan market. Operating from premises in London's Southampton Mews, Peter Pitt, of Austrian ancestry, offered his Moto-Caravan camper based on the Volkswagen chassis as early as 1956, and, whilst this was a fairly basic conversion, it, nevertheless, introduced the modular type of interior fittings. Pitt claimed that his motorhome offered in excess of 30 interior layout arrangements, which included sleeping accommodation for up to four people. Despite its ingenious design, the conversion allowed only 56 inches (1422mm) of headroom, thus occupants, once inside the vehicle, were unable to stand upright. A feature of the conversion was its ability to be quickly and easily rearranged, each piece interlocking with another without need for screws or bolts.

Pitt's interior design meant for great flexibility, the furniture being moved to suit customer requirement. The cooker was housed within the interior side door, so as to make effective use of available space, and, as designs progressed, other features were introduced, the like of elevating roofs, awnings, a fold-away bunk in the cab, and a raised bunk within the body of the vehicle.

Peter Pitt was all too aware that when he introduced his Moto-Caravan, the Volkswagen Transporter was classed as a commercial vehicle and, as such, not only attracted purchase tax but was limited to a top speed of 30mph. Motorhomes were exempt from purchase tax and, therefore, the Moto-Caravan was something of an anomaly. In order to overturn the incongruity Pitt drove his vehicle through Windsor Great Park, from which commercials vehicles were banned, and at the subsequent court hearing argued, and won, the case that his converted Transporter was in fact a motorhome and that it should neither be taxed nor subject to a speed restriction.

Like Devon, Peter Pitt, too, marketed his vehicles to travelling salesmen: early Moto-Caravan brochures promised "Spacious comfort for the living requirements of the man on the road brings the daily expenses into shillings in place of pounds. 1½ minutes' rearrangement gives you a perfect conference table and seating to entertain and conduct your business in your own surroundings. Luggage space to take 16 average suit or sample cases is provided." Indeed, Moto-Caravan publicity material claimed that 1½ minutes was all that was needed to convert the interior "from lounge to dining room, from dining room to sleeper".

An optional extra advertised in Peter Pitt's early publicity brochures was 'The Loft', which when fitted to the roof took the form of a tent in its raised position. Accessed by an external ladder, the loft tent, using the Transporter's roof as a base, accommodated two adults with a degree of comfort. When not required, and with the vehicle on the move, the loft folded flat to form a luggage rack for day travel.

In 1960, the Moto-Caravan carried Pitt's design of elevating roof marketed as the Rising Sunshine Roof. The following year, Pitt Moto-Caravans merged with Canterbury Sidecars Ltd of Romford; thereafter production moved to Romford, vehicles were marketed as Canterbury Pitt Conversions, and two years later the company relocated to South Ockenden in Essex. Pitt's conversions acquired a popular following, the vehicles remaining largely unchanged until production ceased late in 1969, just months after Peter Pitt's death that February. Whilst it had been planned to offer a Bay Window camper conversion, none are known to

have been built other than an example constructed for Peter's personal use.

Just as Lisburne Garage and JP White had formed an association to produce the Devon, so Moortown Motors of Regent Street, Leeds, and Bamforth Joinery of East Heslerton cooperated to produce the MkI Autohome in 1958-9. This was a luxury camper featuring a child's berth in the cab, fitted cooking and washing facilities, coolbox, gas lighting for the living area, and Formica top furniture.

Two years later two new versions of the Autohome were announced, the MkIA and MkIIA, both of which were constructed to the highest standards of craftsmanship. The two models were similarly equipped, the MkIIA offering superior trim finish and, optionally, an awning tent at extra cost.

The Moto-Caravan interior showing the style of layout. During renovation of this vehicle the owner has been careful to retain the period flavour. (Courtesy Ken Cservenka)

The Autohome range was modified in 1962 with two more new models, the MkIB, which was of similar layout to earlier designs, and the MkV, which featured a walk-though layout. Vehicles supplied from 1960 could be fitted with elevating roofs, there being a choice

This Moortown Motors publicity photograph shows the interior of its MkI model Autohome. The table could be stowed away and the washbasin and cooker units concealed within cabinet units when not in use. Did gentlemen really wear suits when on holiday, even in the late 1950s? (Author's collection)

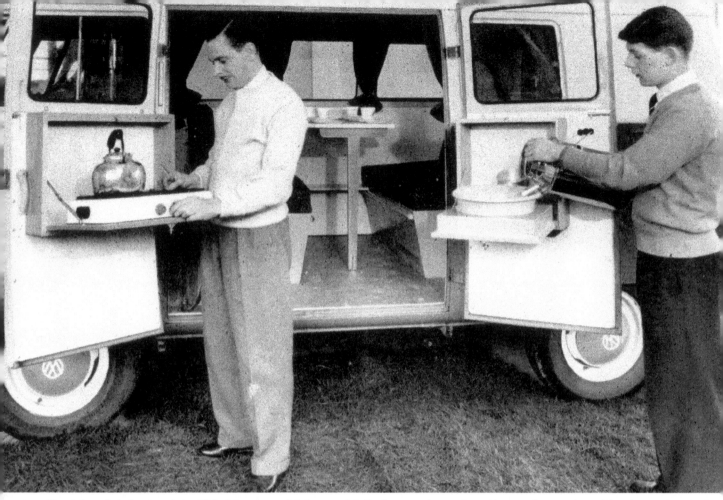

Camping Autohome style. This Moortown Motors publicity image shows how the cooker and washbasin are located on its early models. There is an uneasy feel about this contrived photograph. (Author's collection)

between Moortown's own design and that supplied by Calthorpe which was a windowed, domed affair.

Moortown's conversions accommodated four people, there being a double bed arrangement in the body of the camper, and two singles, one of which was situated above the engine compartment, the other across the cab section. In the latter case the bench seat opened out to what was essentially a cot, with the bulkhead forming one side and the squab, laying flat, acting as the mattress; the seat cushion formed the other side and tilted against the steering column. Essentially for child use was an optional and an easily assembled 'stretcher berth' located above the foot of the double bed. In common with a number of conversions, the Moortown, though of high quality, was short-lived and fell into obscurity before the introduction of the Bay Window Transporter.

Split-screen rarities

A number of camping conversions appeared in the formative years of the Transporter, some, such as those already mentioned, being of enduring construction and fitted with high grade furnishings and quality fittings. Some other offerings enjoyed only a fleeting appearance with often few examples sold, their survival to the present day being rare. These rarities included the like of the Service Mota-Caravan, Slumberwagen and Caraversions Hi-Top.

"For Holidays and Travel – The All Star Holiday Home" was the marketing message broadcast by Service Garages of Colchester when advertising the Service Motor Caravan, which was known as the Mota-Caravan. Priced at £825, this rather basic and unsophisticated conversion was said to sleep a family of four but, in practice, only accommodated two adults. Compared to other conversions that were available, and which offered much more in the way of comfort and convenience, the Mota-Caravan might well have appeared somewhat unrefined. Within just over a year of its introduction, the Service was being advertised in the motoring Press at the reduced price of £797, an indication of limited demand. In order to promote sales, Service offered a range of

THIS IS a motorised caravan which can be [con]verted very simply into [a s]mall, temporary home, [w]ith every need readily available. The famous [Volk]swagen chassis needs [n]o introduction for its wonderful service and reliability.

EUROPEAN CARS LTD

129 OLD BROMPTON ROAD

SOUTH KENSINGTON SW7

TELEPHONE FREMANTLE 7711

Maurice Calthorpe's unique style of elevating roof was fitted to a number of motorised caravans, including the Slumberwagen marketed by European Cars Ltd. of London's South Kensington. (Author's collection)

competitively priced options, such as a walk-through cab, elevating roof, sliding sunroof and awning. None of these helped increase orders by any significant margin and, by 1966, production ceased.

Volkswagen dealer, European Cars Ltd of South Kensington, offered the Slumberwagen in 1959, the Deluxe version costing £950, while a model featuring the Calthorpe elevating roof commanded a further £100. Slumberwagen publicity cleverly depicted vehicles solely fitted with the Calthorpe roof in the raised position, thus giving rise to the belief that Calthorpe roof models were the mainstay of production. The

Slumberwagen, incidentally, was the first Volkswagen camper to feature an elevating roof, and predated Dormobile and Devon models with elevated roofs by at least two years.

Maurice Calthorpe's elevating roof was first utilised on the 1957 Bedford-based Calthorpe Home Cruiser. It proved to be a robust domed metal elevating affair which added both natural light and height to a vehicle's interior: advertised as being completely weatherproof, the Calthorpe roof could be raised or lowered within a few seconds and was among the best designs of elevating roofs tested by *The Autocar*.

Features of the Slumberwagen

were its 6ft 4in (193cm) well-upholstered double bed, children's double bunk, full length wardrobe, and quality furnishings and fittings. European Cars Ltd, which specialised in converting Bedfords and Commas to motorhomes, evidently made a good job of the Transporter, and incorporated to the interior design a degree of storage space mostly absent on other conversions.

The confinements of the Transporter led some converters to devise permanently extended roofs, and a particularly interesting arrangement was that offered by Caraversions, whose premises at Lexham Gardens Mews in South Kensington were in near vicinity to rival European Cars. With

143

its vast, upturned bath-shape roof, marketed as the HiTop, fitted to the Transporter, the arrangement did little for aesthetics, and considerably less for the vehicle's handling characteristics and streamlining. With an overall height of 8ft 2in (2489mm) and a lot of wind resistance, the claim by Caraversions that the conversion was capable of 59mph (94kph) cruising speed and 28-30mpg (10-9 litres/100km) fuel consumption is hardly credible.

Designed for world-wide travel, the HiTop, introduced at £1190 and increasing to £1240, had as standard features, an Electrolux gas refrigerator, a two-burner and grill gas cooker, stainless steel sink with water pumped from a 12 gallon (54.55 litre) under-floor tank. A comprehensive array of utensils was provided, including two saucepans, a frying pan, the ubiquitous teapot, and a full set of crockery and cutlery. There was sleeping accommodation for two adults in a double bed in the body of the vehicle, and two adult single beds built in tandem in the loft which, along with fitted clothes cupboards, was reached by a two-piece ladder. There was seating for three, and sufficient space to stand upright, even with all beds made up. Additionally, the louvred windows built into the HiTop allowed for ventilation and prevented condensation, even when raining. An indication of Caraversions' high specification was that each bed and seat had individual lighting, the upper beds when not required could be used for storage purposes, blinds were fitted to the rear and side windows, and the cab could be curtained off from the living quarters.

A letter dated 28th May 1964 sent by Caraversions and addressed to S Burrell Esq of Halifax in Yorkshire confirmed that the converter was introducing a 'low-roof' version of the HiTop, and that it was identical to the standard model except for the absence

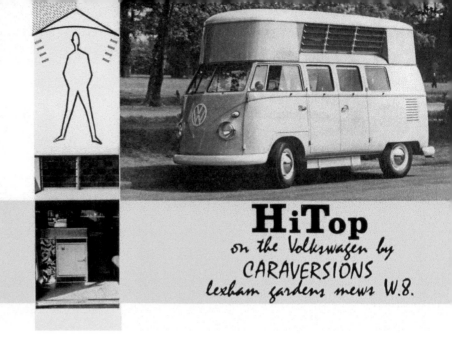

HiTop
on the Volkswagen by
CARAVERSIONS
lexham gardens mews W.8.

There can be few camper conversions that are more unusual than the HiTop which was sold by Caraversions of west London. For all its unconventionality it was, nevertheless, highly practical, even if it was ugly, limited the Transporter's speed, and was difficult to handle in strong crosswinds. (Author's collection)

of all the units above the original VW roof, which remained intact. The conversion, priced at £975, was designed for two adults and a child and featured the same high standard of furnishings and fittings as the HiTop model which, incidentally, reverted to the original price of £1190. There is no indication that the new model ever materialised.

More Bay Windows

The introduction of the Mark II Transporter, along with a rapidly growing demand for motorhomes, persuaded a number of new converters to enter the motor caravan market, such as the Catford Motor Caravan Centre with its Cavalier, Richard Holdsworth, Oxley Coachcraft and Viking Motorhomes. The Cavalier was sold through the Catford Motor Caravan Centre at Catford Hill in south London, and featured a permanent high roof fitting, complete with front and side windows. Simple in design and layout, the Cavalier was, nevertheless, equipped with high quality

fittings and accommodated two adults in comfort. Specification included teak finish furniture with Melamine 'white clean' surfaces, double sided vinyl and cloth upholstery, coolbox or optional refrigerator, and stainless steel cooker and sink units. Contemporary publicity material claimed it was possible to transform the interior seating into a large double bed in less than 10 seconds!

Richard Holdsworth Conversions first appeared in 1967, but it was not until the early 1970s that the firm had become established, and moved from Ashford in Middlesex to larger premises near Reading in Berkshire. Two levels of specification were offered by Holdsworth: Layout 1 being the basic model, and Layout 2 the deluxe. Marketed as a multi-purpose vehicle rather than a motorhome, Layout 1 was available with an optional elevating roof, with its two tapered bunks designed for child use, the dinette arrangement converted to a low level double bed, and there was sufficient room for a child to sleep above the engine compartment.

Richard Holdsworth Conversions offered two layouts on its Bay Window campers. This is Layout 1 which is a basic arrangement showing the interior configuration: the cooker, mounted on top of the refrigerator, can be removed from the vehicle and used outside. The sleeping quarters are also shown; children are accommodated on the engine deck, there is a low level double bed suitable for adults and, in this instance, two tapering bunks are housed in the optional elevating roof. (Author's collection)

Holdsworth's Layout 2 was designed is all the more luxurious compared to Layout 1, and includes a 72in double bed that folds out from over the engine deck. (Author's collection)

Layout 2's emphasis was on luxury, and comprised built-in water supply, stainless steel cooker, and a coolbox, though a refrigerator was optional. A large double bed folded out from over the engine deck to maximise interior floor space, the optional elevating roof providing two further bunks.

Holdsworth conversions are highly regarded and have, on a number of occasions, won awards for quality and design. The company remains a forerunner in motorhome design and construction, the Wedge, T4 and current designs being enthusiastically received.

Oxley Coachcraft of Craven Street in Hull was already recognised as a long standing caravan and commercial coachbuilder when the firm entered the motorhome market in the early 1970s. Two models based on the Panel Van were offered, one being the Airflow HT, with its standard fitment high top roof, the other the Rheinlander, which featured an elevating roof complete with windows and central opening roof light.

The Airflow was fully equipped with a kitchen unit comprising a cooker, washing facilities, water container and coolbox. The dinette arrangement seated up to five people, and easily converted to a double bed, while provision existed for two further single bunks and a large cab bunk. Furnishing was to the highest quality, and, while the low-line high top roof afforded adequate headroom, it also provided additional light and ventilation from its transom windows.

The Rheinlander was similarly equipped to the Airflow but accommodated up to six people, there being a dinette-cum-double bed conversion, a child's bunk, two large roof bunks and an optional cab bunk. Both models were comprehensively specified to include aluminium window frames, louvred windows, quilted gold nylon upholstery, and even teak curtain pelmets. There was a wide range of accessories, too, including a radio, refrigerator and side awning.

When Viking Motorhomes of Berkhampstead launched its camper conversion in 1970, contemporary publicity material claimed it to be an entirely new concept in motor caravan design. With its elevating roof and optional Isabella awning, said to be the most fabulous side tent ever made by man, the Viking's accommodation increased from four people (the camper provided for a double bed and two roof bunks) to seven. With the accent on quality fittings, Viking Motorhomes further claimed that the vehicle's galley was the most revolutionary and well equipped to be found on any Volkswagen camper.

By 1974, Viking Motorhomes had changed its name to Motorhomes International and moved to new premises in Stanbridge, Bedfordshire. A new model, the Spacemaker, appeared soon after, there being two versions available, the Viking and Pioneer, to offer a choice of interior layout. Significant about the Spacemaker was its full-length elevating roof which, by all standards, was huge and easily accommodated two adults in separate bunks.

Motorhomes International devised an elevating roof to incorporate semi-automatic lifting courtesy of gas-filled struts, thus making it simple to operate. Furthermore. the innovative design made the most from a little space, and to make space where none had existed. Recognising that most elevating roofs compromised bunk space, Viking engineered its roof to be side-hinged so that it opened to overhang one side of the vehicle, and then sought an overhang feature along the opposite side. In

that way, the bunks moved outwards over the sides of the motorhome to leave more room inside. Motorhomes' design evoked controversy within the motorhome industry by Volkswagen publicly criticising the roof's design and

claiming it made the vehicle unsafe. Motorhomes rejected the claim and invited Volkswagen to undertake a full appraisal of the vehicle, but when the motoring Press took the view that Volkswagen's marketing policy

ioneer

y motor caravans

Following the style of the Danbury, the Viking motorhome offered forward-facing seating which converted quickly and effortlessly into either a dining area or sleeping quarters. A feature of the Spacemaker, which is illustrated with roof in the raised position, is that the roof overhangs the side of the vehicle to give maximum space within the roof section. (Author's collection)

Motorhomes' products were well received and continued to sell until well into the Wedge era. Competition from other types of motorhome, as well as other Volkswagen-based conversions, meant that Motorhomes' market share diminished, and production ceased in the mid-1980s.

had been largely responsible for the censure, that matter became all the more involved, especially when the company advertised it was possible to retrospectively fit the Spacemaker to an existing vehicle. Moreover, Volkswagen's criticism was seen to be employed towards other type of roof conversions, thus a battle between Volkswagen, and the three official converters on one hand, and other conversion specialists on the other, waged for some time.

Campers from around the world

Camper conversions were as popular in mainland Europe and beyond as they were in America and the United Kingdom. Holland was a vibrant

The Karmann Mobil appeared in 1934 and its caravan-type body set a trend in the design of later motorhome development. (Courtesy Ken Cservenka)

market, especially with Ben Pon's influence selling Volkswagen from the outset. In 1978, however, the Ben Pon dealership promoted the Devon range of vehicles under the Eurec name, the relationship between the two organisations remaining through the Bay Window and Wedge eras. Another Dutch firm involved with importing camping conversions from an early date was Amescador which, until, the arrival of the Bay window model, was Westfalia distributors. During the 1970s, Amescador constructed Bay Window conversions with a range of pop-up and elevating roofs.

Also from Holland was the Bilbo camper which was a conversion based on ex-army and police Transporters. A small business converting a limited number of Transporters, Bilbo's proprietors moved to Reigate in the United Kingdom during the mid-1970s, where they continued their business. The Marlfield, a Bay Window conversion, was named after the area in which the Bilbo factory was situated, and in the Wedge era there appeared the Arragon and Weekender models, along with a new version of the Marlfield. Today, Bilbo is forefront in motorhome design, constructing a range of vehicles on different chassis, and, having won Volkswagen approval, continues building motor caravans on the Volkswagen T5 platform. When tested by *Which Motorcaravan* in November 2004, the T5-based Bilbo Celex was voted as being the best-

The Karmann Gipsy featured an over-cab extension when constructed on the T25 platform. (Courtesy Ken Cservenka)

148

equipped VW-based camper available on the United Kingdom market.

When the German-built Karmann Mobil appeared in 1974, a connection with the Karmann-built Beetle Cabrio and Karmann-Ghia was established. Based on the Bay Window model, the Karmann Mobil was influenced by the South African Jurgens Auto Villa, with its purpose-designed body and over-cab extension. Though the Karmann Mobil, licensed by Jurgens, did not feature an over-cab extension, the vehicle itself, with its caravan type body, set a trend that has evolved as the modern day coachbuilt motorhome. When the T25 platform was introduced, Karmann updated the Mobil's dimensions accordingly, changed the model name to Karmann Gipsy, but left the interior layout largely unaltered.

The Jurgens Auto Villa motorhome on which the Karmann Mobil was based was quite revolutionary when introduced in 1973. Featuring a coachbuilt body incorporating an over-cab feature that was built on a Bay Window Pick-up platform, the Auto Villa followed caravan construction practice, with its extruded aluminium framework and lightweight aluminium panelling, all of which gave the vehicle its required strength. Ingeniously devised and fully equipped, the Auto Villa's features included a separate cloakroom with foot bath and chemical toilet, a dining

With its over-cab extension, the South African Bay Window Jurgens Auto Villa was luxuriously equipped. With the body constructed on the caravan principle, strength was derived from its extruded aluminium framework and aluminium panelling. (Courtesy Ken Cservenka)

The demountable camper was popular in North America but generated only limited sales in Europe. The Tischer Demountable as depicted on a Bay Window chassis was also available on the T25 platform, but such vehicles are rare. (Courtesy Ken Cservenka)

area that converted to a double bed or twin berths, a kitchenette, and plenty of storage space. Thanks to the vehicle's design, there was sufficient headroom in which to comfortably walk around, and, being a full four-berth motorhome, a second double berth was accommodated above the cab, access to which was gained via a removable ladder.

The Auto Villa was powered by a 2-litre engine with manual transmission: an automatic version had been proposed but trials had been unsuccessful owing to the vehicle's weight, performance and handling characteristics.

Several short-lived conversions appeared during the Split-Screen and Bay Window eras, some of which were built in impressive numbers, while others enjoyed only limited production. One of the more successful offerings was the POBA from Denmark, which was based on the design of Westfalia's Camping Box, the interior design continuing over to Bay Window models before the firm fell into obscurity.

Of the other short-lived products, the Tischer Demountable, is of particular note because it followed a practice popular in the USA and Canada but largely ignored in Europe. The idea of carrying one's motorhome piggyback style to a chosen area, and then unloading it as a stand-alone caravan, while the slave vehicle was used as a touring vehicle, never really caught on in Europe. The Tischer Demountable achieved a degree of success with designs suitable for the Bay Window and T25 Volkswagens, all of which were luxuriously appointed with fitted kitchens and shower rooms, and with high quality furnishings.

Camper conversions were also constructed in Australia, the first models being sold through Adelaide Volkswagen dealership Lanock Motors; later examples were marketed by Volkswagen Australia. South African conversions, before the emergence of

The T4 chassis was popular with a wide range of converters, including Compass, whose Calypso model is illustrated here. (Courtesy Ken Cservenka)

the aforementioned Jurgens Auto Villa and Karmann Mobil, were constructed from CKD parts sent from Hanover. These, as well as vehicles built under the administration of Volkswagen South Africa, along with other foreign built vehicles, are to be found elsewhere in this book.

Volkswagen campers in the new millennium

When Volkswagen introduced the T4 Transporter, Kombi vans, base and chassis cabs were made available to approved converters, including Auto-Sleepers, Autohomes, Auto Trail, Compass Caravans, Cockburn Holdsworth, and the Swift Group. Three vehicle types became available: van conversions with elevating roofs; fixed high-top van conversions; and coachbuilt motorhomes.

Elevating roof van conversions were ideally suited for two people,

and, as well as ideally performing as compact motorhomes, could also be used as multi-purpose everyday vehicles. Fixed high-roof conversions also ideally accommodated two people, though the vehicle's additional height provided interior standing space as well as extra berths and storage capacity. Being constructed on a base or chassis cab, coachbuilt motorhomes allowed for a range of body styles, with larger vehicles providing more in the way of amenities and luxury.

The same formula has been extended to the T5 range, and, with it, converters have been able to devise innovative and imaginative interior designs and layouts to make as much use of space as is possible. Advancing technology has meant that power-operated roofs and other luxury items have become commonplace, and purchasers have come to expect an element of customisation when it

comes to fitting useful, practical and high quality furnishings and appliances. Responding to demands of a new generation of motorhome enthusiasts, who expect more from their vehicles than their peers, and who enjoy greater amounts of leisure time, converters build into their vehicles features that were once associated with only the most luxurious caravans. Thus, the modern camper has become home from home.

For the dedicated enthusiast who wants to combine tradition with the latest technology, there is now an opportunity to purchase a new Bay Window camper. Having acquired the rights to use the Danbury name in 2002, Beetles UK undertook converting Type 2 Transporters that are currently built in Brazil. Though the Brazilian-built Transporters appear very much the same as their historic counterparts, they, nevertheless, feature a number

of minor external and interior design differences, including a slightly higher roofline, redesigned bumpers and cab door bottoms, alloy wheels, and thick-rimmed steering wheel. In the summer of 2006, Beetles UK was offering the last of the air-cooled Bay Window models. Powered by a multi-point fuel injected 1600cc air-cooled engine, the new Danbury has a catalytic converter and front disc brakes. Complete with a three-year warranty, two versions of the Danbury are sold, the Rio being of multi-purpose design, and the Diamond a camper par excellence.

With its removable middle seats and an interior layout that allows the vehicle to be utilised as a practical everyday vehicle or occasional camper, the Rio is equipped with a pull-out bed, dining table, two-hob cooker, cool box,

sink, pumped water, and generous storage space. When fitted with the optional elevating roof, two hammock bunks provide additional sleeping accommodation.

Replacing the Surf that was introduced at the same time as the Rio is the Diamond. The interior design has the benefit of seating five people in comfort, while the well-equipped kitchen is mounted horizontally across the front of the vehicle, to the rear of the cab seats. The kitchen specification includes a self lighting stainless steel hob and grill, and there is a matching stainless steel sink, complete with water pumped from a removable onboard container. Wastewater is disposed of via an external socket. There's an electric coolbox, but a chest type refrigerator which can be used as

Production of the air-cooled Transporter ceased in 2005, after which the vehicle, retaining Bay Window styling, was fitted with a 1.4-litre, water-cooled engine. The vehicle illustrated is one of the last air-cooled Bullis to enter the United Kingdom for conversion to a campervan. For Bulli enthusiasts, such vehicles will become collectors' items. (Courtesy Ken Cservenka)

Bay Window campers were still available in 2006. Air-cooled Transporters built in Brazil were imported and converted by Beetles UK using the Danbury name which the firm acquired in 2002. (Courtesy Ken Cservenka)

a freezer is optionally available. In the kitchen area, there's a removable table and, alongside, a seating arrangement that cleverly converts to a large double bed. A child's cab bunk is optional.

The Diamond's elevating roof gives an internal roof height of 2m (6ft 6in) when raised, and also provides sleeping accommodation for two adults in a double bed. The roof canvas is fully waterproof, and incorporates a ventilation panel. For use in cooler climates, there's an independent blown-

air petrol heater, which can used when the vehicle is moving or in camping mode.

It's possible for the Diamond to be personalised to customer specification: kitchen units are finished in marine grade, moisture resistant, light wood finish ply, with black rolled-edge worktops. Upholstery is either vinyl or fabric to choice, and, for luxury, there's the alternative of hide, while curtains are supplied as standard. Flooring is either wood-effect vinyl or black rubber. Accessories include a flat screen television and DVD player, mains electricity hook up and bike rack, along with a choice of two-tone colour schemes. Performance and equipment-wise, Bay Window Transporters were never as good as this!

Prices for the Diamond started at £19,707 for right-hand drive models (£1000 less for left-hand drive), and, if one were to have all the accessories and upgrades, such as awning, bike rack, roof rack, elevating roof and double bed, alloy wheels, porta potti, mains hook up, child's cab bunk, flat screen television and DVD, full repaint in specified colours, lowered suspension, and much more, be prepared to spend a further £23,000!

The 2006 Bay Window Model built in Brazil is fitted with a 1.4-litre water-cooled engine that is designed to run on alcohol, and which, according to Volkswagen, is quieter and more fuel efficient than its predecessor. For the purist, this move towards modernity might be too much to contemplate ...

Chapter

8

Transporters from around the world

The Transporter arrived in Australia thanks to the efforts of Lionel Spencer, whose company, Regent Motors, trading under the name Spencer Motors, established a continent-wide dealer and distribution network. When the importation of vehicles from Germany proved inadequate in terms of demand, arrangements were made to commence building Bullis locally from CKD kits sent from Wolfsburg. Assembly of Transporters, such as the example shown, was conducted in association with coachbuilder Martin and King located at Clayton, a Melbourne suburb. (Courtesy Ken Cservenka)

The Australian Transporter

There is mention in the previous chapter of the Australian Volkswagen dealership Lanock Motors of Adelaide being instrumental in marketing a camper conversion. The vehicle, sold as the VW Kombi Van Caravanette, appears to have been nicely executed, but there is little indication as to the numbers sold. Though Lanock Motors' conversion first appeared in 1958, the Transporter was no stranger to Australia, the first vehicles having been exported to the continent five years earlier in 1953.

The Transporter's arrival in Australia was largely due to the efforts of two people, Lionel Spencer and Baron KD Von Oetzen. It was the same Von Oetzen who had accompanied Porsche and Hitler when they met in 1934, the Baron's work with Auto-Union having taken him to Australia before the war where he met Spencer, who, being the owner of Regent Motors (Holdings) Ltd, was the appointed Auto-Union franchise holder for Melbourne. Spencer and Baron Von Oetzen were to become firm friends, and it was the latter, who, having joined Volkswagen in 1950, was responsible for introducing Spencer to

Volkswagen made headline news in Australia when examples were submitted to some rigorous endurance testing as part of the 1955 Redex trials, then considered as being arguably the most demanding rally anywhere in the world. The result was unprecedented demand for both the Beetle and the Bulli. CKD assembly of the Transporter failed to meet the flood of orders and, ultimately, Volkswagen (Australasia) Ltd was formed, and with it came fully localised production with a substantial number of the vehicle's components being sourced from within the continent. A feature of the Australian-built Bulli is the design of cooling louvres, which, because of the hostile climate, are of larger configuration to those seen on German-built vehicles. (Courtesy Ken Cservenka)

the marque. When visiting Europe in the early 1950s, Spencer was invited by the Baron to visit Wolfsburg where he was cordially received, taken on a tour of the Volkswagen empire, and shown Beetles and Transporters being constructed.

Lionel Spencer was so impressed by what he saw at Wolfsburg that, in 1953, Regent Motors emerged as Australia's Volkswagen distributor. More than being merely a sales outlet, Regent Motors, trading under the name of Spencer Motors, undertook responsibility for importing Volkswagens

to Australia and establishing a country-wide dealer and distribution network which would operate in compliance with Volkswagen's strict policies. No fewer than four Transporters and 27 Beetles were delivered to Australia by the end of 1953; plans also materialised for the assembly of CKD Beetles at Clayton, a suburb fourteen miles from Melbourne, courtesy of coachbuilder Martin and King, working under contract to Regent Motors.

So, what put Volkswagen in touch with Australian motorists who were more used to vehicles of

considerably greater power and size than Wolfsburg's product? Regent Motors' general manager Allan Gray sought to do exactly what other motoring personalities had achieved in earlier times by submitting vehicles to some pretty harsh endurance testing and reliability trials. And what a surprise there was for those Australians who might have been dismissive towards the Volkswagen to see it taking on Goliath: in the 1955 Redex trials which were staged throughout Australia, and which were accepted as being the most demanding anywhere, they saw

Regent's Volkswagens take first and second place.

Figures for 1954 show that some 700 Transporters were exported to Australia, and, once assembly of CKD units shipped from Wolfsburg are taken into account, the evidence is that a combined total of around 1000 vehicles were sold. Volkswagen had captured a tiny proportion of Australia's commercial market, but it was one that was going to increase substantially. Those customers who had the foresight to buy a Volkswagen, with its air-cooling and minimal maintenance, realised it to be ideal for the Australian climate and terrain.

The demand for Volkswagens was unprecedented and, by 1958, it was clear that within a short period of time, the marque would account for ten per cent of the Australian car market, and six per cent of national commercial sales. The truth was that the existing sales and distribution arrangement had become inadequate, and if the rate of demand were to continue there would have to be a major strategic rethink.

The answer was much in the same idiom as the United Kingdom's approach to building 'foreign' vehicles whereby, for example, Renaults, Citroëns and Fiats were assembled using a high percentage of locally sourced components, each locally based filial being a wholly owned subsidiary of the parent concern. In that way Volkswagen (Australasia) Pty came into being, with Volkswagen owning 51 per cent of the shares. The new company not only acquired Martin and King, but invested $A24 million in expanding the works and installing new presses. Higher demand meant even further expansion, and, by the mid-1960s, Volkswagen (Australasia) Ltd was established.

In time, Australian-built Beetles comprised 90 per cent locally sourced parts, while Transporters, known colloquially throughout Australia as 'Kombis' regardless of the actual model, managed 40 per cent. Nevertheless, the content of Australia-sourced components for the Transporter included a number of items, such as shock absorbers, exhaust systems, seat belts and trim items, many of which carried a series of emblems unique to Australian-built vehicles. The insignia sometimes featured the VW emblem together with a Kangaroo, and on others the letter A preceded the encircled VW, or in some instances simply an outline of Australia was evident. Clayton-assembled vehicles were modified in accordance with specification changes introduced in Germany, albeit with a delay of around three months.

Clayton-assembled vehicles were exported to New Zealand, Fiji, Papua New Guinea, British Soloman Islands and Western Samoa. Owing to the importance of assembling Volkswagens in Australia – the term assembly being loosely used as many parts were actually being manufactured – vehicles were being purchased by fleet customers who would not normally have ordered 'foreign' makes: additionally, Volkswagen was increasingly specified by State Government departments. The Snowy Mountains Authority acquired a single vehicle for evaluation purposes and promptly ordered a batch of one hundred: Australian-built Transporters were purchased by the Australian Army, the first order that was placed being for 46 Bronze Green Microbuses. Orders were forthcoming from the Royal Australian Air Force for Microbuses and Panel vans for use at RAAF stations. Other customers included the continent's ambulance services, the Australian Post Office, Tasmanian Hydro Electricity Service and other electricity generators, Qantas Airways, Rothman Cigarettes, and HG Palmer Electrical.

Owing to Australia's climate, particularly the harsh outback environment, there were some differences between the locally produced vehicles and those constructed at Wolfsburg. The air vents positioned above the swage line for engine cooling purposes were larger than was usually the case, and, from 1961, there were two rows of vents instead of one. The 15in wheel size was retained for Australian vehicles when German production specification changed to 14in in 1963. Except for a very few vehicles which had 12-volt electrics, all were fitted with 6-volt systems. Full manufacturing at Clayton ceased in 1968, and, thereafter, CKD assembly resumed, the kits being sent to Melbourne direct from Hanover and Wolfsburg.

Some Volkswagen dealers introduced modifications either to their own design or to customer requirements. Unique to Australia was the Clayton-built high-roof Panel van, which, being 50cm (19.6in) higher than the standard Transporter, allowed a person of average height to stand upright inside the vehicle. To prevent engine failure owing to excessive intake of dust from Australia's mainly unmade outback roads, it was common practice to fit devices intended to protect engines from the effects of the tough environment. These included heavy duty oil bath air cleaners, including the Cyclone air filter which was an official Volkswagen special equipment item. For use in countries with high levels of road dust, another Volkswagen special fitment primarily intended for Pick-ups allowed clean air to be collected from the front of the vehicle and piped to the engine. The arrangement negated use of the low level ventilation panels at the rear of the platform which had a habit of sucking up debris which was then deposited in the engine. This design was adopted in 1962 for all Australian Pick-ups and was factory-fitted.

Clayton-built Transporters were furnished with two rows of cooling louvres from 1961, as seen on this Panel Van. Australian Transporters retained their 15in wheels (the alloys as fitted to the vehicle illustrated are a recent modification) when European specification Transporters were fitted with 14in types. (Courtesy Ken Cservenka)

Australian Transporters were fitted with a unique type of locally sourced speedometer. (Courtesy Ken Cservenka)

For Australians intent on seeing their country at ground level, the Transporter was accepted as being the vehicle in which to explore the continent. It was also the choice of many overseas visitors arriving on Australian soil who, having already experienced the joys of the Bulli in their native countries, were in want of nothing else with which to explore the world's largest island.

Many of the forefront camper conversions found their way to Australia, especially the like of the Westfalia. The Dormobile was manufactured in Australia under licence, and this, together with the Clayton-produced Campmobile, satisfied demand. With cessation of Transporter manufacture at Clayton, the Melbourne works converted back to CKD assembly, this leading to the introduction of the Adventurer.

Australia's version of the Campmobile, the Adventurer, was offered in three model designations, all of which were produced by E Sopru and Company, in conjunction with Volkswagen Australia. The Adventurer was the economy model featuring a seating-cum-bed arrangement, minimal furnishing and washing facilities, and lacking a cooker or coolbox. It did, however, have a mains electricity hook up. The Traveller, the intermediate model, did include a two-ring gas cooker and a refrigerator, while

157

In addition to the double row of cooling louvres, Australian-built Bullis featured a number of technical differences to their German siblings, notably the type of heavy-duty air cleaners that were designed to meet the demands of the country's tough environment. The example illustrated, which is owned by Ray and Margaret Ashcroft, is one of the last split-screen Bullis to be built. (Courtesy Ken Cservenka)

the Adventurer Deluxe was furnished with cloth trimmed seating, a hotplate, built-in sink unit and bottle rack, the latter no doubt fitted to store supplies of Australia's wines! The Adventurer Deluxe was also supplied with an awning, mosquito nets, screened windows, sun visors, towbar, and an optional roof-mounted dust-free air-cleaner. All Adventurers were fitted with

The Ashcroft's Bulli displays a number of features peculiar to Australian construction, namely the type of bumpers, 15in wheels and, out of sight, the design of facia switchgear and components. (Courtesy Ken Cservenka)

kangaroo bars, nose-mounted spare wheels, and elevating roofs, which incorporated ventilation skylights.

A number of other conversions were available, the main ones being SunCamper, which remains in business, Sunliner, and Trakka. The previously mentioned Lanock Motors continued in business converting vehicles into the Bay Window era, after which the firm appears to have disappeared.

Transporters in South Africa

The Transporter is as much at home in the continent of Africa as it is Australia. Miles of deserted bush roads and a searing climate perfectly test the Bulli's tough character.

The fact that the Transporter was built in South Africa is largely attributable to the decision to assemble and distribute Studebakers from a purpose-built factory at Uitenhage in 1946. It was not only Studebakers that were assembled at Uitenhage, Austins, too, were built there, and from 1951 Beetles were driving off the assembly lines again courtesy of the efforts of Baron von Oetzen. The works at Uitenhage, overseen by one of Studebaker's presidents, became known as South Africa Motor Assemblers, and, in 1956, Wolfsburg acquired a controlling interest in the plant, thereafter production was solely Volkswagen. Ten years later the factory and assembly operation was renamed Volkswagen of South Africa.

The Transporter arrived in South Africa when a batch of 24 vehicles was exported there in 1952. Assembly of CKD Transporters commenced at Uitenhage in 1955 and, in common with those produced in Australia, had right-hand drive. Like the Clayton operation, that at Uitenhage saw Transporters being assembled with a high proportion of locally sourced components.

Similarly to Australian-built vehicles, those assembled at Uitenhage were uniquely fitted to combat South Africa's harsh terrain and environment. Heavy duty air cleaners were specified, and differences were again evident in respect of engine design and of cooling ducts. The entire range of Transporters was built at Uitenhage, and, in some instances, there were some hybrids,

Volkswagens were constructed in South Africa in purpose-built premises once administered by Studebaker at Uitenhage. Construction of Transporters, from CKD parts imported from Germany, commenced in 1955, the camper conversions being of Westfalia Campmobile design, as represented in this photograph. (Courtesy Ken Cservenka)

one being the Fleetline bus which had the frontal appearance of a Bay Window vehicle combined with the Split-Screen's loading doors and tailgate.

The majority of camper conversions supplied for South Africa were Westfalia Campmobiles despatched from Germany in CKD form and locally assembled at Uitenhage. Only when the Bay Window model was introduced did Volkswagen of South Africa produce its own version of the Campmobile, which was marketed as the Kampmobile and designed as a multi-purpose vehicle. Components were either authentic Westfalia or items produced locally to a similar pattern: vehicles were fitted with the Westfalia type of front-hinged elevating roof, a purpose-built rear positioned roof rack, an interior that converted to a double bed, and provision of a cab hammock for child use. Accessories included birch ply interior panelling, dinette style furnishings, a luggage net above the central living area, an icebox and built-in water supply. There was no provision for a built-in cooker, but mosquito nets and louvred windows were standard, though an awning was an optional extra. A restyled version of the Kampmobile, called the Kombi Kamper, appeared in 1974, and was basically specified, there being little in the way of luxury items, though a refrigerator, roof rack and tent awnings were available as options.

Transporters in Mexico and Brazil

With the United States being Volkswagen's biggest market outside Germany, it is seemingly odd that the company never supported a dedicated manufacturing facility (one was proposed but failed to materialise). It was, therefore, left to Mexico and Brazil to enjoy a long history of building Volkswagens in the Americas. The

*Transporters were built at Puebla in Mexico from 1954 until 2003, during which time 253,926 examples left the works. The vehicle shown here is a late model, the Bay Window design being retained until production ceased in 2003, complete with water cooling, hence the radiator grille panel and small VW motif.
(Courtesy Ken Cservenka)*

Mexican plant at Puebla opened in 1954, and it was there that the Transporter was built until 1998 when production was transferred to Brazil. Old-style Beetles were also built at Puebla until 2003, and currently the factory builds the new Beetle. In 2006,

*Assembly of Transporters in Brazil commenced in the mid-1950s, though, before then vehicles were imported from Germany. Initially, only five vehicles per day were built, mainly Kombis. This period advertisement evocatively characterises the Brazilian Transporter market.
(Author's collection, courtesy Dorival Piccoli Jnr)*

the Bay Window Transporter remains in production in Brazil, along with other Volkswagens.

The importance of Brazil as a market is evident by the fact that in the 1960s, every other car sold carried the Volkswagen emblem. The assembly of Volkswagens made from parts imported from Germany began in Brazil in 1953, when Dr FW Schultz-Wenck, a German who became a Brazilian citizen, established Volkswagen do Brasil SA on 23 March at São Bernado do Campo. Four years later, after some 2800 vehicles had been assembled, Dr Schultz-Wenck's factory became a fully operative manufacturing facility, and was at the time Volkswagen's most important foreign subsidiary.

Transporters imported from Wolfsburg began arriving in Brazil in 1950, and, by 1954, more than 800 vehicles had been sold. Though seemingly an insignificant number of vehicles, Transporter sales were, nevertheless, encouraging, and were the precursor to localised assembly of CKD kits from Germany. With the greater proportion of production centred at São do Campo, a lesser number were assembled at an existing factory located at São Paulo. The output of Transporters assembled in Brazil was at first modest, totalling some five vehicles daily, the majority of which were Kombis.

Volkswagen do Brasil SA was eventually incorporated as Volkswagen

Brazil, and, in 1956, production of Beetles and Transporters was relocated to a newly constructed factory that was purpose-built at São Paulo near the existing works. The new São Paulo factory was officially opened on 7th January 1959, the ceremony performed by the President of Brazil, accompanied by Heinz Nordhoff and other dignitaries. Volkswagen's interest in Brazil had come about through its policy of supporting Third World economic development, and the creation of a proper vehicle manufacturing facility was completed in partnership with the Brazilian government.

It was not until 2nd September 1957 that the first fully-fledged Brazilian-built Transporter left the new production line. An auspicious occasion, the Kombi had been constructed from parts locally sourced to the tune of 50 per cent, an achievement that was to have far reaching consequences. A manufacturing infrastructure to support the Volkswagen factory was, therefore, initiated, and with daily output of Transporters reaching 71 at the end of the first year of manufacturing, this nearly matched the number of Beetles being produced. The demand for Volkswagens meant that Brazil's dealer network, initially numbering 21 agents in 1956, rapidly flourished; within three years it had expanded to 134 dealers, and, by 1962, had nearly doubled to 250.

Production of Transporters reached a landmark in 1960 when the 500,000th Transporter was constructed, the historic vehicle rolling off the Brazilian assembly line on 28 December. It is also pertinent to note that, at this time, daily output of Transporters at São Paulo was increased to 200. From 11,299 vehicles produced in Brazil in 1960, the figures increased to 16,315 the following year, but then dipped to 12,378 in 1964 before rising to 15,098 in 1966 and 21,172 in 1967. It was in 1967 that the

Dorival Piccoli Jnr with his pristine fish-eye indicator Kombi Luxo that was built at Volkswagen Brazil's São Paulo factory in 1967. (Courtesy Moises Ribeiro Dos Santos)

Brazilian-produced vehicles had specification differences to those built in Germany. Note the window configuration and tailgate/engine compartment hatch arrangement on this 1967 Kombi Luxo. (Courtesy Moises Ribeiro Dos Santos)

500,000th Brazilian Volkswagen was built at the São Paulo factory, which had grown in stature so that it encompassed its own presses, engine manufacturing and chrome plating plant, along with separate assembly shops for different Volkswagen models. Three years later, in 1970, Brazil produced its millionth Volkswagen.

In 1979, Volkswagen acquired a share in Chrysler Motors do Brasil, and, from March 1981, operated under the name Volkswagen Caminhoes Ltda., São Paulo. In November 1986, Volkswagen issued a Press statement to the effect that a new holding company was to be established in South America to cover the activities of Volkswagen do Brasil S.A. and Ford do Brasil S.A., both concerns remaining legally independent business enterprises. It was also announced that the Argentine subsidiaries of both firms would merge and be based under the holding company in Brazil as Autolatina, Volkswagen having a 51 per cent share.

In addition to Kombis, Brazilian output included special-bodied vehicles, such as taxis, fire tenders, ambulances, breakdown trucks, refrigerated vans and camper conversions that were based on the Westfaila design. The design of Brazilian Transporters was always at odds with Wolfsburg and Hanover production, largely as a result of components that were locally sourced and, therefore, of slightly different pattern to those supplied to Germany. There was also a problem, in that materials sent from Germany did not always compliment production then current in Brazil. Thus, the situation often arose that vehicles that were

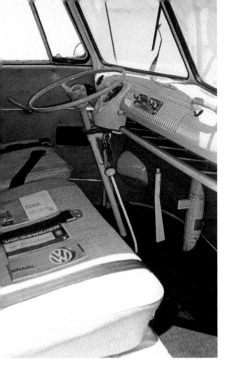

Interior of a Brazilian-built Kombi Luxo cab. (Courtesy Moises Ribeiro Dos Santos)

Interior of a Brazilian Kombi Luxo passenger compartment showing the seating arrangement. (Courtesy Moises Ribeiro Dos Santos)

Brazilian Volkswagen production has accounted for in excess of 1,406,000 Transporters, the 500,000 vehicle having left the works in 1976 and the millionth in 1991. The body configuration of Dorival Piccoli's 1967 Kombi Luxo is similar to that of the Samba Bus. (Courtesy Moises Ribeiro Dos Santos)

seemingly representative of a particular era were adorned with fittings, such as doors and trim items, from previous models.

There were a number of anomalies concerning Brazilian-built Transporters in respect of styling arrangements being peculiar to other models. Hence, some Bay Window Microbuses were fitted with side and rear windows of a pattern similar to those seen on the Split-Screen Samba. Specific to Brazilian production was a water-cooled Bay Window diesel-engined model, complete with an external radiator fixed to the nose of the vehicle!

Brazilian-built Transporters are still in production in the 21st century. What is interesting about them is that they take the form of the time honoured Bay Window vehicle, though Bulli enthusiasts will note the presence of body furniture that spans different generations of vehicles. Whilst they appear as something of a time warp, Brazilian Transporters, nevertheless, employ the latest technology, the 2006 specification including a 'Total Flex' 1.4-litre water-cooled engine that's designed to run on alcohol and has digital multipoint fuel injection.

163

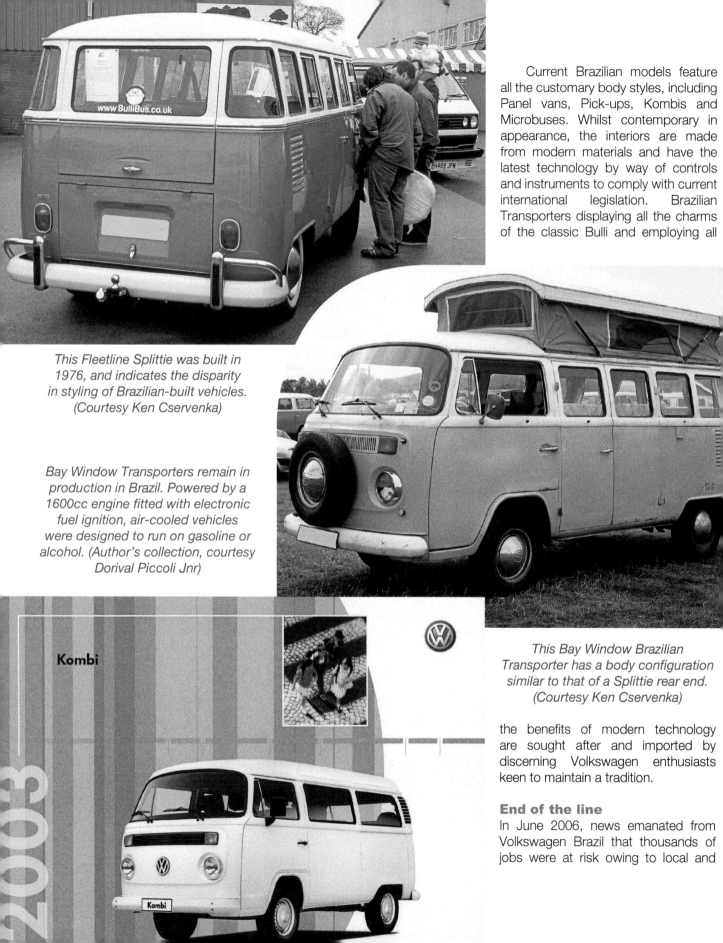

Current Brazilian models feature all the customary body styles, including Panel vans, Pick-ups, Kombis and Microbuses. Whilst contemporary in appearance, the interiors are made from modern materials and have the latest technology by way of controls and instruments to comply with current international legislation. Brazilian Transporters displaying all the charms of the classic Bulli and employing all

This Fleetline Splittie was built in 1976, and indicates the disparity in styling of Brazilian-built vehicles. (Courtesy Ken Cservenka)

Bay Window Transporters remain in production in Brazil. Powered by a 1600cc engine fitted with electronic fuel ignition, air-cooled vehicles were designed to run on gasoline or alcohol. (Author's collection, courtesy Dorival Piccoli Jnr)

Kombi

This Bay Window Brazilian Transporter has a body configuration similar to that of a Splittie rear end. (Courtesy Ken Cservenka)

the benefits of modern technology are sought after and imported by discerning Volkswagen enthusiasts keen to maintain a tradition.

End of the line

In June 2006, news emanated from Volkswagen Brazil that thousands of jobs were at risk owing to local and

2003

world economic factors, and, not least, competition from rival manufacturers. The issue is not an entirely parochial affair, as Volkswagen's problems in Brazil are reflected throughout the global motor industry, having already affected those car makers in mainland Europe and America.

Changes as far as the Type 2 Transporter are concerned mean that as from the end of 2005 Brazilian-built Bay Window models were no longer fitted with the 1.6-litre air-cooled engine. In its place, the 'Total Flex' 1.4-litre water-cooled unit is designed to run on alcohol, and is, according to Volkswagen, quieter and more fuel-efficient than its predecessor.

This Brazilian ambulance featured at the 2000 Salon do Automovel. (Courtesy Dorival Piccoli Jnr)

Air-cooled Bay Window Transporters were produced until 2005, this being the last brochure published for the vehicle. Thereafter, the Bay Window design remained in production with a 1.4-litre, water-cooled engine, thus necessitating the addition of a radiator grafted onto the nose of the vehicle. (Author's collection, courtesy Dorival Piccoli Jnr)

The badging that is unique to Volkswagen Brazil's final air-cooled Bus model which was announced in December 2005. With production limited to 200 vehicles, dedicated Bus enthusiasts were eager to acquire these very special examples. (Courtesy Snr Sossela/ Dorival Piccoli Jnr)

In December 2005, Volkswagen Brazil acknowledged the ending of the 'air-cooled' era by producing the Kombi Série Prata, a special edition run-out model that was limited to 200 examples. Each vehicle was finished in a silver colour, along with green tinted windows. (Courtesy Snr Sossela/Dorival Piccoli Jnr)

Volkswagen Brazil's Kombi Série Prata showing interior arrangement. (Courtesy Snr Sossela/Dorival Piccoli Jnr)

For the 2006 model year Volkswagen Brazil introduced a new model Bay Window Transporter. The large rectangular air intake indicates water cooling courtesy of a 1.4-litre Total Flex engine that is also used to power the Brazilian-built VW Fox. (Courtesy Snr Sossela/Dorival Piccoli Jnr)

Below & overleaf: Volkswagen Brazil produces the new water-cooled Transporter in a number of model configurations, including the Kombi, Minibus and Ambulance. (Courtesy Volkswagen Brazil/Dorival Piccoli Jnr)

Kombi

2006

Kombi Escolar

The interior of Volkswagen Brazil's new water-cooled ambulance: note the jump seat positioned alongside the side door and adjacent to the stretcher. (Courtesy Volkswagen Brazil/Dorival Piccoli Jnr)

Kombi Ambulância

Chapter

Type 2 ethos, the hippie trail and surfing culture

For many people, the sight of a Splittie or Bay Window Transporter brings to mind an immediate association with the Swinging Sixties, Flower Power and peace movements, such as the Campaign for Nuclear Disarmament. Transporters also developed a synonymy with certain political persuasions, particularly left wing militancy, and what can be referred to as the 'angry brigade'. The Transporter, certainly more so than the Beetle, became the signature for the hippie and surfing cultures: quite simply this vehicle will forever be known as the hippie bus.

Of course, it could just as easily have been the Bedford or Commer that lent themselves as being tools of the hippie brigade, as, sometimes, they did. A Morris or Land Rover could have fulfilled the role, as might, perhaps, East Germany's Trabant. So, too, could the classless Renault 4 or Citroën 2CV, and, especially, the latter's big brother the corrugated H-Van. But it was the Transporter, with its gentle styling, friendly face, and welcoming presence that was adopted by the peace and freedom movements. Thereafter, the Transporter became synonymous with

the beatniks, a term coined by San Francisco newspaper columnist Herb Caen in 1958. It was, nevertheless, the Bulli that forged an association with the music of Bob Dylan, Joan Baez, The Beatles, Marianne Faithful and The Rolling Stones. It echoed Allen Ginsberg's poetry, the writing of Jack Kerouac – said to be the Godfather of all hippies – the art of Paul Huxley, the wearing of kaftans and beads, and strumming of guitars.

That the VW Bus provided the means of travelling the world is evocatively illustrated in this Dormobile advertisement dating from the late 1960s and early '70s, the height of the hippie era. (Author's collection)

Open up new frontiers in a Dormobile

Dormobile Ltd., Folkestone, Kent. a member of the Martin Walter Group.
Printed in England. Gen. 70 H.O. 50 m.

It stood for religious expression and inspiration, and the search along The Silk Road for ancient communities, whether Buddhist, Christian or Hindu, all of which enjoyed a peaceful, if somewhat fragile, cohabitation. In his book *Magic Bus,* Rory Maclean recalls hippies driving their Volkswagen Campers aboard the rusty Bosphorus ferry, having first sampled sweet delights purchased from Instabul's famous pastry shops, thus leaving Europe behind bound for Asia and the Indian sub-continent in search of spiritual enlightenment. Today, the hippie trail is covered by the cloak of warfare; the hippies, too, have moved on, but the Bullis remain, surviving the hostile environment without protest.

The Bulli was as much part of the Sixties' culture as left-wing students from the London School of Economics or the Sorbonne, the fashion scene along Carnaby Street, the philosophy of Bertrand Russell, anti-American involvement in Vietnam, and, not least, a society coming to terms with marijuana. The Bulli, too, was the paragon of the then modern age, which stood rebellion, provocation, protest against the establishment, and demonstrating for every cause. The Bulli was adopted by the new society for many reasons then, but particularly because it allowed communal and affordable transport.

Woodstock wouldn't have been the same without the Transporters (nor would Glastonbury today), many of which are still ornately adorned with flowery decals and stickers.

The surfing resorts of Australia's Bondi and California's Laguna Beaches, not to mention Cornwall's Newquay, Devon's Croyde Bay and the vast stretches of sand along the Welsh Gower Peninsula, are home to the Transporter. For surfers heading to any of these places, there's only one vehicle in which to be seen. It is for this reason that the British Surfing Association teamed up with Volkswagen Van Centre,

It was not only the hippie brigade with which the Bulli was associated. Skiing trips, too, were all part of the Bulli culture. (Volkswagen publicity material/author's collection)

Carrs of Truro, in Cornwall in 2005 to provide a T5 Transporter with which to promote its activities, especially as the Bulli has had such a long history with the sport.

Surfing was as much part of Southern California's way of life as the hippie scene itself. As surfers gathered along their tropical playground it was the fashionable Bulli, painted in psychedelic colours, that matched wearers' flowery shirts, carried their surfboards, and loudly exhaled the rhythmic beat of The Beach Boys. When, a generation or so later, surfing was rediscovered, it was the VW Bus that heralded its resurgence; still it broadcast The Beach Boys, Buddy Holly, Elvis, Pink Floyd and The Rolling Stones.

Ever since its introduction, the Transporter has been the bus that has travelled the world. Its hunger for long and arduous overland treks has been fuelled not only by its extraordinary ability but also the extent, internationally, of the

Volkswagen network, comprising both official and independent specialists. By the time that Flower Power made its presence felt in the mid-1960s, an era, it is said, that aped the regime then in full flow in California, Splitties were roving the world's iconic arteries, and their successors have continued to do so. The trail to end all trails was arguably that stretching 6000 miles (9600km) across six countries from Instabul to Katmandu. But there are others, including Scandinavia's Arctic Highway, leading from the heart of Europe to the northern latitude of Nordkapp and the Land of the Midnight Sun; America's Route 66; Australia's Pacific Highway, following the continent's eastern seaboard, which, on its way north to Cooktown and the topmost part of Queensland, skirts the Sunshine Coast with its hedonistic Surfers Paradise and crosses the geographically important Tropic of Capricorn.

These are only a handful of the

Surfing culture was also the Bulli's domain, as shown by the sticker in the window of this Bay Window vehicle advertising Gordon & Smith Classic Longboards. (Author's collection)

GORDON & SMITH
CLASSIC
LONGBOARDS

Awesome

routes along which Bullis, Bay Windows and Wedges trundled in search of destiny. Young Americans set forth to explore their huge country, taking in New England, Florida and The Everglades, the breathtaking grandeur of the Grand Canyon and the vast interior that is Montana, Wyoming, Idaho, Utah and Nevada, before arriving at their Mecca; the golden state of California.

The Transporter was, and is, the choice of young Australians intent on travelling the length and width of their country, from green Tasmanian pastures to crocodile infested Northern Territory, from Adelaide to Ayers Rock and beyond to the Wheat Belt and Perth's coastal plain. The same applies to Europeans, Canadians, New Zealanders and South Africans, as well as South Americans and Asians, each wanting to penetrate their own lands and conquer the world.

As far as Australians and New Zealanders are concerned London

VW Buses bedecked with decals and eccentric paint designs were all part of the hippie scene. This Bay Window Bus pictured in New York's Greenwich Village in 2004 recaptures a colourful era. (Courtesy Bill Wolf)

171

The VW Bus's tenacity allowed it to travel over terrain that was often out of reach of other vehicles. It became the ideal choice for those intrepid travellers whose desire it was to discover the world.
(Volkswagen publicity material/author's collection)

was, and still is, the gangplank to discovering the British Isles, Eire and mainland Europe. Young people – and on occasions the not so young – would, on arriving in the United Kingdom, follow a tradition and head for Earls Court, historically a large Antipodean community. They also headed for the vicinities of New Zealand House in Haymarket or Australia House at the top of The Strand where trading in Transporters, particularly camping conversions, was conducted around street corners or in back thoroughfares. The asking price for a vehicle largely depended on its age and condition, and to a great extent the buyer's and vendor's bargaining skills and determination to strike the best deal. Hence, it was commonplace to see Bullis and Bay Windows in differing states of completeness and cleanliness, painted in a variety of colours and bedecked with graphics, each wearing

AUS and NZ stickers, being examined – not always too closely – before heading off on the grand tour.

Months later the same vehicles would return. They were usually even more graphically endowed and bore all the evidence of a harsh life, having been treated, if lucky enough, to only the most essential maintenance: such was the engine's tired grumbling, its gasping for breath and smoky exhaust. An oil change, tyre inflation and superficial valet to remove dust gathered from the outreaches of Europe were all that was needed before the willing workhorses changed hands for the umpteenth time, after which, in familiar fashion, they departed on yet another tour. To a great extent, therefore, the Transporter is the symbol of freedom and free expression; it is the passport to everywhere.

The Antipodean connection wasn't the only place where a camper could be acquired. Every month in North London

on land along Market Road, between York Way and the Caledonian Road, travellers would gather to trade their Campers in an atmosphere pertaining to an auction or car boot sale. Here, vehicles were offered in a variety of conditions, from the pretty with all mod cons to the pretty awful that needed so much love and attention that one felt guilt at passing them by. Like their siblings being traded in the back streets surrounding Haymarket and The Strand, sorry-looking Kombi-campers with telephone number mileages found willing customers in exchange for a fistful of money and no questions asked.

Typically, the globetrotting Bulli wears a tired expression. It is mud-splashed and grimy, the result of being directed along miles of hostile roads where dusty potholes are the norm, and any hint of tarmac is a welcome luxury. Not uncommonly such vehicles bear evidence of having been loaded to capacity, at least the roof rack will have supported spare wheels and tyres, water containers and probably a bicycle or two. Still attached to the roof rack may be the threadbare relic of a makeshift washing line on which the most essential of clothing items would have been washed in some muddy creek before being hung out to dry. Inside the Bulli its long faded and sun ravaged spartan furnishings, complimented by worn and meagre fittings, are testament to constant use and abuse; frayed gingham curtains hang limply at windows, themselves masked with layers of gunge.

Epic journeying was all part of the Transporter ethos from the very beginning of the vehicle's career. With its penchant for tenacious stability and disregard for extremes of temperature, and not least a proven track record for reliability and longevity, the Transporter ventured with enviable courage and ability. There is the story of the taxi driver

who, in 1957, clocked-up 100,000 kilometres (62,500 miles) taking skiing parties over Austria's notorious Grossgiockner Pass to the foot of the ski runs. The daily runs demanding that the fully laden bus tackle the Grossgiockner's steep gradients, calling for long distances to be covered in second gear and then subjected to long and cruel braking, was well within the vehicle's capabilities.

The strength of the Bulli is no better exemplified than with the account of a vehicle being savagely attacked by an elephant. The occupants of a Microbus were driving through a game reserve in what was then Rhodesia when a herd of elephants blocked the road; threatened by the Volkswagen's presence, a cow elephant protecting her calf decided that attack was the best form of defence and charged at it with full force. The Transporter's occupants having exited the vehicle with little time to spare watched as the Bulli was turned on its side, then its roof, and on its other side before the animal had decided it no longer posed a threat. Bearing the marks of the attack, including several six-inch diameter tusk-holes in its floor and sides, the Transporter, once righted, started at the first attempt and continued to do so for some long time after.

Too many stories have been told about Bullis exploring the ends of the Earth; each is an adventure in itself and one has only to look at the internet and travel books to discover feats of unbelievable endurance. Today, the Transporter, whether it be a Splittie, Bay Window or Wedge, remains the firm favourite among the younger generations when selecting a vehicle with which to roam. That there is camaraderie amongst travellers in their Bullis is obvious, merely go to any ferry terminal or tourist resort and you'll see Transporter owners congregate as if by magic.

Nearly half a century on since the hippie culture made its mark on society, it is not unusual to see now ancient Bullis still bearing the signs of an era past, with their painted and florally decorated exteriors and time-warp interiors. Nor is it bizarre to discover that the occupants of these vehicles have become lost in time: hippies they were, and hippies they remain.

The Bulli hasn't always been associated with hippie culture, but rather was adopted by it. Designed to provide freedom of travel and getting away from the constraints of work and everyday living, the Transporter established a cult of its own from the very beginning, following in the tyre tracks of those already decrepit buses that served a Top Deck view of the world. It served, and serves, as an artist's canvas; it was, and is, a mobile studio,

Hostile terrain proved too much for some vehicles, even a Bulli. This exhausted example was pictured in 1996 at Ukutu near Mombasa in Kenya. (Courtesy Rod Grainger)

The Transporter remains the choice of vehicle for young adventurers as well as the young-at-heart. Pictured at Brazil's Autoshow in 2000, this then current model Bulli reflects the romanticism of Flower Power. (Courtesy Dorival Piccoli Jnr)

and its persona helped and helps instil creativity; it was and continues thus the choice of craftspeople and artisans.

Take a look down memory lane to see those wonderfully emotive brochures, courtesy of Volkswagen and associated camping conversions depicting carefree family scenes. See, too, the social contrast: colour images of a relaxed and affluent American lifestyle, the monochrome snapshot of a Britain emerging from austerity. Holidaying with a Transporter opened new opportunities, broadened horizons and kick-started a fashion that half a decade later would support a massive motorhome and leisure industry.

The Westfalia and its contemporaries portrayed poignant images of worry-free days spent playing tennis amidst peaceful surroundings, and sunbathing by tranquil waters. Sportsmobile idyllically immortalised the home from home, as did Devon, Danbury and others with their comforting imagery of seaside scenes complete with deckchairs, beach games and, so quintessentially British, a table laid for tea. Who could have resisted the

temptation to rush out and buy a VW Camper and follow the sun to happy summer vacations? And there wasn't a hippie or surfer to be seen!

Pre-surfing culture as depicted in this wonderfully evocative 1960s scene. And there's not a hippie in sight! (Devon publicity material/author's collection)

Chapter 10

The custom scene

Travel stained Transporters are a familiar sight, whether on the roads of Europe or the Australian Outback, the African Bush or the Americas, on the roads to Madras or Mandalay. The fact that the Bulli knows few boundaries or frontiers is all part of its essential recipe, as is its appetite for gobbling up distances counted in tens and hundreds of thousands of miles or kilometres. From humble beginnings, the Transporter has developed an international status, either in its purest form or customised to serve a specific purpose.

There are always a number of issues when it comes to customising any vehicle, and there is always a faction which believes it to be an unnecessary and unwanted practice. A counter view would argue that the practice holds little or no harm, especially when a vehicle might otherwise be scrapped. To complicate matters, there is often debate on the level of customisation: a Kombi given a new interior to afford enhanced comfort and modern facilities

The Bulli lends itself to elaborate and artistic paint schemes ...
(Courtesy Ken Cservenka)

would probably be acceptable, as might be the addition of supplementary instrumentation; altering its exterior and overall appearance, let alone its technical specification, might be a very different matter.

From the very beginning of its career the Transporter lent itself to being customised in some way or another, not least by those intrepid travellers described in the last chapter, who covered their vehicles with a profusion

175

Volkswagen recognised that sign written vehicles would be a niche marketing opportunity. (Courtesy Ken Cservenka)

Whether Volkswagen would have approved of this adaptation is open to conjecture. The ears on this dog food advertising van are removed when travelling! (Courtesy Ken Cservenka)

of decals and stickers that indicated the different countries visited worldwide. A more familiar aspect of customising appeared when companies, in choosing the Bulli as a highly versatile multi-purpose vehicle, had it decorated with corporate advertising designs. The Transporter's overall shape and size was ideal for this purpose, especially as the vehicle attracted a good deal of attention wherever it went. Volkswagen's publicists went as far as advocating that substantial savings in advertising were possible by having a Transporter suitably signwritten. An interesting, and highly successful, sales ploy was instigated in Germany when Volkswagen offered the use of Transporters to selected businesses on an extended trial basis. By using the Bulli to project the image of their merchandise, managers were quick

two Transporters, a number of hybrid vehicles have appeared. These include examples fitted with crawler tracks, while a number of double-deckers

A number of hybrid vehicles have appeared over the years. This long wheelbase Transporter is the product of Kemperink, a firm known for its long wheelbase Pick-ups built to special order.
(Courtesy Ken Cservenka)

to appreciate the effectiveness of the arrangement.

Owing to its versatile design, it wasn't long before the Transporter was lending itself to some extremely diverse applications, the majority of which would not have received official Volkswagen approval.

When a Californian scrap metal merchant cut a Microbus in three, removed the middle section and welded the front and rear sections together, he increased his publicity enormously by running around in a Bulli that was considerably shorter than a standard Beetle saloon. The mini Transporter had a number of virtues, among which it was easy to park courtesy of its 46 inch (1.7m) wheelbase and 20 foot (6.1m) turning circle. The front of the vehicle was so light that, not only was it possible for a person of average strength to lift it, but all that was needed to have the bus skating along on its rear wheels with the front off the ground, was a sudden burst on the throttle.

Together with stretched buses that were built from the bodies of at least

The Coffee Bug is an unofficial conversion which perfectly suits its purpose.
(Courtesy Ken Cservenka)

having been constructed from two vehicles, one on top of the other, and some comprising a standard Kombi or Microbus with the cabin of a Beetle saloon grafted on it to form a permanent roof extension. Conversion of Transporters into trailer units is another popular adaptation, especially when a vehicle has suffered frontal damage and the cab area has been removed from the rest of the body. A visit to any one of many Volkswagen enthusiasts meetings will reveal a huge variety of innovative and intriguing ideas.

Customising a Transporter

The shape and size of the Transporter, as well as its charisma, makes for an ideal conversion by those enthusiasts who want more from their Bulli than a Panel van or Kombi would seemingly offer. There are numerous reasons why owners feel the need to adorn their vehicles with special paintwork and exotic interiors: some desire the creativity that the customisation process affords, while others may wish to give their vehicles a particular identity. Whatever the reason, owing

to the Transporter's popularity and the impressive number of vehicles that were produced, there's no shortage of vehicles to which enthusiasts can apply their artistry.

The business of customising vehicles is accepted as a serious art form, and with it has emerged a whole industry aimed at satisfying the demands of discerning enthusiasts. A glance through any of the Volkswagen related periodicals will reveal the extent of interest that customising Transporters, and Beetles as well as Karmann Ghias for that matter, commands.

Customising the Transporter took on a new direction with the extrovert trend of the 'Cal-look' which emanated from California in the early 1970s, though personalising Bullis has been popular since the 1950s. Before the Cal-look era the extent of customisation was confined mainly to engine tuning, and came about largely as a result of endeavours surrounding Beetle racing. An industry aimed at making Volkswagens perform far more spiritedly than either the designers or engineers had ever thought possible blossomed:

as well as treating their Transporters with tuning kits, twin carburettors, modified crankshafts and close ratio gearboxes, owners began adorning their vehicles with wide wheels, additional brightwork and dazzling colour schemes.

Customising techniques in the way described ultimately gave way to a somewhat less brash attitude which saw the Transporter's, and other air-cooled Volkswagens' styling enhanced. This was achieved by removing bumpers and trim items to create a smooth shape, and then giving the vehicle an intensely deep and glossy coat of paint, preferably in a pastel shade. That was only part of the effect as the idea was to continue the theme inside the vehicle by affording it a new and smooth-line facia along with new seating and interior furnishings trimmed with colour-matched upholstery. The whole image was enhanced by the fitment of one-piece windows, usually with tinted glass, sun roof and alloy wheels, not to mention interior lighting and sound systems befitting a night club.

This fashionable tendency was coined the Cal-look in the mid-1970s

Customising a vehicle can extend to more than just a paint job: lowering suspension and fitting high-powered engines is all part of a highly specialised process. These 'Rat-look' Splitties pictured at a Van Fest will not appeal to all enthusiasts. (Courtesy Ken Cservenka)

Lowering a Transporter's suspension calls for some expertise and should be undertaken carefully; the result will alter a vehicle's handling characteristics. (Courtesy Neil Barker)

after it was debated by Jere Alhadeff in *Hot VWs* magazine, after which the trend rapidly proliferated throughout the international Volkswagen scene. The arrival of the Cal-look was the precursor to enthusiasts having their vehicles fitted with resculptured body panels and lowered suspension. Nothing escaped the customiser's art: along with Panel vans, Kombis and Microbuses, Camper conversions and Pick-ups, too, were given the Cal-look.

It is the Bay Window models that are currently the choice of vehicle for customisation. The reasons are that these vehicles are still abundantly available compared to the Splittie which is regarded as a historic vehicle and a classic in its own right. Customised Splitties are to be found, some having been treated to the Cal-look, but current consensus is that these vehicles should be preserved to reflect their original styling. This doesn't mean to say that a Splittie should not be given a makeover, especially with regards to minor cosmetic treatment, such as the fitting of American market bumpers, alloy wheels and a fresh coat of paint. While even this may be abhorrent to some enthusiasts who are keen not to destroy the vehicle's originality, others

might decide it pertinent to lower the suspension and fit a customised interior.

Accepting, therefore, that many owners are unhappy about the customisation practice, those vehicles displaying worn and neglected interiors might well benefit from some mild bespoke refurbishment. The original fittings can be retained, albeit restored to their former condition, but recovering furnishings in carefully chosen materials and fabrics could enhance a vehicle's appearance. This goes for headlinings, carpets, and side walls, too. Restoration of the interior need not stop there; some owners choose to fit new cab seats which provide greater comfort and support than the original variety, and others may want to fit more comprehensive instrumentation, including an oil temperature gauge and rev counter. Such interior conversions need not be obtrusive if carried out sympathetically.

There is currently huge enthusiasm for Bay Window Transporters, the last of which, apart from those models remaining in production in Brazil, went out of production in 1979 after a career spanning twelve years. These vehicles provide an excellent basis for a custom conversion, their shape and increased size over the Splittie giving the enthusiast much scope. Some owners are happy maintaining originality as far as the external body trim is concerned, but, nevertheless, aim to achieve a unique paint finish. Others may decide to take a bolder approach by removing the VW roundel and fitting flush-mounted headlamps and indicators to provide a styling effect, together with a colour scheme, that is totally smooth. The danger here, is that the end result will have arguably eliminated the vehicle's original character.

The most obvious area of customisation, apart from alteration of the bodywork, is the paint finish

VW enthusiasts often prefer to customise a Bay Window model rather than a Splittie because of the former's styling and its more commodious body. (Author's collection)

and colour co-ordination of bumpers and mirrors, etc., which should be professionally undertaken to achieve the best result. Transporters can be seen parading the most extrovert colour schemes, including wild psychedelic patterns, but caution should be exerted as fashions change, the Sixties' Flower Power being an example, and adoption of new themes could well prove to be very expensive.

Lowering a vehicle's suspension is one of the more popular customising techniques, and whilst resulting in a less bus-like appearance it does radically alter handling characteristics. Under normal use on smooth surfaces lowered suspension may improve a vehicle's handling, particularly when alloy wheels and low profile tyres are employed. On rougher surfaces and unmade roads, having lowered suspension could well present a problem: the consequences of off-road driving could be disastrous as ground clearance almost certainly will be less than adequate, resulting in serious damage being sustained to both the suspension and the underside of vehicle. Modifying a vehicle's suspension calls for precision and

expertise, and should be skilfully carried out to eliminate potential danger.

At all times, any customisation, whether to bodywork or mechanical specification, should comply with current legal and safety legislation. An example concerns the lighting arrangements following suspension lowering; headlamps, fog lights, indicators and rear lenses should satisfy height requirements.

Some owners choose to fit body styling kits to their vehicle, particularly in conjunction with lowered suspension. The extent to which such kits, which can include air dams and side skirts, are used will depend on individual preference, and budget.

Before embarking upon a customisation project, it's advisable to price the job thoroughly, as it's easy to become over-enthusiastic, the result being disappointment when a task has to be delayed or abandoned owing to over-spend. It's also essential to calculate a realistic timescale in which to complete the project, as, again, there will be disappointment when the working schedule overruns.

Customising may well include

modifying the original engine to afford more power, or exchanging it for a more powerful type. In any event there are several options. Modifying an existing engine will require employing one of many tuning kits, and this could include fitting replacement barrels and pistons to afford a cubic capacity of up to 3-litres. Such modifications can be expensive, both initially and in terms of running costs, though enthusiasts could argue the reward is a level of performance previously unknown. Somewhat milder tuning modifications could, however, prove to be more affordable. The ultimate modification might be to achieve 600bhp for racing purposes, though such an adaptation is highly specialist and not intended for road use.

An alternative is to fit the power unit from, say, the Type 4 Volkswagen, or to install something very different, such as a 2-litre Ford engine, or even a V8. A popular choice is to fit the Porsche flat-six, but whatever course is followed it will almost certainly involve extensive mechanical modifications. Gearboxes can also be modified or exchanged, some owners electing to fit a 5-speed unit. Undertaking any mechanical modification will more than likely require upgrading braking and suspension systems, and should, therefore, be professionally carried out.

For those enthusiasts unwilling to change the classic styling of the Splittie or Bay Window, they may prefer to customise a Wedge model. A certain amount of interior customising was undertaken on these vehicles by Volkswagen when the Caravelle and Syncro models were introduced, which gave customers hitherto unparalleled comfort and traction. For unusual customising projects, a vehicle such as the double-cab Syncro Pick-up could have huge potential. The 'Eurolook' is the latest custom technique and concerns those vehicles built after

This modified Splittie interior is as far as many enthusiasts are prepared to go in order to customise their vehicles. (Courtesy Ken Cservenka)

use on special occasions, the expense of the project has to be weighed against the degree of pleasure derived from the vehicle, together with the amount of time it will spend unused. In any event it has to be accepted that, in the event of accidental damage, repairs will be vastly more expensive than for an original vehicle.

Customisation is a practice just as fashionable in Europe as it is in America, and enthusiasts go to extraordinary lengths to derive individual and innovative designs. Notwithstanding its widespread following, and the huge industry customising has created, there are countless enthusiasts who believe the Bulli should remain in original form as testimony to being a dependable workhorse.

1980. Originating in Germany in the mid-1990s, the look has now become established in Britain. Eurolook is about bold pastel colours combined with smooth, tasteful body kits painted to match the Transporter's overall colour scheme. Modifications include replacing standard headlamp assemblies with four round or square lights and fitting spoilers normally found on the VW Golf; engines, too, are replaced, usually with the 16 valve Golf Gti unit or the VR6. It is customary to lower suspension height by around 45-65mm (1.5-2in) and to fit 16-17 inch (410-430mm) or 18 inch (460mm) alloy wheels and low profile tyres. Interior modifications emphasise luxury and comfort along with hi-tech sound systems.

With the customising project complete, the owner will have to decide whether the vehicle really is suitable for everyday use. If it is, the quality of work will have had to be executed to a sufficient standard for the Transporter to withstand the rigours of current road use and driving conditions. Should the vehicle be intended as a showpiece for

The effort that went into customising this T25 Wedge model exhibited at Bristol Volksfest is clear for all to see! (Courtesy Ken Cservenka)

Chapter

Living with a Transporter

Ben Pon could have little known that his box-on-wheels, the outline of which he sketched in 1947, would, sixty years on, remain in production and have become an international icon. Nor could he have imagined that nearly one and a half million Transporters would have been sold by 1967, a further three million by 1979, and more than two million thereafter.

Exactly what makes the Bulli inspire so much affection is difficult to define. Its shape suggests security and its frontal profile has a distinct 'face', both of which present more than a good measure of individuality. In Kombi and Camper guise especially, the majority of owners tend to regard their Transporters as a natural extension to home and family lifestyles.

Additionally, the Bulli's uniquely

resilient and durable nature allows it to perform untiringly its role as an eminently practical commercial vehicle which is highly adaptable to so many uses. That the Transporter has discovered the elixir of life is evident by the number of elderly vehicles remaining in active service. As regards current generation Transporters, although much of the technology has advanced from that of the early models, the fundamental concept is unchanged; as a market leader it pioneered and led a design that was adopted by rival manufacturers.

While commercial variants of the Transporter create much interest within enthusiast circles, it is the Kombi and Camper conversions that have the widest appeal to existing and prospective owners.

As a desirable classic vehicle, the Bulli has few equals, and all three generations of models, Splitties, Bays and Wedges, add significantly to the international Volkswagen movement. So, what is it that makes what is essentially a workhorse so attractive? The answer is simple: in an age of similarity when it comes to styling trends, the Bulli's unique design promises pleasure of ownership as well as affording driving satisfaction. Unlike a lot of classic vehicles, fifty or more years of age, even the earliest surviving examples of Transporter are perfectly suited to daily use, which means that there is a heavy demand for Split-Screen and Bay Window Bullis.

Kombi and Camper models often remained with the same owners over relatively long periods, unlike many

For the majority of Bulli owners their vehicle is an extension to their home. Harry Cook and his family travelled extensively with their Peter Pitt Moto Caravan, seen here on a camping holiday and towing a caravan for additional accommodation. (Courtesy Harry Cook)

saloon and estate cars that were exchanged every couple of years or so. The reasons for this included initial price, sound basic design, reliability, and ease of maintenance. Not least is the fact that vehicles were characteristic of their owning families. Typically, a family purchasing a Transporter would maintain it over several years, using it as a family runabout, as well as for weekends and holidays when it became a home from home.

Harry Cook of The Wirral, Merseyside, emerged as being an archetypal Transporter enthusiast. Having purchased a Canterbury Pitt conversion in the mid-sixties, Harry used it on a regular basis for more than thirty years, during which time he amassed more than 100,000 miles (160,000km). Only on three occasions did the vehicle break down: at 80,000 miles (128,000km) an engine valve failed which resulted in a reconditioned unit being fitted, and on the other two occasions the faults were traced to hairline cracks on the rotor arm and distributor cap, respectively.

Buying advice

Having decided that life is incomplete without a Bulli, there comes the task of finding a suitable vehicle. Though there is no shortage of Transporters, locating one that fulfils every requirement in terms of age, body configuration and condition, not least the price asked, may well result in inspecting several vehicles before deciding on a particular example. Finding a very early type will be considerably more difficult than sourcing later examples, nevertheless, models dating from the early fifties do occasionally appear for sale. It's fortunate that, in the majority of instances, with the exception of very early vintages, prices are relatively affordable.

Usually a glance in any of the motoring magazine classified columns, especially those catering for classic Volkswagens, will reveal a healthy selection of vehicles. For greater choice it is recommended that one of the dedicated marque journals be consulted, or alternatively specific internet websites, and, should the

There are many ways in which to purchase a Transporter. This example was offered for sale at the famous Beaulieu Autojumble. Note the American specification bumpers. (Author's collection)

enthusiast be seeking a particular model, or indeed a rarity, it's worth joining one of the many recognised owners clubs. Fortunately, Volkswagen owners are served by an enormous number of enthusiast clubs throughout the world.

For the potential buyer unused to the Transporter, the myriad of vehicles on the market can present something of a problem, especially as they will reflect vastly varying conditions. Owing to the fact that some vehicles will have had a hard working life, and others, because of their size, will have been exposed to the elements rather than cosseted in a garage, it is only to be expected that a percentage of Transporters offered for sale will be in less than pristine condition. Such an example, even if it looks reasonably sound on the surface, is liable to have some serious defects. In order to avoid disappointment, and possibly financial disaster, prospective purchasers who are lacking mechanical or specific model knowledge are well advised to approach a reputable specialist who will be only too pleased to provide reliable and sensible advice for a fee. Some vehicles will carry a price premium because of rarity or condition, but ultimately, any additional outlay will be money well spent. It will not be so much the price paid for the right vehicle that is remembered but more the pleasure and usefulness it provides.

Owners of Split-Screen Transporters will argue that their vehicles are the most charismatic; Bay Window owners will contend theirs to be equally attractive and enjoy added functionality, while Wedge enthusiasts campaign theirs to be the pinnacle of achievement. Volkswagen-related magazines and the internet will reveal a plethora of Splitties, both right- and left-hand drive, and because they are so international expect them to be offered from mainland Europe as well

as America and elsewhere. Surprisingly, Scandinavia, despite being noted for its harsh winters, has for some time produced some interesting examples of early Transporter, the impressive survival rate being due to the region having been a popular destination.

It goes without saying that all variations of Transporter are extensively sought-after, whether in commercial guise or as Kombi or camper conversions. The most popular types are the latter as these offer the greatest versatility and comfort. Many regularly use their Bullis as family runabouts and as the means of enjoyable family weekend breaks and holidays.

Buying a Split-Screen Bulli

As well as having historical and desirable values, Splitties enjoy an attraction all of their own. They are also uniquely distinctive in appearance, especially with the large VW roundel on the nose.

When buying an example in the United Kingdom expect to pay between £2000 and £5000 for something in need of total restoration. Vehicles in a better state of health will command higher values, and a usable example with a test certificate should carry a price tag of around £5000-£7500. Even for this amount of money the need for some tidying of the vehicle's exterior and interior must be expected. Mint condition Bullis will be correspondingly more expensive: be prepared to pay £10,000-£12,000, and for a concours Samba or deluxe Microbus the ceiling is around £25,000. Purchasing a dilapidated vehicle at a minimum price and having it totally restored to pristine condition might appear to be an attractive proposition. The downside to this is that the cost could be prohibitive and, long term, the likelihood of the investment being recovered in any subsequent sale is remote.

Buying a Bulli calls for extensive deliberation. Checking a vehicle's provenance is as important as knowing that it is mechanically sound, and that the body is without decay. (Author's collection)

Whilst a vehicle may appear to be in need of attention, it's gratifying to know that there exists a huge industry aimed at keeping these vehicles alive. All body panels are available, as are mechanical items, though some parts for the earliest vehicles may require some sourcing. (Author's collection)

Even if the bodywork and mechanics of a vehicle appear to be in good condition, take a close look at the interior. Make sure that all the equipment installed in a camping conversion is sound and in working order, and that furnishings are in as good a condition as can be expected, considering age and use. Check that all bedding equipment – and that includes folding stretcher bunks – converts to sleeping accommodation as intended. The elevating roof, when fitted, should be carefully examined to ensure that it operates correctly and, in particular, look for evidence of water leaks, stained woodwork and worn carpets in its vicinity. Any work that is required in repairing and replacing fabrics, roof mechanism and utensils can be time-consuming and expensive.

A vehicle's external condition should be fairly easy to judge. All panels are replaceable and any obvious repair work is most likely to be contained to the lower areas, such as the front valence, which is obscured by the bumper and

collects mud and road debris. Check the condition of sills, wheelarches and door bottoms, all of which can show signs of corrosion. Look, too, beneath the vehicle for signs of fatigue on the front floor pans; lift the engine cover to investigate the inner rear wheelarches and to ensure there is no damage from leaking battery acid. There are two other areas that are prone to rot: one is the leading edge of the roof, the other immediately beneath the windscreens, and, in the case of the latter, check for any dampness in the cab floor footwells. The chassis should also be carefully checked, and, while it is ruggedly built the outriggers are prone to corrosion. This is not as serious as it sounds as outriggers can be easily replaced, and it is rare to see the main longitudinal rails affected by rust to any degree.

Potential purchasers should be wary of vehicles offered for sale and not being quite what they appear. Returning a customised vehicle to its original specification may require the correct body trim (which might be

expensive if the original items have not been retained) and a new coat of paint. Unless a purchaser is happy buying a customised Transporter displaying lowered suspension, add-on body kits, and modified interiors, such vehicles should be left well alone.

It is advisable to check on a vehicle's history and, therefore, the vendor should be able to produce evidence of servicing history and MoT test certificates: any model that is offered for sale in dubious circumstances or without registration documents should be treated with the utmost caution or avoided entirely. The best advice is to pay as much as can be afforded in order to obtain the best possible vehicle.

There is comfort in the knowledge that the running gear of early Split-Screen Transporters is virtually the same as on early Beetle models. Practically all parts are available from marque specialists, though those relevant to very early models may take some sourcing, and there are certain parts that can only be supplied on a re-manufacturing basis but, as there is a remarkable industry dedicated to keeping older Volkswagens alive, there should be little difficulty in locating even the most obscure items. The same applies to body panels and trim items, with specialists such as Alan Schofield, Karmann Konnection and Just Kampers catering exclusively for this market.

A Splittie's engine doesn't have a great deal of power, which means that, not only is the speed at which a vehicle can travel limited, full use of the gearbox is needed. Evidence of engine wear is blue smoke when accelerating, itself a sign of oil being burned owing to worn piston rings or cylinder bores. The best option here is to fit a reconditioned engine, the cost being around £1000, though a short-term remedy is to fit a used unit, which, costing substantially less, may not be in much better condition than the one it replaces. Some owners have fitted larger capacity engines from later models, but there is potential danger of eventual serious wear caused through high revving, a consequence of having rear hubs designed to be fitted with reduction gears. To avoid this problem, it's necessary to replace the rear axle with the independent rear suspension fitted to post-1967 models, for which there is available a specialist kit. Most owners, however, prefer to leave the reduction gears in place and take care not to over-rev the engine.

Before choosing a Splittie in preference to a Bay Window model, there are some factors to consider. Firstly, should body panels be needed for repair or restoration, these are likely to be more expensive than for other models. The same applies to mechanical components, especially if re-manufactured in small-batches. The maximum speed at which one can safely drive will usually, subject to weather and traffic conditions, be between 55-60mph(88-96kph) and do not expect

fuel consumption to be better than 18-25mpg (16-11.5litres/100km). Once maximum speed has been achieved, braking can be a problem as the drum brakes have a tendency to fade, the option here being to employ a disc brake conversion. Gearchanging can be awkward, especially when the bushes of the remote control system start to wear. Ventilation is notably poor, particularly when condensation adds to the problem in winter: interior heating is also somewhat less than Saharan, often resulting in owners fitting non-original heat exchangers in order to achieve sufficient warmth. Splitties can be noisy although applying sound-deadening material around the engine housing does alleviate the problem. In the case of camper conversions, interior soft furnishings tend to absorb much of the excessive noise.

Apart from the very last Splitties that were built with 12-volt electrics, all other early models will have been

fitted with 6-volt systems. While this is perfectly adequate for a lot of the time, it can present a problem in winter, particularly when lighting is required over long durations. Many owners convert their vehicles to 12-volts, an operation requiring the replacement of all electrical items, including bulbs and component parts of the charging system. The reward is worth the effort and results in bright lights and easier starting instead of glow-worm power and risk of complete battery discharge should the engine fail to start immediately. When converting a 6-volt Split-Screen vehicle to 12-volts, be prepared for a search for the correct 12-volt windscreen wiper motors and fuel gauges.

Fitting flashing direction indicators to a Bulli equipped with semaphore signals is a worthwhile and important safety measure. Do ensure that flashers are in keeping with the vehicle's design, and a move that is worth considering

Early Splitties relied on semaphore signalling but, in the interest of safety, it's wise to fit discreet flashing indicators. Some enthusiasts prefer to mount indicators to the bumper, but in this instance flashers have been fitted to the front panel in similar style to the bullet-type lights introduced in 1955 for American specification vehicles and 1960 for the European market. (Courtesy Charles Trevelyan)

is the installation of amber indicators within the headlamp assemblies.

It is by understanding the pitfalls of Split-Screen ownership that the vehicle's character can be fully appreciated, along with their historic value and status, and not least the driving pleasure they afford.

Taking a close look at the Bulli

When looking at Transporters there are several factors concerning bodywork and general wear that need to be considered. The Bulli is as susceptible to the vagaries of decay as any other vehicle, and many prospective owners will, therefore, decide in favour of a vehicle that has been restored, but not before carefully checking that the work has been completed to a satisfactory standard. A Transporter that has received expert attention will mostly carry some photographic evidence of the restoration process, and should be accompanied by bills and a work schedule.

Obviously, it would be unwise to settle on the first Transporter selected from a list of potential vehicles, even if it does appear to be an attractive proposition. It is far better to examine a number of examples in order to gauge the disparity between those nicely presented and others that are less so. Always beware the fresh coat of paint which can hide rust and decay, and even camouflage plastic filler and accident damage. The most vulnerable areas of a Bulli's structure are the platform, outriggers and sills; front wheelarches; the front panel, especially around the valence, cab floor and windscreen pillars; accommodation area floor, and the section around the battery support tray. Other parts prone to wear and rot are the body seams, door bottoms, jacking points and windscreen channels.

The platform and outriggers are noted for their strength but that does not mean they are immune to corrosion, especially on a vehicle that is fifty or more years old. At worst, the chassis rails will have cracked, usually at the point where they meet the outriggers. Unless repairs of this nature have had specialist attention and have been properly executed, serious distortion of the platform can occur. Severe damage to the platform is likely to be found only on vehicles that have been subjected to obvious abuse and uncaring ownership. If the corrosion is purely superficial it may be that a measure of preventative maintenance, such as a thorough cleaning, rust treatment and painting, is all that's necessary. Always take care to inspect the load area floor which could have endured severe wear; any restoration necessary in this respect is likely to be extensive, and therefore expensive.

The front panel, by virtue of its size, is susceptible to damage from stone chippings; if this is left untreated rot will set in which, as well as being unsightly, will quickly spread so that repairs will be both difficult and expensive. Replacing the sheet metal in this area will be beyond the capabilities of most enthusiasts. The front of the Bulli is vulnerable to minor accident damage sustained from parking and manoeuvring in tight spaces, and, if only for appearance sake, should be repaired. The double skin construction of much of the front panel prevents easy repair; knocking dents out from the inside is usually impossible and could involve welding new sheet metal in place. The valence, which is hidden by the bumper, is very prone to decay, and, in severe cases, will mean that new panels and box sections will have to be welded in place.

The ingress of water through the double-skinned wheelarches can be the cause of extensive rotting of the cab floor. In extreme cases the floor can give way entirely owing to the continual up-spray of water, salt and road dirt from

When inspecting a Bulli, take a look behind the bumper. Road dirt and water can rot the valence, which will mean some restorative work.
(Courtesy Keith Hocking)

the wheels over a lengthy period. While examining the cab floor, also inspect the base of the windscreen pillars, as these are vulnerable areas and any signs of decay will mean replacement sooner or later.

Any corrosion around the bottom of cab doors should be thoroughly investigated, the cause usually occurring when water cannot escape because of blocked drain holes. It is also advisable to check further along each side of the vehicle; the side doors are vulnerable to rusting along the lower edges and, if rot is detected, it's a good indication that the area around the jacking points will also be affected. The reason for considerable decay in this area could be due to water making its way to the floor, and spreading, from the elevating roof. In extreme cases it means that the vehicle is unfit for restoration.

Front and rear wheelarches and quarter panels may also reveal signs of rust damage. Often it is too late for localised renovation as the rot can penetrate from the inside to the exterior. As rust spreads it's usual for it to affect the body seams which will require even further restoration work. Making one's way round to the rear of the vehicle, assume that if there is general evidence of corrosion elsewhere, the rear panels, including the engine compartment door and tailgate, will be in need of some tidying.

The roof is the one remaining section of bodywork that could determine whether the vehicle is worth considering. Carefully check the guttering along both sides as it can display serious defects. If the seams are badly corroded, holes will be evident in the surrounding metalwork and specialist attention will almost certainly be necessary to effect a successful repair.

Attention should be paid to items of body trim, such as headlamp surrounds, door handles, seals and window frames. A vehicle that – apart from possible renewal or refurbishment of these items – is otherwise sound should not be entirely dismissed, as this is not a major task, nor will it be excessively expensive. However, if it's recognised that the vehicle requires restoration work, the cost of the work should be allowed for in the overall budget.

Buying a Bay Window Transporter

To a large degree, many of the points to consider when deciding upon a Split-Screen Bulli also apply to Bay Window models. At one time it was the Splittie that was the most sought after of models, but more recently the Bay has achieved a cult status of its own, and is highly desirable.

Prices of Bay Window models are catching up with those of Splitties, but it's possible to acquire a complete restoration project for around £1000. Don't expect much for your money, though, as the vehicle will undoubtedly show evidence of neglect and advanced all-round corrosion: unless the vehicle is special-interest, such a purchase is unlikely to be financially viable.

For a nicely presented vehicle that is ready for use, expect to pay around £5000. Anything less than this will in all probability require some cosmetic work within a reasonably short period of time. It's probable, too, that some welding might be required, together with replacement of some body panels or floor sections. For a pristine or concours example it will be necessary to pay up to £10,000. For this price one can expect the vehicle to be in first class structural and mechanical condition, with an interior specification to match. Unlike Split-Screen Panel vans and Pick-ups, which have a curiosity value as well as historical interest, Bay Window commercial variants will command vastly lower prices.

Enthusiasts purchasing a Bay Window Transporter will appreciate the vehicle's comfort, its improved visibility and greater power compared

In recent years Bay Window Transporters have achieved cult status. Vehicles like this late model make ideal everyday and go-anywhere vehicles. It is always important to check that elevating roofs operate correctly and don't allow water into the vehicle. (Author's collection)

Kombi and camping conversions are the most popular types of Transporter. They provide comfortable accommodation and are a favourite vehicle with traders who attend autojumbles. The spare wheel is located within the plastic box mounted on the nose of this Westfalia conversion. (Author's collection)

to the Splittie. There is comfort in the knowledge that Bay Window models are all the more available than their predecessors, and thus there will be greater choice. There are several ways of finding the right vehicle; through the medium of an enthusiasts' club, the classified advertisements in any one of the many classic car journals, or via the internet.

Kombi and camping conversions are generally the preferred choice of vehicle, not least for the level of comfort and performance they afford. For a good all-round vehicle that can be used on a daily basis it's wise to avoid a vehicle that has been customised, though naturally a vehicle with an original specification exterior but displaying a bespoke interior might just be an attractive proposition.

Performance-wise, a Bay Window model will have a comfortable maximum speed of around 65mph (105kph) while fuel consumption will be no better than 22mpg (13 litres/100km).

At one time it was not uncommon to see Bay Window Transporters in various states of disrepair, sometimes degenerating in gardens and on driveways, sometimes even by the roadside. Such vehicles presented a sorry sight; stone chipped paint having been left to decay thus resulting in ugly patches of rot which eventually crumbles away leaving unappealing holes. Evidence of corrosion along door bottoms and sills, around wheelarches and the roof matched interiors that were stained and threadbare, floors damp and long rotted. Happily, renewed interest in these vehicles means that preventative maintenance can ensure that a well-used Transporter can be kept in good condition.

The number of surviving Bay Window types of all ages and in sound condition serves as reassurance enough that the original build quality was excellent, although it has to be recognised that the techniques of rust-proofing were not as good throughout the motor industry during the fifties, sixties and seventies as they are now.

The great majority of Bay Window models in everyday service are most likely to have been built during the mid-seventies, and can be easily identified by the high-level positioning of the front turn indicators, a feature introduced for the 1973 model year. There are, nevertheless, many earlier examples in excellent condition, which continue to provide exemplary daily use.

Enthusiasts keen to combine traditional values with the benefits of a more modern vehicle can choose between an air-cooled Wedge model or move right up to date and acquire one of the Brazilian-built Bay Window models being made available in the United Kingdom and mainland Europe. In the case of the former, vehicles are in abundant supply, and a good example will be relatively inexpensive. At present there are many commercial variants in daily use and these will command lower values than a Kombi or camping conversion. The advantage of the Wedge is its ample size and high level of trim and accessories, features not found on earlier types of bus.

The Brazilian-built models have been discussed elsewhere in this book and, as has already been mentioned, can be the means of enjoying a modern vehicle coupled with the pleasures of driving a classic Volkswagen. When importing a vehicle from Brazil other than through a recognised supplier, it is important to ensure that it conforms to United Kingdom (or specific country) regulations and that it is suitably rust and corrosion proofed.

Under the skin – what to look for

A Transporter's exterior state of health will give a clue as to its mechanical condition, hence a vehicle displaying a tatty appearance will almost certainly have an engine compartment that clearly denotes neglect. Unlike the bodywork, which might indicate the

A vehicle's general appearance will be an indicator of overall condition. Watch for decay along the roof and around the windscreen, and for signs of accident damage on the front panels, which will be difficult and expensive to repair.
(Author's collection)

presence of rot, and, therefore, be time consuming and expensive to renovate, the mechanical aspect of the vehicle is much easier to restore.

A vehicle with an engine compartment that is swathed in oil and grime but is otherwise well presented should not be immediately disregarded unless one is seeking all-round perfection. The enterprising purchaser could use this as a bargaining tool to good advantage, thus negotiating an attractive price.

A fundamental aspect of the Bulli is its robust engineering and capacity for endless hard work, even under the most demanding conditions. The plentiful supply of parts has already been mentioned, so don't be put off by stories of Volkswagen engines having limited life. Whilst it has been known for engines to require rebuilding after 70,000-80,000 miles (112,000-128,00km), this mainly applies to those units which have abused and mechanically neglected. With no other precautions other than careful and regular maintenance, together with a sympathetic driving attitude, there is no reason why an engine should not provide continual reliability for well in excess of 150,000-200,000 miles (240,000-320,000km). Engines fitted to post-1960 vehicles will not require any adjustment for running on unleaded petrol but earlier types will require an additive.

Notwithstanding the foregoing, Volkswagen engines do have weaknesses, and the earlier series can be prone to valve failure, which is usually confined to the 3rd cylinder. The problem can be mostly attributed to the exhaust valve which will have been subjected to overheating, and is exacerbated by excessively long periods of flat-out driving. Failure can occur when the valves, which are constructed from two separate components and welded together, are damaged as a result of overheating, and when this happens there is no alternative but to fit a reconditioned engine.

In instances where a more powerful engine than originally specified has been fitted, in the case of Split-Screen models, the reduction gear hubs have been left in place, there is a tendency for the motor to over-rev which, in time, can cause irreparable damage. Such damage can be avoided by either removing the reduction gearing and converting the rear axle to independent suspension, as fitted to Bay Window Transporters, or simply regulate engine speed.

Don't be surprised to see some oil around the engine; the air-cooled boxer is notorious for leaking small amounts of oil but anything more than a spoonful every 1000 miles should be investigated. The reason for the seepage is that oil can ooze past a rubber seal on the push-rod tubes; rectification of the problem means dismantling the engine in order to replace the seal. Should the oil leak be far worse than described, it is probable that the trouble will be traced to a perished seal on the engine flywheel, in which case the engine must be removed to effect a successful repair.

The gaiters on the inbound ends of the driveshafts should also be checked for wear. These are known to perish at regular intervals to allow oil to seep out, and, while this should not present too much of a problem as long as the gearbox oil level is maintained, serious problems will arise if the gearbox runs dry.

Air-cooled engines are inherently noisier than water-cooled units, but don't accept any argument that an unduly raucous engine is normal. A deep growling sound may indicate crankshaft bearing wear, in which case check the crankshaft pulley for excessive play. To do this, grasp the pulley with both hands; any backward or forward movement will indicate wear in the bearings, the remedy being fitment of a new or reconditioned engine.

With the engine running at normal temperature, any sluggishness could indicate a cracked cylinder head. Although a compression test is the only positive way of confirming one's worst fears, such lethargy could indicate the engine is in need of a complete overhaul. Unless a vehicle has been standing idle for any length of time, there should be no reason for the exhaust to emit blue smoke. If this is the case suspect the cause to be more serious than oil having collected in the cylinder heads merely burning off. These are classic valve wear symptoms and the only remedy is a complete engine overhaul.

When examining the tail section of a vehicle, take care to investigate any exhaust problems. The replacement of an entire exhaust system complete with new heat exchangers will be a costly enterprise. Nevertheless, if a faulty or worn system is left untreated, it will, in time, allow unpleasant fumes to enter the vehicle through the heating system.

While the engine compartment cover is open, check for any discernible fuel leaks from the carburettor. Leaks could present a fire risk so you'll need to fit a new carburettor (a fairly simple and inexpensive task). It's wise, also, to check the fuel line from the petrol tank to the front of the engine. The cotton-sheathed rubber hose can split with age and heat and should be changed annually. You should also inspect the wiring from the battery to the starter motor; it should be supported by rubber grommets where it passes through the engine bulkhead, and should not be chaffed or touch the metalwork.

Check the gearbox, which is noted for being exceptionally rugged and reliable. A gear change displaying a lot of play will indicate a worn gear linkage coupling, something that is easy and inexpensive to repair. Should a vehicle have a propensity to jump out gear, the problem could be more serious, indicating severe wear of the differential and crown wheel and pinion, in which case there will be accompanying grinding of cogs. There is no alternative in this instance but to fit a replacement or reconditioned gearbox. Overhauling and rebuilding a gearbox is a demanding operation and is best left to a specialist.

A clutch can last for in excess of 100,000 miles (160,000km) with sympathetic use. A common cause for a slipping clutch is a sticking cable, which might not be attributed to the clutch mechanism at all. Should a clutch show serious signs of wear, don't be put off buying the vehicle if it's in otherwise acceptable condition. Clutch renewal is straightforward for owners who are happy to undertake such a task, but it does entail removal of the engine. Owing to the weight of the engine it is recommended removal and installation is tackled with two pairs of hands, not least to avoid dropping the unit and risk damaging the crankcase.

Finally, before taking the vehicle for a test drive that is of sufficient duration in order to get a proper feel for it, check the steering and, in the case of a Splittie, the condition of the king pins. These vehicles are renowned for king pin wear which, at around £200 per wheel, is costly to remedy. Any play when rocking a wheel could indicate a worn wheel bearing, this being adjustable. When test driving a vehicle firstly try out the brakes: the pedal should not have far to travel, will not have a spongy feel, and will stop the vehicle without the steering being affected. The steering should be light and accurate, and the ride quality good, but beware a vehicle that demonstrates tight spots as the steering wheel is turned; any work to be done on the steering box is best left to a specialist, especially as a steering box rebuild kit will cost in the region of £500. Don't get carried away by believing a little cosmetic renovation will turn a mechanically sound vehicle into a concours winner; it won't! Nor will it be easy or inexpensive to tidy up an interior that looks slightly scruffy.

Using a Transporter to its full potential

With the purchase of the chosen vehicle complete it's only natural that the owner will want to use it to its full potential, which means careful attention to servicing and preventative maintenance. Assuming that a vehicle is in first class all-round condition, there is every reason to keep it that way: as well as carrying out periodic servicing, the bodywork will have to be regularly examined and any stone chips treated to prevent corrosion from getting a hold. During winter months, all road salt should be thoroughly washed away from the under chassis and body panels, and any ingress of water through the wheelarches, along the gutters and around the sunroof or elevating top is checked for. The interior of the vehicle should also be periodically inspected so that any staining or water spillage to upholstery, carpets and fittings is treated.

Owners of 6-volt Bullis will be aware of the necessity of keeping the electrics in good condition and free from damp. Though air-cooled engines are immune to freezing in winter, a couple of fruitless turns on the starter is sufficient to flatten a battery. For this reason many owners of early Transporters keep a ready-charged battery in case of emergency.

There is little problem regarding the availability of mechanical parts or body panels, and specialists exist to supply everything that is required to keep even the earliest vehicles in a good state of health. All specialists provide a mail order service and many attend the major enthusiast meetings, so it's a good idea to get to know the field of expertise that is offered. It will, therefore, be easy to obtain such items as cab floor repair panels, chassis outriggers, sills, front and rear wheelarches, and windscreen channels. Mechanical components, including front and rear brake shoes, master and wheel cylinders, handbrake, clutch and accelerator cables, complete wiring looms, and heat exchangers are also easy to obtain from specialist suppliers.

Even the best prepared Transporter will, at some time, require replacement parts. Whether maintenance is carried out on a DIY basis or entrusted to a

A vehicle in good condition will give lasting pleasure. The high mounted indicators show this to be a late model Bay Window with the step into the cab concealed by the door, an arrangement introduced when the Transporter was given added frontal protection in the event of an accident.
(Author's collection)

specialist, it's essential that only the best quality components are fitted, as to compromise on servicing is a false economy and can be detrimental to overall safety and longevity of the vehicle. In the event of uprating a vehicle's performance, extreme care has to be taken to ensure modifications are properly carried out: for example, to increase power without modifying the braking system would be foolhardy.

Where a vehicle has been customised, there will be need for caution as some mechanical components may not be as originally specified, especially if different running gear has been implanted. Different body panels may also have been introduced which, in the event of undertaking repairs, may cause problems.

Ownership of a camping conversion may well involve replacing some of the interior equipment from time-to-time, especially if the vehicle is used regularly for holidays and long trips. It will not always be possible to

replace items of the original design, and many enthusiasts are happy to devise modifications of their own.

Restoration

At some time in a Transporter's life the difficult decision may have to be faced concerning restoration. The ravages of time and the elements, as well as general wear and tear, may mean the end of a vehicle in its existing condition. There are usually two options: sell the vehicle on at a price commensurate with its age and condition, thus letting the new owner take on the responsibility of restoration, or to personally oversee the project. Mechanical restoration will prove a lot easier than renovating the bodywork. When working on the bodyshell there are many unknown quantities and, until work is commenced there is often little opportunity to assess the full extent of the project. Where decay is extreme, it's possible that a successful restoration might be either uneconomical or impossible, but as

long as the bodywork can be easily repaired, all mechanical components can be replaced or reconditioned.

When having a vehicle professionally restored, discuss with the specialist the extent of the project, its duration, and likely cost. It is usual to make stage payments as agreed between the two parties, and a reputable firm will keep the customer informed as to progress. Care is needed when choosing a specialist, and, unless the customer knows a particular restorer and is happy to entrust the work to them, it is advisable to visit several companies and obtain quotations before making a decision. Enthusiast clubs will often be able to make recommendations, and inspecting the quality of work undertaken on members' vehicles will help with making the final choice.

If attempting a DIY restoration, it must be appreciated that special tools and equipment will almost certainly be required. Ideally, the work should be carried out in suitable premises, and remember that completing the project could take longer or prove to be more expensive than anticipated.

The following is not a step-by-step procedure, nor is it a guide as to how to undertake a restoration project as it's presumed the enthusiast will have some experience of restoration techniques. Instead, its purpose is to indicate what to expect when restoring a vehicle, and how to avoid arriving at a situation where loss of interest results from flagging enthusiasm.

Any lack of enthusiasm will probably occur after the first wave of excitement when the vehicle has been stripped of body trim, oily components and all interior fittings. As well as looking in a forlorn condition, what is left is a mix of decayed metal which, as soon as prodded with a screwdriver, will crumble to the floor. Cutting out all traces of rot can be a dismally extensive exercise, but this is the time to make a detailed list of all the items that need replacing, and those that can be salvaged, even if it means sending them to be expertly renovated.

All items that are to be renovated should be labelled so that they can be identified later; all traces of oil and dirt should be eradicated and, presuming the vehicle is to be repainted, the metalwork should be suitably prepared. This is a painstaking job that will require wearing protective overalls, gloves, face mask and goggles; when using chemical cleaners ensure that the manufacturer's instructions are followed, particularly where there is need for ventilation. Depending on the state of the vehicle, it might be prudent to employ specialist steam cleaning and sand-blasting techniques.

As has been described elsewhere, the main areas most likely to have succumbed to rot are the wheelarches, cab floor, sill, chassis outriggers and chassis floor, as well as the lower rear quarter panels. Additionally, the front panel will probably need rubbing down completely and, owing to its double skin construction, filled where necessary; the front valance, once the bumper assembly has been removed, may be found to be so badly corroded that it is necessary to weld replacement sheet metal panels into place. Before that, though, take a good look at the chassis box section behind the valance, as there is a strong possibility that this will also require replacing. On Split-Screen models, the amount of rot around the windows might demand that new channels be fitted and, often, it will be necessary to cut out and replace the windscreen pillars. Water collecting in the door bottoms will often have been responsible for extensive damage here, but it may be possible to cut away the lower panels and weld in new sections; if this is impractical there may be no other solution but to obtain replacement doors. The same applies to the rear hatch and engine compartment panels.

A vehicle in need of total restoration will require an amount of welding work and, according to the number of replacement parts needed, this is likely to be both extensive and expensive. Unless an enthusiast has the expertise that is necessary to undertake such an operation, it might be best to leave such a task to a professional, even if it does add to the overall cost. Before attempting any welding work, there are certain safety precautions which need to be taken, including removal of the vehicle's battery and fuel tank to prevent risk of fire.

As part of the restoration process, it will be necessary to use some form of rust protection. It pays to use an inhibitor that is recommended by specialist restorers, and, once this is complete, work can then start on filling weld seams and making good any bodywork imperfections. Any amount of time taken at this stage is well-spent in ensuring a satisfactory finish.

Preparing for, and applying, the finishing coasts of paint requires expertise and, until recently, there has been a choice of using two-pack isocyanate or cellulose paints, the former needing special requirements to meet health and safety conditions, and, as such, is likely to need specialist application. Regulations state that cellulose paint cannot be manufactured after January 2007, nor used in the community from January 2008. Whether there will be any exclusions in the case of historic vehicles is, at the time of writing, open to conjecture. Recent developments in paint technology include HVLP application (high volume, low pressure) and the availability of certain water-based materials, both of which require specialist advice before use.

During time of otherwise inactivity, such as waiting for body panels to arrive, work can progress with the preparation of mechanical items. Most components will need to be cleaned or reconditioned; items of trim may require refurbishment as might seats, furnishings and roof fittings. In any restoration project it is often the finishing touches that take the most time and effort. Attention to window glass, door handles, mirrors, hub caps, instruments and interior material quality will be worth the effort.

Given the Transporter's size, weight and modest performance, some enthusiastic owners have fitted tuning kits that are available through specialist suppliers. During the fifties, the boxer engine's lack of performance was somewhat redressed by the Okrasa company which marketed a kit that basically comprised a pair of Solex carburettors and twin-port cylinder heads. When fitted, the modification raised the compression ratio, providing an increase of around 30 per cent in power from the 30 and 34bhp motors.

Other conversion kits followed, and the 34bhp engine could be made to deliver punchy performance using larger pistons and barrels. Supercharging enjoyed a spell of popularity, and fitting the Judson, which was one of the favourite designs, a 1200cc engine could be made to deliver power equal to a 1600cc motor. The problem with this was the expense and effort involved, when simply swapping the 1200 engine for a 1600 unit would have achieved virtually the same result.

In order to improve the Transporter's performance simply to the level of today's traffic conditions, a number of relatively simple measures can be taken. These include uprating the carburation system, fitting an all-centrifugal distributor, and modifying the exhaust system, all of which can be done with minimal effort and outlay. The result will not in any way be outstanding, but there will be increased acceleration and a marginally higher top speed. More adventurous methods would be to prepare an engine with larger barrels and pistons, along with high performance rocker and pushrod assemblies. Further tuning can be achieved by fitting specially modified crankshafts and cylinder heads but, ultimately, at the risk of destroying the vehicle's original character.

The number of Transporters in daily use is evidence of the vehicles' practicality and the level of enjoyment they afford. For many enthusiasts, owning a Bulli would not be complete without membership of one or more of the many clubs that exist worldwide to enhance ownership. Such institutions not only seek to provide a high degree of camaraderie, they serve to make parts and services available to members and to keep them informed of events and ongoing developments aimed at getting the maximum use and pleasure from these highly desirable vehicles.

That the classic Transporter remained in production in Brazil for so long is testament to the vehicle's enduring design. The final traditional VW Bus rolled off the production line in Brazil in 2013. Rumours abound that Volkswagen will at some time, as it did with the New Beetle, introduce a new derivative of the Transporter, possibly displaying retro styling characteristics. Whether such a move will materialise is unknown as this book goes to press ...

Left: Enjoying one's Bulli (in this instance a Westfalia conversion) is the essential aspect of ownership. (Courtesy Ken Cservenka)

Below and below left: The final Type 2 to be built at the Brazil factory. Production ceasing at the end of 2013. (Volkswagen)

Appendix

Production and sales figures

Volkswagen Type 2 production figures 1950-1992

Split-Screen models, March 1950-August 1967	1,477,330
Bay Window models, August 1967-July 1979	3,292,272
Wedge models August 1979-July 1992	1,745,805
Total	**6,515,407**

Brazilian production figures 1957-June 2006

Locally built vehicles	1,361,826
CKD vehicles	44,436
Total	**1,406,262**

Note: CKD assembly began 1971 and ceased 1989
Number of vehicles built between August 1979-June 2006 = approximately 780,882 assuming half of 1979 production (50,337) to be around 25,000 vehicles.
The most productive years were 1976 (62,548 + 3732CKD vehicles); 1975 (53,335 + 6060CKD); 1996 (55,481); 1995 (52,731); 1995 (52,731); 1974 (48,803 + 3540CKD); 1978 (51,239 + 324CKD); 1997 (50,960); 1979 (49,161 + 1176CKD) In 1957, 371 vehicles were constructed; 4819 in 1958; 8383 in 1959, 16,315 in 1961; 21,172 in 1967 and 30,205 in 1970. In 2000, 20,156 vehicles were built, 9708 in 2003, 13,873 in 2005 and 9407 between January and June 2006.
Production figure to 31 December 2013 when last model left the factory 3,200,000 (approx)
Source of information: Volkswagen Brazil.

Mexican production figures 1971-1995

Total production: 253,926 Kombi models for the domestic market.
Annual breakdown of figures as supplied via VW Mexico is unavailable.

United Kingdom sales figures 1950-1992

Year	Transporter	Campervan	Total
1955	1054	-	1054
1956	1181	-	1181
1957	1272	-	1272
1958	1324	-	1324

Year	Transporter	Campervan	Total
1959	1242	-	1242
1960	3029	-	3029
1961	2929	-	2929
1962	3039	-	3039
1963	3488	-	3488
1964	3800	-	3800
1965	1735	1264	2999
1966	1786	1465	3251
1967	2151	1387	3538
1968	1968	2148	4116
1969	2444	2368	4812
1970	3002	3317	6319
1971	3128	5484	8612
1972	6048	9325	15,373
1973	6875	7986	14,861
1974	4489	3133	7622
1975	3297	1676	4973
1976	2800	961	3761
1977	3072	596	3668
1978	3447	899	4346
1979	4316	1277	5593
1980	5026	1583	6609
1981	3799	1087	4886
1982	4414	932	5346
1983	4718	731	5449
1984	4199	836	5035
1985	3668	794	4462
1986	3756	861	4617
1987	2745	779	3524
1988	3242	759	4001
1989	3536	910	4446
1990	2636	950	3586
1991	2671	629	3300
1992	3293	719	4012

Source of figures, Volkswagen. These are official figures and do not take in account those campervans supplied by different converters, eg Canterbury Pitt and Devon etc before 1965.

Production landmarks
The 100,000th Transporter was built 9th October 1954, the 200,000th on 13th September 1956 and the 500,000th on 25th August 1959
The Hanover factory produced the one millionth Transporter in August 1961
When the Mark 2 vehicle replaced the Split-Screen Transporter in July 1967, 1.8 million Transporters had been constructed; by the end of the year the 2 millionth Transporter was produced.
Production of the Transporter reached 3 million in 1971.
Type 2 Transporter production ceased in Brazil, December 2013.

Appendix

Transporter chronology

1947. Ben Pon sees motorised flat-bed trucks in use at Wolfsburg. These remind him of pedal-powered delivery vehicles, known as bakfiets, used by traders in Holland. He sketches an idea that would, in time, emerge as a Beetle-engined commercial vehicle, known simply as the Volkswagen Type 2.

1948. Ben Pon's ideas are translated to detailed drawings for a commercial vehicle on instruction of Major Ivan Hirst who was in charge of administration at Wolfsburg prior to the Heinz Nordhoff's appointment as Volkswagen chief executive.

1949. Tests begin of a prototype vehicle but it became apparent that the Beetle floorpan did not have sufficient strength to withstand the stress imposed by the Transporter's body. A new prototype was designed using unitary construction; tests were positive and Heinz Nordhoff assigned the Type 2 Transporter for production. The vehicle was announced in November.

1950. Delivery of Panel vans begins in March; the Kombi arrives three months later.

1951. The Microbus is launched, and with it the deluxe Samba Bus.

1952. The Pick-up is launched and is immediately a favourite with tradesmen. The design of the vehicle meant re-engineering the drivetrain layout.

1953. Engine capacity increased from 1131cc to 1192cc. Production commences in Brazil.

1954. 100,000th Transporter built. Right hand drive available on all models. Assembly commences in Australia. VW factory opens in Mexico; Transporter production ceases at the plant in 1998.

1955. Styling modifications include opening tailgate, made possible by lowering of engine deck. Peak above windscreen allows for improved ventilation system. Smaller wheels fitted, along with hydraulic shock absorbers. New, full-width dashboard. Assembly begins in South Africa.

1956. Production transferred from Wolfsburg to Hanover.

1958. Pick-up available with double-cab, known also as 'crew cab'

1959. 1192cc engine redesigned to afford increase of power to 34bhp at 3700rpm. Gearbox improved with synchromesh on all ratios.

1960. Bullet-shaped flashing indicators fitted in place of semaphore signals.

1961. The millionth Transporter is built. High-roof Panel van introduced.

1962. Cab seating improved.

1963. 1497cc engine introduced; power increased to 42bhp at 3800rpm. Lighting system improved, larger flashing indicators fitted. Sliding doors optional; larger rear hatch, payload increased to one tonne.

1964. Windscreen washers fitted.

1965. 1497cc engine uprated to provide 44bhp at 4000rpm.

1966. 12-volt electrics introduced.

1967. Major styling changes – Bay Window model introduced. All models have sliding doors; 1.6 litre of 1584cc engine provides 47bhp at 4000rpm. Revised transmission sees and end to reduction gear hubs.

1968. Glass-fibre roof on high dome models.

1969. Stronger doors and collapsible steering column fitted.

1970. 1584cc engine delivers more power: 50bhp at 4000rpm.

1971. 1.7 litre engine (1679cc) fitted to produce 66bhp at 4000rpm.

1972. Automatic transmission available on all models except Pick-up. Cab floor has safety 'crumple zone'.

1973. Engine enlarged to 1.8 litres, 1795cc to produce 68bhp at 4200rpm. Cab step repositioned; front indicators moved to new position on sides of grille.

1975. 2-litre engine introduced; capacity 1970cc providing 70bhp at 4200rpm. Payload increased to 2500kg.

1979. Wedge model introduced to reveal larger and more accommodating bodywork. Change from torsion bar suspension to coil springs.

1982. Diesel engine introduced. Demise of air-cooled vehicles in favour of water-cooling.

1986. 2110cc engine specified.

1991. Fourth generation (T4) vehicles introduced with front wheel drive. Engine size increased to 2459cc.

2003. Fifth generation (T5) vehicles introduced.

2005. Air-cooled Type 2 still in production in Brazil. Examples being imported to UK via Beetles UK Ltd. and Surf and Diamond campervan conversions constructed by Danbury Conversions.

2006. 1.4 litre water-cooled engine replaces air-cooled unit in respect of Brazilian production.

Appendix

Original specifications

Split-screen models

Length	163in/4150mm
Width	65in/1660mm
Height	75in/1900mm
Wheelbase	94.5in/2400mm
Track, front	53.9in/1370mm
Track, rear	53.5in/1360mm
Unladen weight	2150lb/975kg
Ground clearance	7.75in/200mm
Engine	4-cylinders, ohv, air-cooled, horizontally-opposed, 1131cc
Bore and stroke	75x64mm; compression ratio 5.8:1, 25bhp at 3300rpm
Maximum speed	56mph/90kph
Transmission	4-speed gearbox with reverse, swinging half-axles, spur wheel reduction gear to rear wheels
Gear ratios	1st: 3.60:1; 2nd: 2.07:1; 3rd: 1.25:1; 4th: 0.80:1; reverse: 6.60:1
Final drive	1:6.2
Clutch	Single dry plate
Chassis	Unitary construction; ladder-type frame
Front suspension	Transverse torsion bars, parallel trailing arms and double-acting telescopic shock absorbers
Rear suspension	Transverse torsion bars and parallel trailing arms; double-acting telescopic shock absorbers & swinging half axles
Steering	Worm and peg; unequal length tie rods and king pins
Turning circle	39 feet/12metres (approx)
Brakes	Hydraulically operated drums all round; mechanical parking brake acting on rear wheels
Wheels and tyres	16in/406.4mm wheels with 5.60x16 tyres
Fuel tank capacity	8.75 Imp gals/10.6 US gals/ 40 lts
Fuel consumption	25mpg/11.32lts per 100km
Electrical	6-volts

Right hand rive models with the 1192cc engine for the UK market came available in 1954, the specification differing as follows:

Bore and stroke	77x64mm, compression ratio 6.6:1, maximum power 30bhp at 3300rpm
Transmission	Synchromesh on 2nd, 3rd and 4th ratios
Gear ratios	1st: 3.60:1; 2nd: 1.88:1; 3rd: 1.23:1; top: 0.82:1; reverse: 4.63:1

Mark II (Bay Window) models

Length	174in/4420mm
Width	69.5in/1765mm
Height	77in/1956mm
Wheelbase	94.5in/2400mm
Front track	54.5in/1384mm
Rear track	56.1in/1425mm
Unladen weight	Panel van: 2590lb/1175kg; Kombi:2789lb/1265kg
Ground clearance	7.25in/1840mm

Engine	1.6 litre (1584cc), 4 cylinders, air-cooled, horizontally opposed
Bore and stroke	85.5x69mm
Maximum power	47bhp at 4000rpm
Compression ratio	7.7:1
Maximum speed	65mph/104kph
Transmission	4-speed gearbox with reverse and synchromesh on all ratios
Gear ratios	1st: 3.80:1; 2nd: 2.06:1; 3rd: 1.26:1; top: 0.82:1; reverse: 3.61:1. Final drive: 5.375:1
Clutch	Single dry plate
Chassis	Unitary construction
Front suspension	Transverse torsion bars, parallel trailing arms and double-acting telescopic shock absorbers
Rear suspension	Transverse torsion bars, trailing arms and double-acting shock absorbers
Steering	Worm and roller
Turning circle	40 feet/12 metres
Wheels	5.5Jx14 with 7.00x14 crossply or 185R14C radial tyres
Brakes	Hydraulic; dual circuit drums all round; parking brake operating on rear wheels
Fuel tank capacity	15.8 gals/71.83 lts
Fuel consumption	24.8mpg/11.41ts per 100km
Electrical	12-volts

Mark II (Wedge) models

Length	179.9in/4569mm
Width	72.6in/1844mm
Height	77.2in/1961mm
Wheelbase	96.9in/2461mm
Unladen weight	3290lb/1492kg
Ground clearance	7.5in/1900mm
Engine	4-cylinders, air-cooled and horizontally-opposed. 1970cc
Bore and stroke	94x71mm
Compression ratio	7.3:1
Maximum power	67bhp at 4200rpm
Maximum speed	80mph/128kph
Transmission	4-speed synchromesh gearbox with reverse or 3-speed automatic
Gear ratios	1st:3.78:1; 2nd: 2.06:1; 3rd: 1.26:1; top: 1.00:1; reverse: 3.28:1
Final drive	4.57:1
Clutch	Single dry plate
Chassis	Unitary construction

Front suspension	Unequal length control arms, hydraulic shock absorbers, coil springs and anti-roll bar
Rear suspension	Semi-trailing arms, coil springs and hydraulic shock absorbers
Brakes	Front discs, rear drums, mechanical parking brake on rear wheels
Steering	Rack and pinion
Turning circle	34.5 feet/10.52metres
Wheels	5.5Jx14 with 185x14 radial tyres
Fuel tank capacity	13.2gals/50lts
Fuel consumption	21mpg/13.5lts per 100km
Electrical system	12-volts

Mark IV (T4) models

Length	186.6in/4740mm
Width	72.4in/1839mm
Height	75.2in/1900mm
Wheelbase	115in/2921mm or 131in/3320mm
Engine	water-cooled 1.9 litre turbo-diesel; 2.0 litre petrol; 2.5 litre petrol; 2.4 litre diesel or 2.5 litre turbo-diesel
Transmission	5-speed manual gearbox or automatic
Clutch	Single dry plate
Chassis	Unitary construction
Front suspension	Double wishbones and torsion bars
Rear suspension	Coil springs and semi-trailing arms
Brakes	Front discs, rear drums, ABS optional; mechanical parking brake on rear wheels (later models have all-round discs)
Steering	Power-assisted rack and pinion
Electrical	12-volt

Mark V (T5) models

Length	192.5in/4890mm
Width	75in/1904mm
Height	77.52in/1969mm
Wheelbase	118.1in/3000mm or 134in/3400mm
Engine	1.9 litre or 2.5 litre turbo diesel
Transmission	5-speed gearbox
Chassis	Unitary construction
Clutch	Single dry plate
Suspension	As T4
Brakes	Front and rear discs
Steering	Power assisted rack and pinion
Electrical	12-volt

Appendix

Clubs and specialists

Clubs

Throughout the world there exits a countless number of clubs and associations dedicated to the cause of the VW Type 2 Transporter and Bus. The following organisations mainly refer to the United Kingdom but for more information it is advisable to refer to the internet or check details in the many Volkswagen Type 2 related magazines. The contact information shown is subject to change.

Association of British VW Car Clubs
C/o John Daniel, 76 Eastfield Road, Burnham, Bucks SL1 7PF
Tel 01628 205624

Historic Volkswagen Club
Rod Sleigh, 28 Longnor Road, Brooklands, Telford, Salop TF1 3NY
Tel 01952 242167
www.historicvws.org.uk

London and Thames Valley
VW Owners Club
jack.thebug@ltv-vwc.org.uk

Volkswagen Owners Club of Great Britain
www.vwocgb.com
VW Type 2 Owners Club
www.vwt2oc.co

Split Screen Van Club
Robert Meekings, 21 Nabwood Road, Shipley, West Yorks, BD18 4AG
www.ssvc.org.uk

Specialists

There are numerous specialists throughout the world offering services to owners of air-cooled Volkswagens, the Type 2 in particular. The following is only a small selection of firms and it is recommended that for more information that reference is made to the internet or the many VW-related magazines.

Aircooled Parts (USA)
www.aircooled.net

Alan H Schofield
Unit 14 Dinting Lane Industrial estate, Glossop, Derbyshire SK13 7NU
Tel 01457 854267
www.alanhschofield.com

Bernard Newbury
1 Station Road, Leigh-on-Sea, Essex, SS9 7ST
Tel 01702 710211
www.bernardnewbury.co.uk

Bluebird Customs
www.bluebird-type2.co.uk

Bus Brothers
www.busbrothers.com

Bus Depot (USA)
www.busdepot.com

Calypso Campers
18 Paul's Dene Crescent, Salisbury, Wiltshire, SP1 3QU
Tel 01722 327081
mob: 07720 167603
www.calypso-campers.co.uk,
jon@calypso-campers.co.uk

Cool Air (GB) Ltd
Unit 4 Bilton Road, Erith, Kent DA8 2AN
sales@coolairvw.co.uk. www.coolairvw.co.uk

Dubtricks,
Low Hall Farm, Dacre near Harrogate,
N Yorks. HG3 4AA
Tel 01423 780147
dubtricks@hotmail.com

Jacks Garage
20-22 Kingsdown Close, London
W10 6SW
jacksgarage10@gmail.com
www.jacksgarage.co.uk

Java. Jonny Abbott
Unit 6A Blythe House Farm, Lichfield
Road, Hawstall, Staffs, WS15 3QQ
Tel 01889 504080
www.vwjava.com

Just Kampers
Unit 1 Stapeley Manor, Long Lane,
Odiham, Hants RG29 1JE
Tel 01256 862288
www.justcampers.com

Karmann Konnection
289 Victoria Avenue,
Southend-on-Sea SS2 6NE
Tel 01702 340613
www.karmannkonnection.com new

Kingfisher Kustoms
Unit 5 Oldbury Road, Smethwick,
West Midlands B66 1NU
Tel 0121 558 9135
www.kingfisherkustoms.com

Now VW Heritage
Tel 01273 444000
www.vwheritage.com
See details of VW Heritage elsewhere

Old Skool
82 Bunting Road, Northampton
NN2 6EE
Tel 01604 930082
www.oldskoolvw.com

Parts Emporium
Unit 1, Netherfield Mills, Calder Road,
Dewsbury WF13 3JS
Tel 01924694401
www.partsemporium.co.uk

Rainbow Camper Hire, Skiddaw
Grove, Vicarage Hill, Keswick,
Cumbria CA12 5QB
Tel 017687 80413
 info@vecamperhire.net
www.vwcamperhire.net

RCC Import/Export
Rhiwlas Farm, Llanbedr,
Denbighshire LL15 1US
Tel 01824 524003
sales@rccimort.co.uk
www.rccimport.com

Retrodubs
Unit 4 Killwherries Industrial Estate
Tel 01872 561194
retrodubs@btinternet.com
www.retrodubs.co.uk

A.H. Schofield
see entry listed as Alan H Schofield

Status VW Parts
See Just Kampers

Volksheaven (Salvage and Parts)
Greenacre Farm, Hop Hills Lane,
Dunscroft, Doncaster DN7 4JX
Tel 01302 351355
email: mailbox@volksheaven.co.uk

Volkspares
Branches throughout London and
Kent
For further information call
020 8778 7766 www.volkspares.co.uk

Volkswagen Emporium
Tel 020 8407 2106 email: chris@
volkswagenemporium.co.uk

Volkswares
Unit 1B, Metal products Business
Park, Prospect Road, Burntwood,
Staffs WS7 0AE
Tel 01543 671614
sales@volkswares.com

VW Books
28 Longnor Road, Telford, Shropshire,
TF1 3NY England
Tel 01952 245345
sales@vwbooks.co.uk
www.vwbooks.co.uk

VW Bus Junkies
www.busjunkies.com

VW Campers
VW Campers UK, PO Box 5848,
Milton Keynes MK4 1WS
www.vwcampers.co.uk

VW Heritage
Hollands Lane, Henfield, West Sussex,
BN5 9QY
Tel 01273 495800
sales@vwheritage.com

VW Junkies
www.vwjunkies.com
VW Relics Air-cooled Salvage co.
Lavericks Industrial Estate,
Elvington, York
Tel 01904 608535
www.vwrelics.co.uk

VW Vanshack
Unit 3 Wharf farm, Cassington,
Oxon OX29 4DB
crew@vanshack.com
www.vanshack.com

Wolfsburg VW, 45 Sandringham Drive,
Brinscall, Chorley, Lancs PR6 8SU
www.wolfsburgvw.com

A stunning record of the VW Transporter's first 40 years. Using the same lavish artistry and photography employed by Volkswagen over the decades, model history and range development are outlined, and specifications and performance discussed, with a particular emphasis on marketing and advertising strategies.

ISBN: 978-1-845845-80-3
eV4580 • Fixed layout • Base price* £8.99 UK / $9.99 US / €10.99 EU

*Vendor prices may vary.
For more info on Veloce titles, visit our website at www.veloce.co.uk • email: info@veloce.co.uk • Tel: +44(0)1305 260068

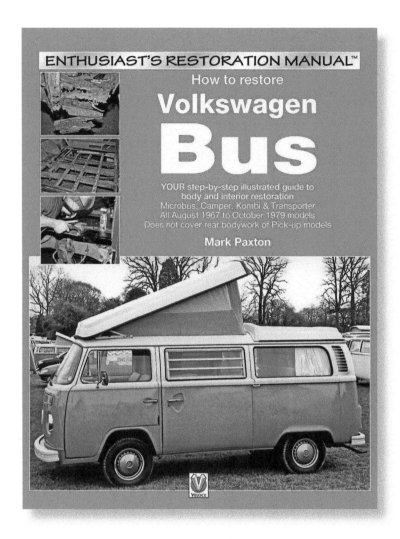

A complete guide to the restoration of your VW Bus, with full coverage of body and chassis repairs, suspension, steering and brakes, plus trim and paint. It also covers the tools, equipment and workshop techniques needed to make your Bus look like new once more.

ISBN: 978-1-845840-93-8
Paperback • 27x20.7cm • £50* UK/$85* USA • 272 pages • 1110 colour and b&w pictures

For more info on Veloce titles, visit our website at www.veloce.co.uk • email: info@veloce.co.uk • Tel: +44(0)1305 260068

* prices subject to change, p&p extra

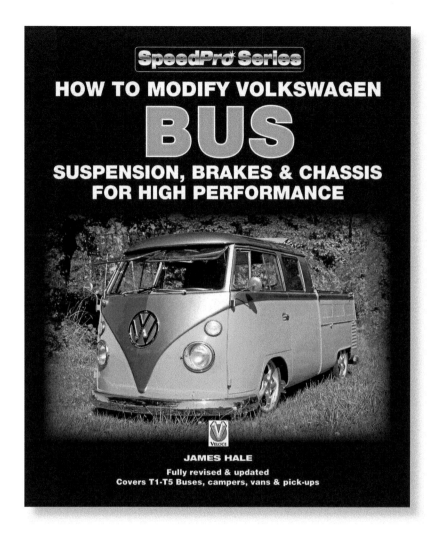

A unique volume dedicated to three generations of VWs legendary Transporter.
Meticulously researched with many model specific photographs reproduced to illustrate a
genuinely informative text.

ISBN: 978-1-845840-22-8
Paperback • 19.5x13.9cm • £12.99* UK/$25* USA • 64 pages • pictures

For more info on Veloce titles, visit our website at www.veloce.co.uk • email: info@veloce.
co.uk • Tel: +44(0)1305 260068
* prices subject to change, p&p extra